*THE FIRST AMERICAN REVOLUTION*

# Milton Lomask

# THE FIRST
# AMERICAN
# REVOLUTION

FARRAR, STRAUS AND GIROUX

*New York*

*For Ray Neville*

Library of Congress Cataloging in Publication Data

Lomask, Milton.
The first American Revolution.
Bibliography: p.
1. United States—History—Revolution—Juvenile literature.
[1. United States—History—Revolution]    I. Title.
E210.L65    973.3    73-90972
ISBN 0-374-32337-2

# Contents

The sun never shone on a cause of greater worth. 'Tis not the affair of a city, a county, a province, or a kingdom; but of a continent, at least one eighth part of the habitable globe. 'Tis not the concern of a day, a year, or an age; posterity are virtually involved in the contest and will be more or less affected even to the end of time by the proceedings now.

THOMAS PAINE, 1776

# PART ONE

---

# THE REVOLUTION

---

# 1

# Thirteen Clocks

R EVOLUTIONS OFTEN END on battlefields, but John Adams of Massachusetts always said that the American Revolution did not begin on one.

Thirty years after it was all over he was arguing the point with an old friend.

"What do we mean by the Revolution?" he wrote in 1816 to Thomas Jefferson of Virginia. "The War? That was no part of the Revolution. It was only an effect and consequence of it."

According to Adams the Revolution began in "the minds and hearts" of the American people. That development had run its course long before the windy April morning in 1775 when on the green of a Massachusetts village a British soldier in scarlet regimentals—or was it a New England farmer in wrinkled homespun?—fired the opening shot of the American War of Independence.

John Adams had begun life a subject of the King of England. He had lived long enough to be the first Vice President and second President of the United States of America. Brooding over his memories in the quiet of his high-gabled house in Braintree, Massachusetts, the old man looked back in wonder at the changes he had seen.

He remembered how rancorously divided the thirteen colonies had once been. He remembered how they had thrown their differences aside to join in opposition to British rule. By some miracle, he wrote, "thirteen clocks were made to strike together."

But how had the "miracle" come about and when did it begin? Brilliant, crotchety John Adams had no certain answers to those questions. The family quarrel between colonies and mother country had boiled up toward the end of an earlier war during which British grenadier and American militiaman had fought shoulder to shoulder. That was in the 1760's, but by then the ingredients of rebellion had been accumulating for 150 years.

It was in the early 1600's that the first permanent English settlements began to appear on the craggy backsides of coastal bays or at the mouths of tidal rivers along the Atlantic shores of North America. To some of their inhabitants these crude plantations were religious havens. To others they were an escape from the grinding poverty that in the Old World was the fate of more people than not.

All were commercial ventures. In England a group of businessmen would obtain from the King a grant of land in "His Majesty's Overseas Dominions." Then they would persuade people to colonize the land in the hope of developing a new source of raw material for England's factories, a new market for her goods.

Not many people wanted to cross the turbulent Atlantic in leaky wooden vessels to start new lives in an unknown wild. Few would make the journey until a solemn promise was written into the charters underlying the governments of their colonies. The promise was that in the New World they would "HAVE and enjoy all the Liberties, Franchises, and Immunities" of "free-born Englishmen."

Beautiful phrases! His Majesty's government never troubled to define them, but His Majesty's transatlantic subjects knew exactly what they meant. One of their earliest acts was to set up bodies of elected representatives in the wilderness. These were copies of the House of Commons, the lower branch of the Parliament that assembled with pomp and ceremony every fall in the drafty chambers of Old Westminster Palace on the banks of the Thames River in London.

Great Britain regarded the creation of these miniature parliaments in the indulgent manner of a mother watching her offspring playing at being grownups. It had no objections to the colonials making a few laws for themselves—just so long as they remembered that the last word must always come from Westminster.

For several decades the little plantations in America were too unproductive for England to bother with much. Then, in the early 1680's, one of her kings noticed that in the northern colonies the people were acting as if their general courts and assemblies—their legislatures—were as important as Parliament itself.

That, decided proud King Charles II, would never do. His subjects on the far side of the Atlantic must be reminded that it was not they but he and his ministers who called the tune. But before Charles could do more than send some stern demands and a few investigators to Boston and other colonial capitals, he was dead. It then fell to his brother, King James II, to finish the job. Beginning in 1685, James worked quickly. By the spring of 1688 all of the colonies from Maine to New Jersey had lost the charters that previous kings had given them. All had been lumped together into a single province called the Dominion of New England. Over this commonwealth King James placed a governor responsible only to London.

The colonists didn't like it. They were used to their little general courts and assemblies. They meant to keep them. Connecticut farmers and Narragansett Country (Rhode Island) rum distillers reached for their muskets. In Boston there was an armed uprising. Revolution would have followed had not a change of government in London brought an end to this first attempt by Great Britain to limit "the Liberties, Franchises, and Immunities" of her American subjects.

In 1689 King William III ascended the throne. Busy with problems at home and eager to avoid trouble in America, William disbanded the New England dominion and permitted the colonies to return to their old governments.

For the next seventy-five years Mother England spared the rod. Not that she neglected her American dependencies. She was devoted to the principles of mercantilism. According to these notions colonies were "cows to be milked"; they existed for the purpose of enriching the parent country.

Dutifully Parliament passed the necessary laws. Acts of Trade and Navigation they were called, or more commonly, "the trade acts." Some of them forced Americans to buy certain goods only from England. Others placed some American products on an "enumerated list." An enumerated item could be sold only to the mother country or to one of her possessions. Still other trade acts put heavy duties on foreign goods, especially on those imported from the French West Indies.

Every new commercial restriction loosened angry tongues in the colonies, but these wails were muted and of short duration. The Americans grudgingly conceded that England was within its rights. It had an empire to manage; it must frame laws to that end. Even "external taxes" (duties on foreign imports) could be endured, provided they were imposed only for the purpose of regulating trade, *never* for the purpose of raising a revenue for the use of the English government.

America's lawyers were given to much discussion of this point. They said that all funds going from the colonies to the British government should take the form of a gift. When His Majesty wanted money from America he must come to the provincial assemblies, crown in hand as it were. It was up to those exalted bodies to let him have it or not as they saw fit.

England's reasonable rule notwithstanding, the growth of the colonies was at first slow and painful. An incredible amount of sweat and personal sacrifice—and blood, for the frontier was close and Indian raids frequent—went into every clearing to emerge from the forest, into every building that went up. At the turn of the century fewer than 400,000 British Americans were living on a strip of land along the ocean, only fifty miles across at its widest.

Then came the great immigrations of the eighteenth century.

Heretofore most of the pioneers had come from England. Now they began pouring in from every corner of the Old World: Germans from the little principalities along the Rhine, Scots-Irish from the northern counties of Ireland, French Huguenots fleeing from the persecutions of Catholic France, Jews happy to leave behind them the ghettos of Prague and Frankfurt. Some stopped at the seaports to become merchants, professional men, and laborers. Others trooped westward. Felling trees and Indians as they went, they built up the "backcountry" and pushed the frontier to the Appalachian Mountains.

By 1750 British America had over a million people and was doubling in size every twenty years. Visitors coming from England for the first time were startled at what they saw. Many expected to find a barely literate populace living in mean little communities bounded by ferocious animals and hostile Indians. They found instead cultivated fields, neatly-laid-out villages, comfortable roadside inns, princely country estates, six respectable colleges, thirty public libraries, and four seaports as busy and opulent as any towns back home outside of great London itself.

With close to 25,000 inhabitants, two swiftly growing suburbs, and the second busiest waterfront in the British Empire, Philadelphia was colonial America's urban showplace. After it, in size, came cosmopolitan New York with twenty thousand inhabitants, cultured Boston with fifteen thousand, and aristocratic Charleston, South Carolina, with fourteen thousand.

For many years boundaries shifted frequently. Smaller provinces merged into larger ones or larger ones divided. Well before the middle of the eighteenth century, however, British America had become the thirteen colonies we remember so well.

Each had its legislature. It consisted as a rule of a lower house made up of delegates elected by the people and a smaller upper house or council whose members were usually named by the King or, as in Pennsylvania, by the "proprietor," to whom the sovereign had given the lands where the colony stood. Each had a governor, appointed by crown or proprietor, except in

Rhode Island and Connecticut, where this official was chosen by the voters.

Over the years the elected lawmakers had become much more influential than England had intended them to be. In theory, to be sure, the royal governors had great power. When they were displeased with what the elected legislators were doing, they could prorogue or dissolve the assembly by ordering its members to adjourn and go home. They could also veto legislation or send it to England to be disallowed by the King.

In practice they exercised their authority sparingly. The colonials insisted that only their elected representatives had the right to pay royally appointed governors and other officials. Most of the governors needed their salaries. Few of them argued overmuch with the purse-holding tribunes of the people.

When they did argue, they often lost. The colonial era offers numerous examples of confrontations between royal governors and elected lawmakers with the crown-appointed dignitaries backing off in the end.

For generations these disputes came and went without putting an undue strain on the ties that bound colonies to mother country. A contented people for the most part, few Americans resented being the subjects of a distant monarch.

Then, in 1754, came the last of the Old French Wars. Known in Europe as the Seven Years' War and in America as the French and Indian War, it was the fourth conflict within the century to find Great Britain and France battling for the upper hand in North America.

On the eve of the struggle, New France (the domain of the Bourbon kings in America) was extensive. The fleur-de-lis flew over most of what is now Canada. On the Gulf of Mexico, guarding the mouth of the Mississippi River, stood the little French city of New Orleans. Between New Orleans and the Great Lakes the French beaver trappers and fur traders trod the lush forests of the Mississippi and Ohio River Valleys with the arrogance of men convinced that they were on their own premises.

Bad blood between British America and New France was as old as they were. Religion was responsible for much of it. The people of New France were Roman Catholic, and to American Protestants "papacy"—their name for the Catholic Church—was a synonym for tyranny. Another source of mutual dislike was France's unending effort to occupy areas west of the Appalachian mountain ranges which the Americans regarded as belonging to them. Still another was the skill of the French in attracting to their cause the original occupants of the land, the Indians.

Both groups traded with the Indian. Both trespassed on his hunting grounds and cheated him in transactions for the purchase of his goods. On the whole the English were fairer to him—but the French were warmer. To the average British American the feather-bedizened king of the woods was an inferior being, to be dealt with only when necessary and at arm's length. The hardy French hunters and traders treated him as an equal. They shared his lodgings, adopted his customs, and married his women. Their priests patiently converted him to Christianity. Their governors in the fortress-capital of New France at Quebec welcomed him into their council chambers.

Some of the tribes avenged themselves on the English by pillaging and burning their border communities. They rewarded the French by becoming their military allies. To dwellers on the frontiers of British America the most chilling sound in the lonely wilderness night was a war whoop. The greatest affliction was a band of rampaging Indians, drunk on French rum and armed with French guns.

The last of the Old French Wars began when in western Pennsylvania a band of French soldiers clashed with a detachment of Americans commanded by a twenty-two-year-old Virginian named George Washington. Not until 1756 did France and England make the contest official. Thereafter it was an international war. In Europe it was primarily Britain against France. In the New World, England and her American subjects confronted the French and their Indian allies.

For three years both struggles went badly for the English. Then the tide changed, thanks largely to the administrative genius of William Pitt, England's wartime Prime Minister. In 1759, on the Plains of Abraham high above the St. Lawrence River, an English army captured Quebec. With the signing of the peace treaty four years later Britain became the ruler of a vastly expanded empire. Among its new possessions were Canada, with sixty thousand French inhabitants, and all but a tiny corner of what is now the United States between the Appalachians and the Mississippi River.

There were celebrations on both sides of the Atlantic. The English rejoiced because after a century of warfare they had broken the power of France in the New World. The colonials rejoiced because their old enemy to the north was gone.

Neither the English nor the Americans would have lifted the brimming tankard in jubilant toast had they been able to foresee the future. It was the problems spawned during the last of the Old French Wars that only a little more than a decade hence would inspire the "thirteen clocks . . . to strike together."

## 2

# The Not So Gentle Shepherd

I N 1763 a dry little man named George Grenville became
Prime Minister of England and doggedly set about trying to
rescue his country from the mess into which her glorious victory
over France had got her.

The war had doubled England's national debt to 140 million
pounds. A postwar economic depression showed no signs of
abating. An effort by the government to raise funds by taxing
cider, a favorite drink of the common people, had brought cries
of distress from the rural poor, threats of violence from the
unruly street mobs of London.

Awesome burdens rested on George Grenville's bony shoulders, already stooped by chronic arthritis. Somehow he must
refill His Majesty's coffers without further taxing His Majesty's
already heavily taxed subjects.

Under British tradition the head of the government came
from either the House of Lords or the House of Commons.*
Grenville sat in the Commons. When he rose to speak there,
even his most faithful followers stretched out to snooze on the
green cloth of the tiered benches along the wall.

He was a man of many words, all of them delivered in the
bleating voice that had earned him his nickname, "The Gentle
Shepherd." King George III shuddered whenever Grenville
came to visit him at St. James Palace.

"First he talks at me steadily for two hours," His Majesty

* Today all are members of Commons.

complained, "and then he looks at his watch to see if he can spare the time to weary me for another hour."

In short, the leader of the British government had no flair for leadership. What he brought to his high office was a talent that in 1763 was even more badly needed. Grenville knew more about the mysteries of finance than any man in England.

Unfortunately all he knew about the Americans was that they had benefited greatly from the French and Indian War. It followed that they should help pay for it. At the very least they should support the ten thousand regular soldiers Great Britain had left in the New World to discourage France from reclaiming her lost territories and to help put down the Indian troubles still flickering along American frontiers.

Financial stringency was not new to England. Twenty years before, another prime minister had been urged to relieve an economic crisis by taxing the colonials. Canny old Robert Walpole waved the suggestion aside. He noted that the Americans purchased a third of England's exports, about 16 million pounds' worth a year. He said that taxing his country's best customers would have to be done by a government head "less fond of commerce and more courageous than I am."

Now the step that one prime minister had sagely avoided another all too courageously undertook. Even stubborn George Grenville might have refrained had it not been for the presence on his desk of twenty-six flourishingly inscribed documents.

These documents were reports that British leaders had requested from the royal governors in America. Why was it, they asked the governors, that the duties taken in by the British customs officers at colonial seaports were not even large enough to cover the costs of collecting them?

The governors' answers were long and heavy with statistics. All of them, however, could be summed up in a single word: smuggling.

According to one governor the colonial merchants were "natural-born smugglers." They evaded paying British-imposed duties on imports in one of two ways. They sneaked the forbidden goods past the customs officers who were honest and bribed those who were not.

"If Care be not soon taken to cure this growing Mischief," one governor lamented, "the proper Dependence" of the colonies "on their Mother Country will . . . 'ere long be lost."

One can imagine the "tut-tuts" fluttering George Grenville's thin lips as he read these revelations. Clearly the time was at hand to show the impudent colonials that Mother England was still in charge.

Across the sea went orders that converted British warships in American waters into revenue cutters. Soon sixty-four-gun vessels were poking their wooden bows into thousands of little inlets along the Atlantic coast. Customs officials roamed the colonial waterfronts, hunting for illegal goods. In their hands were the dreaded writs of assistance—general search warrants that permitted them to break into a man's warehouse or home at any hour, on any pretext, without warning.

Previously, save for a short time during the French and Indian War, England had been lax about enforcing her Acts of Trade and Navigation. At first her sudden surge of efficiency stunned the colonial merchants into silence. When they recovered their voices, protest rolled across the American landscape.

The threnody of complaint enlarged as it became apparent that the Gentle Shepherd had only just begun to chastise his American flock. Out of Parliament tumbled a sheaf of new laws. One of them, called the Sugar Act, reduced a long-detested import duty, but standing out from its thick legal terminology were words offensive to every American—the unequivocal statement that the purpose of the Sugar Act was *to raise a revenue for the use of His Majesty's government!*

Howls coursed the colonial world when the Sugar Act appeared. Audible as these responses were, they were whispers compared with those that arose when word reached the colonies that Parliament was about to pass what would become the Stamp Act of 1765.

Here was England's first and only attempt to extract money from the American people by means of an "internal" or direct tax. The law ordered the colonists to use stamped paper for all legal and commercial transactions. No suits could be filed in court until the parties had bought stamps for every document involved. No vessel loaded with Rhode Island rum or Virginia tobacco could leave an American wharf until the captain's clearance papers bore the requisite symbol. None of the colonies' twenty-seven newspapers could appear without displaying a handsomely designed stamp showing the royal insignia, the crown and the orb, and the legend, *Honi soit qui mal y pense*, "Shame on him who thinks evil of it."

The people of England had been paying such a tax since 1694. Sale of the stamps had proved a good source of income for the government. George Grenville was cheered by the thought of what a similar levy might produce in prosperous America.

Late in 1763 he began conferring with Benjamin Franklin of Philadelphia and other spokesmen for the colonies in London. Did they think the Americans would accept a stamp tax? Some thought they would, some were dubious. Even those who anticipated resistance were staggered by the size of that resistance when it came.

# 3

# Crisis

DURING THE OPENING WEEKS of May 1765, Williamsburg, Virginia, tiny capital of the largest of the thirteen colonies, was all sunny contentment and pastoral quiet.

In an airy chamber on the first floor of the wine-red capitol the House of Burgesses, elective branch of the legislature, was in session. Ordinarily this event sent the population from two thousand to twice that many, crowded the town's taverns, and agitated the tongues of its politically minded inhabitants.

But it was common knowledge that this session of the assembly would be dull and brief. So far as anyone knew there were only two orders of business.

One was a financial bill, so complex that it was of no interest to the local gossips. It was disposed of quickly.

The only other important matter was a measure intended to help the tobacco growers. The tobacco market had been bad in recent years, and the tall, big-boned representative from Frederick County, George Washington,* was pleased when the bill passed the House, received the approval of the Council of State (the upper branch of the legislature), and went on to the palace to be signed by the royal governor.

At this point most of the Burgesses began leaving Williamsburg for their homes—Washington among them, it would seem,

---

* Washington's home, Mount Vernon, was in Fairfax County, but in 1765 he was still sitting for Frederick, where he also owned property. Later he ran for Fairfax, and represented that county for the remainder of his fifteen-year legislative career.

since we have no comment from him on the sensational events about to take place.

Of the 116 Burgesses only forty were in their seats when on the afternoon of the twenty-sixth one of them moved that the House consider the "resolutions of the . . . Commons of Great Britain relative to the charging of certain Stamp duties in . . . America."

The quickly spreading news of this motion smote the ears of the people of Williamsburg like a clap of thunder. No one had expected a development of such magnitude during this lack-luster gathering of the legislature.

During the session of the year before, word had reached the little capital that Prime Minister Grenville was drafting a Stamp Act. The Burgesses had promptly sent His Majesty a polite petition stating that all Virginians would regard such a levy as subversive of their "Liberties, Franchises, and Immunities."

Since then scarcely another syllable concerning the rumored tax had been heard in Williamsburg. Now suddenly, and without warning, the issue was being noisily argued in the brightly polished chamber of the House of Burgesses.

The first man to speak on it was a newcomer to the House, a ferret-faced young attorney named Patrick Henry from one of the poorer "upcountry" counties.

Henry asked the Burgesses to adopt some proposals that he had scribbled on a blank page of an old lawbook. Four of the resolves encountered no serious opposition. The fifth one created an uproar, and in the course of the debate two more resolves mysteriously appeared, introduced apparently by other men. In the opinion of the soberer heads among the Burgesses, these propositions were a tissue of rudeness. One resolve went so far as to declare that any Virginian who helped enforce a stamp act or even simply went along with it "shall be deemed an Enemy to this His Majesty's Colony."

On the afternoon of the thirtieth, a hot and humid day, Patrick Henry again took the floor, this time to defend the more inflammatory of what had become seven resolves in all.

The House was meeting as a Committee of the Whole. No record of its proceedings was being kept, but the open space between the sunlit lobby of the chamber and its rear benches was jammed with onlookers. A young law student answering to the name of Thomas Jefferson had spent the earlier part of the day showing the sights of Williamsburg to a visitor from France. He and his guest were there and many others.

No verbatim text of Patrick Henry's speech that afternoon exists, but many who heard it later testified to its effect. When the unsmiling statesman from the little upcountry town of Hanover addressed himself to a subject close to his heart, the result was not a speech but a performance. His listeners were lifted out of themselves. Suddenly they were hearing in stirring language what was to become the great credo of the Revolution. Henry said that by the labor of their hands and minds the colonials had earned the right to control their own destiny. A parliament sitting three thousand miles away and ignorant of the problems of Virginia could no longer lay down the law for America.

The name of Jefferson's guest has not come down to us, but his firsthand description of the speech has. "Henery," as the Frenchman spelled the name, asked his auditors to recall that in the 1640's the leader of England's Puritan revolution, Oliver Cromwell, had sent King Charles I to die on the scaffold. Other mighty rulers had similarly fallen.

"Charles I had his Cromwell," thundered the orator, "Caesar had his Brutus, and George III . . .!"

The veteran Speaker of the House, John Robinson, blanched, lowered his gavel, and rapped out a one-word ruling.

"Treason!" he shouted.

Henry's vibrant voice hung momentarily in mid-air. Then: ". . . and George the Third may profit by their example!" he declared. "If *this* be treason make the most of it!"*

---

* The only firsthand account of this speech, that of Jefferson's French guest, does not describe Henry as uttering this defiant phrase. According to the Frenchman, Henry apologized to Speaker Robinson and assured him

For two more days the uproar prevailed. Unaware that the measure they were protesting had already become law, the Burgesses first adopted five of the seven Virginia Resolves. Then, getting cold feet, they settled for the four least defiant of them.

Meanwhile, someone had sped the resolves northward. On June 24 they burst upon the already excited New England public in the columns of the *Newport* (Rhode Island) *Mercury*. Accompanying them was a story that left the impression that the Virginia Burgesses had adopted all seven of them. Picked up by other newspapers, Patrick Henry's proposals were soon the talk of every colony.

From the Appalachians to the seaboard, from Boston to Charleston, a fury of dissent broke out. Merchants canceled existing orders for British goods and served notice that unless the Stamp Act was withdrawn they would stop all purchases from the mother country. Gathering at their clubs and taverns, thousands of people pledged themselves to consume no English products until the baleful excise disappeared.

In every major city rioting throngs poured into the streets, shouting regional variations of a slogan first heard in Mother England a century earlier: "No taxation without representation!" Converging under selected oaks and elms, soon to be known as Liberty Trees, the noisy crowds hanged their royal governors and the Gentle Shepherd in effigy. *Pro Patria,* proclaimed a menacing poster from walls and fences, *The first man that . . . makes use of the Stampt paper, let him take care of his House, Person and Effects. Vox Populi. We Dare.*

In New York the newly appointed commander in chief of the British forces in America, Lieutenant General Thomas Gage, noticed something peculiar about the behavior of the brawling mobs. He reported to his superiors in London that the "plan of

---

that he meant no treason. About fifty years later William Wirt, publishing what purported to be the texts of Patrick Henry's speeches, added the "If this be treason" line. Too bad! If Henry didn't say it, he should have.

the People of property" in New York was "to raise the lower class to prevent Execution of the law."

In every city it was the lower classes who rioted. The few merchants and other "People of property" who participated in the tumults did so in disguise. Mostly they directed the riots from the secrecy of their homes and stores.

Again and again swarms of citizens would appear on the city streets, raise a deafening rumpus, and then suddenly, as though on signal, melt away. Only occasionally did the gangs escape from the control of their hidden masters. In Boston one night, a "hellish crew" gutted the townhouse of scholarly Thomas Hutchinson, lieutenant governor and chief justice of Massachusetts, president of the provincial Council and captain of Castle William, the island fortress in Boston harbor.

In an effort to make the act more palatable, the Grenville ministry permitted the agents of the colonies in London to select the officers who would distribute the stamps and collect the tax. None of the individuals named to these posts ever performed his duties. Infuriated neighbors saw to that. Many of the tax gatherers, having resigned with dignity in private, were forced to do it all over again, humiliatingly, in public.

College students, irked by the two-pound stamp required for both matriculation and graduation, plied their professors with themes entitled "Oppression and Tyranny" and "All Men Are Free by the Law of Nature." Younger women did their part by renouncing suitors who failed to condemn the hated measure, older ones by refusing to make any further contribution to the colonial population until their pro-British husbands recanted and switched sides.

One alarmed crown-appointed officer noted that "the high sons of liberty" included "the ministers of the gospel who instead of preaching to their flocks meekness, sobriety, . . . and a steady obedience to the laws of Britain, belch from the pulpits liberty . . ."

America's independent ministers (those not connected with

the established Episcopalian or Anglican church of England) had been belching liberty for generations. Back in 1750, Jonathan Mayhew had told his congregation at West Church, Boston, that "neither God nor nature has given man a right of dominion over any society independently of that society's approbation and consent to be governed by him . . . disobedience is not only lawful but glorious to those that enjoin things that are inconsistent with the demands of God."

To many colonials, equipped with little or no formal schooling, their churches were halls of learning as well as places of worship. Sitting at the feet of liberal ministers, large numbers of them had long since acquired their most important weapon as revolutionaries—a philosophical justification for resisting the laws of the mother country. The idea of civil disobedience as a proper response to unjust legislation did not originate in the nineteenth-century writings of the American poet-naturalist Henry Thoreau. It was being preached by the independent clergy of colonial America almost two centuries before.

Combing the Scriptures, the ministers found there what they spoke of as "natural law." England's political writer John Locke best stated the essence of this doctrine. God, the doctrine said, had endowed man with certain inalienable rights—"life, liberty and property," according to Locke. A government that respected these rights was good and ought to be obeyed. One that did not was bad and should be resisted.

Not all members of the British Parliament were in favor of the Stamp Act. Under the high, open-beamed ceiling of Old St. Stephen's Chapel—meeting room of the House of Commons—eloquent voices spoke for America.

None was more effective than that of William Pitt. In 1765 the "Great Commoner" was nearing sixty, a tall, gaunt figure with the face of a hawk and the manners of a cultured buccaneer. Gout and melancholia had aged him before his time, but his singular abilities were still in evidence as he arose to remind his colleagues that "the Americans are the sons, not the bastards, of England."

No friend of America at Westminster questioned England's legal right to tax her colonial subjects; but why, Pitt demanded, should the British jeopardize their invaluable trade with the colonies in return for a "peppercorn" of tax revenue? Another parliamentarian, brawny Colonel Isaac Barré, called the aroused Americans "sons of liberty."

Barré's shining phrase sailed across the Atlantic to become the name of the popular societies springing into action in every province. Most of these patriot groups were composed of the lower classes. In Boston their smoky meeting rooms helped supply Sam Adams with the revolutionary street gangs he would later manipulate with telling effect. In Charleston the white-haired merchant-prince, Christopher Gadsden, found among the carpenters, house painters, saddlers, and blacksmiths belonging to the Sons of Liberty the muscle he needed to achieve his long-nurtured desire for an America free of British control.

These popular societies would disappear before the outbreak of war, but the term "liberty boys" would continue to attach itself to active rebels. The Stamp Act crisis brought still other terms into the colonial vocabulary. People began speaking of the patriots as "Whigs," the name of the loose political aggregation chiefly responsible for having shifted the political power of Mother England from the palace of the King to the halls of Parliament. Those who remained pro-British called themselves loyalists—and the Whigs called them "Tories," the name applied in the mother country to the King's supporters.

Even before the Virginia Resolves leaped from the pages of a Rhode Island newspaper, the legislators of Massachusetts had acted. They had called on the other colonies to send representatives to a congress in New York. The Congress was to draw up "a general and united, dutiful, loyal and humble Representation of their Condition to His Majesty and the Parliament," and "to implore relief."

Nine colonies responded. On October 7, 1765—three weeks before the Stamp Act became effective—twenty-seven delegates gathered in a stuffy chamber of Manhattan's City Hall on Wall Street. They had come to the city on horseback or by boat or in high-slung carriages, wearing gold or silver lace on their hats and flaring coats, sky-blue or plum or some shade of drab in color. Almost daily for three weeks they met with the din of New York's roving liberty boys providing a dramatic background to their deliberations.

There was much timidity among the members of this gathering and little unanimity. Not untypical was the New York delegation: two Whigs, two unavowed Tories, and one neutral. Even the delegation from patriotic Massachusetts contained a loyalist. He had been instructed by the royal authorities there to see to it that nothing as disastrous as the Virginia Resolves came out of the Stamp Act Congress.

What emerged was even more drastic. Easily the most important thing about the petition drafted by the Congress in New York was what it did not say. It contained no reference to "external" taxes as distinct from "internal" ones. It simply stated that in America the imposing of *any* tax was the exclusive right of the colonial legislatures.

As a solution to the tax problem George Grenville had suggested that Parliament permit the colonies to send representatives to its elective branch. The Stamp Act delegates "dutifully, loyally and humbly" pointed out that with three thousand miles of ocean to cross, the Americans could not be properly "represented in the House of Commons in Great Britain." Three copies of the petition were rushed to Whitehall, as the offices of the British government leaders in London were collectively known. One was for King George, another for the Commons, a third for the House of Lords.

Crown and Parliament alike ignored them. But Parliament could not ignore a development within the borders of England itself. In the great trading centers of the kingdom—in London, Liverpool, Manchester, and Bristol—fur-hatted merchants were scanning their accounts with narrowing eyes.

Across the sea nine hundred New England, New York, New

Jersey, and Pennsylvania merchants had put their names to an agreement to import no goods from England. No machinery for enforcing their pledges existed; some abided by them and some did not, but the overall effect was devastating. Already American purchases of British products were down almost 50 percent.

Into the House of Commons rolled petitions from frightened businessmen, memorials beseeching that body to eliminate a law that was ruining English commerce.

The Grenville ministry had fallen, a victim of internal politics unconnected with America. To the new ministry headed by the pro-American Marquis of Rockingham fell the honor of asking Parliament to withdraw the Stamp Act.

It happened on February 22, 1766. William Pitt put the motion that "the stamp act . . . be repealed absolutely totally, immediately." Off the statute books it slid.

Copies of the Act of Repeal were in America the following May and in the shops along King Street, Charleston, and Broadway, New York, the demand for busts of the "immortal Pitt" far exceeded the supply. From London to a political crony in Philadelphia came a warning from Benjamin Franklin. He suggested that the rejoicings over repeal be "subdued and seemly" in order to "give the lie" to a spreading feeling among the British that the colonists were forgetting the "filial gratitude" due to the new and pro-American ministry in London.

The merchants of the Quaker City comported themselves accordingly. At a banquet in the statehouse they toasted "the growing greatness of the British Empire." Then they voted to give their homespun suits to the poor and buy new ones "of Broad Cloth made in England" to wear on the King's next birthday.

Elsewhere there were bonfires, parades, and frolics. In Hartford, Connecticut, the fanfaronade cost six men their lives when the schoolhouse where they were making fireworks for the occasion blew up. In New York (if we may trust a loyalist observer) the liberty boys and the Friendly Sons of St. Patrick toasted one another at Fraunces Tavern. Then they took to the streets, to spend the evening hours "throwing Squibbs, Crackers, firing of muskets and pistols, breaking of . . . windows and forcing off the knockers of . . . Doors."

Reports of these delirious antics were soon in England, where they planted bitter seed. In Liverpool and other trading cities the merchants bristled. After all it was *they* who had procured the nullification of the Stamp Act. Now, it would seem the Americans were taking all of the credit. Many a Bristol or Manchester businessman, previously sympathetic to the colonials, began to heed those who were saying that the time had come to put those insolent Americans in their place.

Innumerable Britons were baffled by the insistence of the Americans that a legislative body should reflect the will of the people. In 1765 the English Parliament made no pretense of doing that. It would not even begin to do so for another sixty-seven years.

As the result of a number of internal revolutions, the government of England had long since ceased to be an absolute monarchy—a fact worth stressing if only to eliminate the romantic notion that the American Revolution was a battle against royal tyranny.

This is not to say, however, that in the eighteenth century the government of England was a democracy. Not at all. It was a parliamentary aristocracy. The country was ruled jointly by the King and by the relatively small upper-class group known as the gentry. This situation prevailed even in the House of Commons, whose largely upper-class members represented not individuals but interest groups. Some members spoke for the large landowners or squires, some for other elements of the upper class. Others spoke for the merchants, and a few, at least in theory, represented the country's workers. Many of the larger industrial communities did not even have the right to send delegates to Westminster.

A farmer in Herefordshire spoke for thousands of English yeomen (property owners ranking just beneath the gentry) in a letter to the *London Chronicle*. Signing himself John Ploughshare, he wrote that when he heard that "the Americans were declaring openly that the Parliament of England had no right to tax them" because they were not represented there, he was "as much astonished as if a field where I had sowed barley should turn up pease." Wrote Ploughshare:

I am not represented, and there are millions of Englishmen . . . who have no more share in the elections of Members of Parliament than the Man of the Moon, and I believe that we notwithstanding pay the greatest part of the taxes. I, for my part, don't desire that it should be otherwise. We are very well in this Country if we could but think so. But I fear our folly and restlessness will not suffer us to remain long in our present condition:—If these new-fashioned doctrines get once into the people's heads, they won't be easily got out again.

In America the "new-fashioned doctrines" had indeed wormed themselves into many heads. The crisis having come and gone, the inhabitants of the thirteen colonies would never be quite the same again.

The Stamp Act Congress had made no impression on the British government, but from Portsmouth on the Piscataqua River in New Hampshire to the tiny settlements near the mouth of the Savannah in Georgia, people marveled that representatives of most of the colonies had not only conferred—an event that had happened before—but had actually agreed on something.

For those of us who know only twentieth-century America it is hard to realize how bitter the relations among the original colonies were.

Prior to 1765 there were no Americans in America. There were Virginians and Pennsylvanians. Both of the commonwealths to which these people belonged laid claim to the lands spreading west and north from their mountain borders. When a group of Virginia land speculators organized the Ohio Company and obtained from the King 500,000 acres south of what is now Pittsburgh, the Pennsylvanians trapping furs in that region took umbrage. Circulating among their Indian associates they urged them to murder any Virginians who came west with the idea of settling the Ohio Company's newly acquired territory.

There were New Yorkers, Rhode Islanders, and Massachusetts Bay colonists. To a New York newspaper Boston was "the common sewer of America." To the *Boston Gazette* the little province bestriding beautiful Narragansett Bay was "the filthy, nasty, dirty colony of Rhode Island."

There were New Englanders and Carolinians. In Boston, Hartford, and Newport it was an article of faith that the cavaliers of the South dwelt in the "Stygian darkness of irreligiosity." In high-living Charleston lace-fringed gentlemen shuddered whenever their minds turned to the "well-known addiction" of the New England Puritans to "the ravening sins of levelling and democracy."

Geography contributed much to this divisiveness. Good roads were scarce. The royal postal system remained poky and uncertain even after capable Ben Franklin became its guiding spirit. In an era when people traveled mostly by ship, Charlestonians felt closer to London than to New York.

The Stamp Act crisis did not tumble the barriers between the colonies but it breached them. For the first time the big public markets in the cities began featuring products displaying the word "American." Patriotic housewives testified to the excellence of a new drink labeled "American porter," to the tastiness of a curdled milk known as "American clabber."

"What a Blessing to us has the Stamp Act eventually . . . proved," Sam Adams would say years later. ". . . when the colonies saw the Common Danger they at the same time saw their mutual Dependence."

The fall of the Stamp Act did not remove all points of difference between colonies and mother country. The Sugar Act remained on the books, but alongside the now-vanished Stamp Act this and other unpopular English laws were bearable.

To the law banishing the despised stamps Parliament had attached a reservation known as the Declaratory Act. This measure categorically affirmed the right of the British government to tax its colonial subjects. Americans wondered: Was the Declaratory Act a face-saving gesture or a portent of worse to come?

In Charleston the zealous merchant-patriot Christopher Gadsden summoned a group of workingmen to his "neat cottage, built of cypress." Calling their attention to the Declaratory Act, he urged them to maintain their vigilance against the "designs" of the British rulers. He prophesied that America's troubles with the mother country were not yet over.

They weren't. As the year 1766 waned into its successor, new schemes for getting money by taxing the colonists were hatching in the mind of dapper Charles Townshend, one of the most fascinating (and exasperating) men ever to put his hand to the tiller of His Majesty's government in London.

# 4

# Champagne Charley and Farmer Dickinson

THE SECOND SON of an English peer, a tall and well-built man with luminous eyes in a swarthy countenance, Charles Townshend was brilliant, witty, knowledgeable, charming, and unencumbered by principles. In the coffee houses of London he was known as "Champagne Charley," a fitting nickname for a man of his bubbly good humor. A member of Parliament since 1747, he had maneuvered himself in and out of important government posts, chiefly by managing somehow to be on all sides of all questions at all times.

His big moment came in the summer of 1766 when conditions at Westminster forced the Marquis of Rockingham and his fellow ministers to retire and another band of fumblers to take over the British government.

Repeal of the Stamp Act proved to be a boon to English trade but it left His Majesty's coffers as empty as ever. In an effort to relieve this uncomfortable situation, King George asked the country's most popular man, William Pitt, once again to form a ministry.

Pitt selected Charles Townshend as his Chancellor of the Exchequer, the key cabinet post under the circumstances, as its holder was responsible for financial policy.

In agreeing to head a new ministry, the Great Commoner assured the King that he would devote "his life, body, heart and mind" to solving his country's problems. In 1766, unfortunately, William Pitt's "life, body, heart and mind" all were failing; he was tired and sick, at intervals seemingly demented. Accepting an elevation to the peerage that made him the Earl of Chatham, he retired to the quietude of the House of Lords—and lost control of the ministry he had formed. Into the vacuum thus created stepped breezy, ambitious Charles Townshend.

Townshend's first official act was to propose that the wartime tax on land, four shillings to the pound, be retained. For months the landowning squires who dominated the House of Commons had been clamoring for tax relief. In what amounted to legislative mutiny they ignored the new minister's proposal and lowered the land tax to three shillings.

Tradition decreed that when the Commons defeated an important measure the minister who had sponsored it should resign. But Charles Townshend could laugh off anything, including tradition.

Instead of leaving the cabinet, he put his finger into the air to determine the prevailing wind. He swiftly discovered how things stood with the influential squires. They were beginning to repent of having withdrawn the Stamp Act. Stories reaching London pictured the Americans as wallowing in prosperity—galling news to English country gentlemen overwrought with debts and taxes.

It was plain to Charles Townshend that he could solidify his shaky position by finding some way of making the Americans pay the difference lost to His Majesty's treasury by the reduction of the land tax. To this end he presented to Parliament what would be known officially as the Revenue Act of 1767, unofficially as the Townshend Acts.

Defending his revenue measure, Townshend pointed out that he had avoided George Grenville's mistake. The Gentle Shepherd had asked the Americans to pay an *internal* tax. Townshend's measure called for *external* taxes only—duties on goods that the English merchants regularly exported to the colonies, chiefly lead, paint, paper, glass, and tea. Townshend said airily that the Americans had paid duties before; surely they would do so again.

In advancing this argument, the flamboyant Chancellor of the

Exchequer overlooked the petitions that the Stamp Act Congress had sent to London. Those documents made the American position clear: A tax was a tax. External or internal, if it came from the British Parliament, it faced certain challenge in the colonies.

Perhaps Charles Townshend had never read the Stamp Act Congress declarations. Perhaps no top British official had. On the eve of the Revolution the authorities in London were notably derelict about their homework. Had they legislated less and studied America more, the next ten years might have been less jolting to them—and to England.

The Revenue Act of 1767 was loaded with provisions that its maker should have known the Americans would find unacceptable. One of the most sacred political doctrines among the colonists was that only their provincial legislators had the power to pay crown-appointed officials. Now the Chancellor of the Exchequer proposed to make such officials independent of colonial control by setting aside the proceeds of the Townshend duties to take care of their salaries.

In June 1767 Parliament voted the new revenue measure. The King signed it with pleasure, and in July the Townshend Acts began their westward journey across the Atlantic.

Their creator would not live to witness the consequence of his labors. Even Charles Townshend could not chuckle away the inevitable. In July the City of London honored him at a gala, and in September he died "of a neglected fever" at the age of forty-two.

Although America's reactions to the Townshend duties were eventually as effective as those that had brought down the stamp tax, they developed more slowly and with less hue and cry.

Chiefly responsible for this comparatively hesitant response were the colonial merchants. In 1765 these gentlemen had marched in the vanguard of resistance to parliamentary rule. This time they were slow to mobilize. They remembered too well the drunken frenzies of the Stamp Act mobs. They wanted no more violence and destruction. During the Stamp Act crisis they had been the prime movers in the fight with England, but as colonial resistance to the Townshend Acts gradually took form, they made no effort to lead it. As a result, direction of the opposition fell to adherents of the popular party—to men like Sam Adams of Boston and Christopher Gadsden of Charleston.

The objectives of the merchants were limited. Most of them asked for nothing more than deliverance from British laws that threatened their profits. Men like Adams and Gadsden were looking for something bigger. Their goal was total home rule, and if England would not go along with that, then separation from her.

Adams at his end of the country and Gadsden at his end needled and harangued, but the spark that converted a simmering anger at the Townshend Acts into militant opposition did not come from the independence-minded radicals. It came from a rich Philadelphia aristocrat whose affection for Mother England was only slightly less deep than his hatred of unjust legislation. His part in the battle began on December 2, 1767, when a Philadelphia newspaper, the *Pennsylvania Chronicle,* published the first of a series of articles called *Letters from a Farmer in Pennsylvania to the Inhabitants of the British Colonies.* The articles appeared over a pen name, but every reader knew at once that "the Farmer" was John Dickinson.

No farmer in truth but one of the ornaments of the Philadelphia bar, John Dickinson was thirty-five that winter, a tall and ethereally handsome man with narrow shoulders and a high head. Dickinson's career would win him many critics. He would be called the "Hamlet of the American Revolution," a brilliant but "vacillating" man "who by drawing back from critical decisions" compromised his "potential greatness." This not unjust appraisal rested on his refusal, while a member of the Continental Congress, to vote for the Declaration of Independence on the grounds that the timing was wrong, that an honorable reconciliation with England was still possible as late as 1776.

Whatever Dickinson's shortcomings, cowardice and dishonesty were not among them. During the war of the Revolution he would see action in the American armies both as an officer and a private. When after the war an artist asked permission to do a portrait of him for inclusion in a larger picture of the signing of the Declaration of Independence, he declined to sit. "The truth," he explained, "is that I opposed making the Declaration . . . at the time it was made. I cannot be guilty of so false an ambition as to seek for any share in the fame of that council."

Born to wealth on a Maryland plantation, Dickinson received his early education from private tutors and studied law in London before settling in Philadelphia, where he quickly became a prominent member of the local aristocracy.

The circumstances under which his *Farmer's Letters* reached print are eloquent of the sinuous ways of revolutionary endeavor. One of the backers of the *Pennsylvania Chronicle,* where the articles originated, was hotheaded Joseph Galloway, America's leading loyalist. Galloway's purpose in establishing the *Chronicle* was to provide an outlet for those opposed to any act likely to widen the breach with the mother country.

A newspaper needs an experienced editor and Galloway found one in a printer named William Goddard. He knew that Goddard was "ill-tempered" and "quarrelsome." What Galloway did not know was that he was also a rebel at heart. Taking advantage of a clause in his employment contract that bade him avoid "narrow political partisanship," Goddard gleefully opened the columns of the *Chronicle* to Dickinson's patriotic essays.

Tory Galloway could only fume. "Damned ridiculous . . . more fluff!" he exclaimed when the *Letters* came out. Philadelphia's pro-British aristocrats fumed with him. They called Dickinson a traitor to his class. They predicted that before long he would be egging on mobs and disturbing the peace like Sam Adams of Boston.

Actually Dickinson's *Letters* were bland. Nowhere in the Farmer's deftly reasoned paragraphs was there even a veiled suggestion that the colonies should part company with the parent state.

The portion of his *Letters* that lifted patriot hearts was a lawyer's brief. Going back to Magna Charta, to the Bill of Rights of 1689, and to other written instruments of the British constitution, the genteel Philadelphia attorney showed that under British law itself, acts of Parliament were not binding on the colonies.

It is hard to overrate Dickinson's contribution to the revolutionary spirit. The Protestant clergymen of British America, with their notion of natural law, had provided the colonists with a moral justification for their opposition to British tax legislation. Now Dickinson provided them with a legal justification for it. It was heartening to the rebels to hear from their spiritual leaders that their will was the will of God. It was equally encouraging to be assured by lawyer Dickinson that they stood on firm constitutional grounds.

They showed their gratitude by reading him. All but four of the colonial newspapers reprinted the *Farmer's Letters*. From his seat in the Massachusetts House of Representatives Sam Adams hastened to profit by the excitement that the *Letters* engendered. In February 1768 the archrebel wrote and the House adopted a circular letter urging the other colonies to join Massachusetts in a memorial to the King, denouncing the Townshend Acts as contrary to the "fundamental rules" of English law.

This attempt to unify colonial resistance fared poorly at first. Pennsylvania, where Joseph Galloway was Speaker of the Assembly, pointedly ignored the Massachusetts circular letter. By midsummer only three colonies had endorsed it. Sam Adams's unification movement might have withered away had not the leaders of His Majesty's government in London unwittingly come to its rescue.

The British government had recently set up within the cabinet a new post known as Secretary of State for the Colonies. Its first occupant, the Earl of Hillsborough, was as certain as George Grenville that England must take "no more nonsense from those arrogant Americans."

Hillsborough's response to Sam Adams's unification effort was to dispatch a circular letter of his own to the colonial legislatures. He instructed them to treat the Massachusetts circular letter "with the contempt it deserves."

Sam Adams himself could not have struck a stronger blow for the rebel cause. By the close of 1786, seven colonies had given their support to the Massachusetts circular letter. Even Joseph Galloway's minions in the Pennsylvania Assembly endorsed it, letting it be understood that no British minister could tell them what to do.

Lord Hillsborough sent a special letter to Francis Bernard, royal governor of Massachusetts. No more faithful servant of His Majesty than Bernard was to be found on either side of the Atlantic. Hillsborough told the governor to see to it that the Bay Colony lawmakers rescinded their "most dangerous and factious" circular letter at once.

Obediently Bernard placed the appropriate bill before the House—and in the most heavily attended session of its history, that body turned it down by a vote of 92 to 17.

Stunned by Boston's defiance, Lord Hillsborough took a dramatic step. He sent redcoats to occupy the city. Two regiments came from England, a third regiment, the wing of a fourth, and a train of artillery from Halifax, Britain's naval base in Nova Scotia. Up from New York came the British commander in chief in America, General Gage, to make certain his troops were properly billeted. Before returning to his Manhattan headquarters, Gage assured the people of Boston that their city was not under martial law. The soldiers were there merely to preserve order.

But there was no order. By night Sam Adams's mobsters staged hit-and-run attacks on isolated guard units. Women traversing the dark alleys of Boston would purposely bump into soldiers and then scream "Rape!" Street urchins hung on the heels of redcoats, shouting "Bloody backs!" and "Lobsters for sale!" Wherever Sam Adams went he carried a new atrocity story: An artilleryman had seduced the daughter of a wealthy merchant, a grenadier had beaten up a small boy.

Gage reduced the garrison to two regiments, but even with only one redcoat for every twenty-five citizens, the situation remained volcanic. On the crackling cold night of Monday, March 5, 1770, the unavoidable explosion occurred—the rowdy disorder that John Adams called "the battle of King Street" and that his propaganda-wise cousin, Sam Adams, renamed "the Boston Massacre."

There had been trouble over the weekend: fisticuffs between a private soldier and a ropewalk employee, a pitched battle between redcoats and dockworkers.

On Monday night the streets were full of restless people. On Brattle Street, about eight o'clock, a small boy sighted an officer of the 14th Regiment, a Captain Goldfinch, and took after him. The boy was an apprentice in the shop of Monsieur Piemont, the French barber.

Piemont had been doing a fine business during the occupation, making perukes for the English officers. His only complaint was that some of his high-ranking customers considered it beneath their dignity to pay the bills rendered by "a provincial tradesman." Goldfinch owed him a large sum. "Get the money from him," the barber told his apprentice, "and you can keep it."

Espying his prey, the enterprising boy went baying after him, shouting that the captain was a "cheat and a robber" and that his female ancestors were kennel-connected. There was a crowd on Brattle Street. Not wishing to start anything, the captain tried to give his diminutive tormenter the slip by hurrying over to King Street.

But there was a crowd there too. For an hour or more its members had been entertaining themselves by chucking snowballs, oyster shells, sea coal, and New England epithets at the lone redcoat, Private Hugh Montgomery, standing guard in front of the Town Hall (now the Old Statehouse). Montgomery had already had as much as he could take. The shrill accusations of the young barber's apprentice, still nipping at Captain Goldfinch's heels, was one annoyance too many.

Some stories have it that Montgomery cuffed the boy with his hand. Others say that he merely glared and that the boy ran screaming through the crowd, crying that the "bloody back" had struck him without provocation.

Whatever happened, the boy stirred the people. Closing in on Montgomery, they began yelling, "Kill him! Kill him!" The sentry, having loaded his gun, shouted back, "If you come near me, I'll blow your brains out."

By this time the aroused Bostonians had found a ringleader in a tall and fierce-looking black. This man, Crispus Attucks, was about forty-seven, a native of the nearby village of Framingham, Massachusetts. Early in life Attucks had shaken off the shackles of slavery by running away. He had gone to sea for a while, had then returned to his birthplace to work for a farmer who spoke highly of his abilities. He was a frequent visitor to the Boston waterfront, was well liked there.

On that freezing Monday night in King Street he had a pack of sailors at his heels and a stick in his hand. He kept waving the stick at Montgomery and threatening to separate the sentry from "one of your claws." Frightened and overwhelmed, Montgomery shouted in the direction of the barracks across the street, "Main guard, turn out!"

Out came seven redcoats led by Captain John Preston, the officer of the day. Lining his men up in front of Town Hall, Preston ordered them to prime and load.

A deafening din set in: catcalls, Indian whoops, bellowed curses. Barely audible among them came the commands "Present . . . Fire!" Who uttered the fatal words no one could ever say, only that they did not come from Captain Preston. Party or parties unknown mouthed them, and then the soldiers' muskets blazed.

Probably a dozen people fell, two of them mortally wounded,

three instantly killed—among the latter, big Crispus Attucks. As the last shots echoed away, British drums beat to arms and hundreds of musket-bearing redcoats poured into the street.

A few months earlier the royal governor, British-born Francis Bernard, had gone back to England in disgust, leaving the task of coping with rebellious Boston to his Boston-born lieutenant governor, Thomas Hutchinson. It was Hutchinson who now struggled through the still-muttering crowd and ascended to the Town Hall balcony.

He made a striking figure there, a tall man with a long, bold face and large dark eyes brimming with intelligence. Sam Adams and other Boston patriot leaders hated Hutchinson, but the people of the town still respected him. They fell silent as he began to speak. He assured them that the soldiers involved in this night's work would be placed on trial. Then he asked the people to go home, and they went.

The Battle of King Street was over, but Sam Adams would see to it that no American ever forgot it. For years to come, on the anniversary of the unhappy event, there would be memorial services, long orations categorizing the sins of those responsible for the "horrid massacre."

Sam Adams was a member of the committee that called on Lieutenant Governor Hutchinson on the morning after the tragedy. They made two demands. One was that Hutchinson send all of the British soldiers out of the city. Reluctantly the lieutenant governor ordered the two regiments to withdraw to Castle William, three miles out in the harbor.

The other demand was that Captain Preston and his guards go on trial for murder at once. Hutchinson said the law must take its course. Mercifully the course of the law was slow. The trial, months later, took place in a calmer time. Defended by two patriot attorneys, John Adams and Josiah Quincy, Preston and five of his men were acquitted of all charges. The remaining two guardsmen, convicted of manslaughter, were lightly punished.

Three thousand miles away from Boston—on the very day of

the "horrid massacre"—a British Parliament was doing to the Townshend Acts what a previous Parliament had done to the Stamp Act. Again the colonial merchants, albeit grudgingly this time, had made themselves felt.

Irked by Lord Hillsborough's policies and under constant pressure from Sam Adams's mobs, the Boston merchants had finally taken action. In March 1768 they had drawn up a tentative non-importation agreement. They pledged themselves to buy no English goods, provided the merchants of New York did the same. In April the New York merchants promised to go along as soon as those in Philadelphia did. In February 1769 the Philadelphians fell into line.

In Charleston the patriot leader Christopher Gadsen had been busy. By the time the South Carolina merchants joined the trade embargo in July, however, conditions in England were smoothing the way for the fall of Great Britain's second attempt to raise a revenue in the colonies through taxation.

Once more the merchants of Bristol and Manchester were complaining of falling sales. On February 10, 1770, fat and genial Frederick Lord North* formed the British government over which he would preside as His Majesty's chief minister for a dozen years.

One of the new Prime Minister's first official statements was that the late Charles Townshend's revenue act was "a preposterous measure." In April Parliament agreed with him. When the British lawmakers got through with the Townshend Acts, all that remained was a tiny duty on tea—kept alive as King George sententiously remarked, "to preserve England's right" to tax its colonial subjects at will.

During the ensuing fall most of the American merchants abandoned their non-importation agreements and happily went back to business as usual with England. From Connecticut a delighted royal official wrote home that "the people appear to

---

* The "Lord" was a courtesy title as in 1770 North was still legally and politically a commoner. The second son of the Earl of Guilford, he did not fall heir to the title until 1790.

be weary of their altercations with the mother-country." Even Governor Thomas Hutchinson of Massachusetts* took heart. He informed his superiors in London that he detected on all sides a disposition "to let the great quarrel subside."

Subside it did. What people later remembered as "the era of good feeling," a pleasant lull in the quarrel, had begun. Few Americans saw anything to worry about in the little tax remaining on tea. For the next three years most of them demonstrated their patriotism by eschewing English tea and by refreshing themselves instead with the cheaper brews smuggled in from Holland.

---

* Soon after the Boston Massacre, Hutchinson was promoted to governor.

# 5

# The Grand Incendiary

EVEN WHIGGISH BOSTON relaxed during the so-called "era of good feeling" between America and Mother England that followed the abolition of the Townshend duties in 1770. "In this town," said Governor Hutchinson, "if it were not for two or three Adamses, we should do well enough."

The principal person Hutchinson had in mind was Sam Adams, better known to his Tory opponents as "the Grand Incendiary." When during one of the autumn elections the archrebel came within a few votes of losing his seat in the House of Representatives, Hutchinson and his friends exulted. One of them predicted that the day was near when the archrebel would "vanish into that obscurity to which his vile deeds entitle him."

But Sam Adams was not the vanishing kind. He bent before the prevailing winds, but he kept his eyes on his objective, a Massachusetts free of interference from London.

The seeds of Sam Adams's rebellious nature are visible in his upbringing. His father, usually called "Deacon Sam" to distinguish him from his son, was a leader of the local "country" or popular party. His fine home on Purchase Street, where the younger Sam began life in 1722, was a meeting place for the champions of the people.

A frequent visitor there was outspoken Elisha Cooke, whose "fixt enmity to all kingly government" was well known. Deacon Sam and Cooke hated the Hutchinsons and the Olivers and the other Boston mercantile aristocrats. They hated their "prodigious snobbery," their ability to monopolize the royal patronage in Massachusetts by circulating among themselves the influential appointive jobs that only the King of England could fill.

When His Majesty requested the General Court to provide fixed salaries for the governor and other royal officeholders, the Deacon and Cooke helped beat back what they viewed as an attempt to destroy the legislature's sacred privilege of deciding what emoluments, if any, crown-appointed officials should receive.

They were less successful when they set out to rescue the common people from an economic depression. A chronic difficulty among the poor was the scarcity of gold and silver, aggravated by the refusal of the Boston merchants to let them pay their debts in the paper money issued by the colony.

The solution of Deacon Adams and Cooke was to set up a land bank with authority to issue paper money backed by real estate. Claiming that this scheme would put the political power of the colony in the hands of an "idle and extravagant . . . rabble," the merchants implored Parliament to dissolve the bank.

Parliament did so, an act that almost ruined Deacon Adams, as he had been a heavy stockholder in the enterprise. Young Sam would never forget his father's efforts to help the debtor classes of Massachusetts. Neither would he forget that it was a British Parliament that had destroyed the bank and impoverished his family.

Receiving the first of two degrees from Harvard in 1740, the younger Sam embarked on a sketchy commercial career. He got a job in a countinghouse, and lost it within a few months through inefficiency. His father lent him a thousand pounds to start his own firm. Sam gave half of it to a needy friend and frittered the rest away.

When the Deacon died in 1748, his unbusinesslike son became the owner of the family brewery. The brewery was burdened with debts, and its new proprietor was too busy elsewhere to do much about them. Sam Adams had begun his lifework; he had entered politics.

His first step was to organize a secret society composed of workers. Later he became a member of the inner ring of the powerful Caucus Club, which met regularly in a garret to "smoke tobacco . . . drink flip," and see to it that men friendly to the common people were elected to local and provincial offices.

His own first elective post was that of town scavenger. Later, in 1756, he became one of Boston's tax collectors. Nine years later his account showed a shortage of eight thousand pounds.

Sam's aristocratic foes labeled him "a common thief and an embezzler." After much effort they haled him into court. But Sam was the idol of the Boston masses and no jury would indict him.

Subsequent efforts by the townspeople to recover the moneys he owed were too halfhearted to be more than moderately successful. Meanwhile, the voters had given him another term as tax collector and would gladly have elected him forever had he not refused to run. It was plain to his supporters—and probably to his enemies as well—that none of the missing money ever soiled Sam Adams's pockets. By 1763 he was deeply in debt. His Purchase Street home had become a ruin, and he and the children of his first marriage were living on the generosity of his second wife.

In 1765 when Sam became a power in the Boston town meeting and a member of the provincial legislature, James Otis was the leader of the local radicals. But this Barnstable-born attorney had a strange wild streak. He tended to blow hot and cold on the issues, now attacking Parliament with unparalleled effectiveness, now defending it with equal vigor. When in 1769 he heard that a British customs commissioner had called him a traitor to the mother country, he invaded a club frequented by such officials, declared himself "insulted," and demanded "satisfaction." What he got was a blow on the head. From this injury he never fully recovered, and Sam Adams became the acknowledged leader of the Massachusetts Whigs.

Sunday always found the archrebel at Old South Church, earnestly and sweetly singing the hymns. On workdays his slight and boyish figure could be seen now here, now there, moving unhurriedly from one Boston tavern to another, recruiting wharfingers and other workmen for his rebel street gangs, tirelessly playing the role for which we best remember him, that of the great ward heeler of the Revolution.

He did not confine his powers of persuasion to members of the lower class. He realized that a revolution requires brains as well as brawn, wealth as well as willing hands. His biggest "catch" was John Hancock, whose fine stone house on Beacon Hill had the sweep of Boston Common for its front yard.

On the eve of the Stamp Act crisis, Sam discovered that the young merchant was unhappy in spite of his riches. Nicknamed "the Peacock" because of his strut, Hancock longed for the adulation of the crowds, for the limelight of public office. Sam controlled the votes that the Peacock needed. When the pursy dandy was elected to the legislature, the archrebel told his cousin John Adams that the "town has done a wise thing today . . . They made that young man's fortune their own."

These were not idle words. Soon after Hancock's first victory at the polls, the archrebel talked the wealthy merchant into creating hundreds of jobs on the waterfront by building some new wharves—an act that endeared Hancock to the workingmen of Boston and solidified their allegiance to Sam Adams.

Gossip credited the archrebel with other converts among Boston's "men of consequence." One of them was handsome young Dr. Joseph Warren, who was to give his life for the patriot cause.

Sam Adams did not create the Boston mobs. They were already there. What he did was fuse two long-time rival groups, one from the North End and the other from the South End, into a single and disciplined street army.

For many years November 5 was a hideous day in Boston.

"Pope Day," it was called. Carrying monstrous effigies depicting the leader of the Roman Catholic Church as identical with Satan, the two gangs poured into King Street. There they belabored one another with staves and cudgels, each gang striving to destroy the other's effigies. Cracked skulls and broken teeth were plentiful. Creaking carts carried off the dead.

When on the night of August 24, 1765, one of the Pope Day gangs—or perhaps both—wrecked Thomas Hutchinson's townhouse, Sam Adams was as alarmed as any Boston aristocrat. Mindless destruction, he knew, was not the way to unseat the Hutchinsons and the Olivers; nor was it the answer to British misrule. The word about town was that the ruffians who had overrun Hutchinson's place meant to do the same to the homes of fifteen other crown officials.

The archrebel worked fast. Back and forth he went, from North Boston to South Boston, ingratiating himself with the leaders of both gangs. Early autumn saw an occasion the city would long remember. At a banquet in Faneuil Hall both mobs sat down with the local patriot merchants and politicians to toast an end to their differences.

For Sam Adams and the "cudgel boys" of Boston, the festivities marked the conclusion of a whirlwind courtship, the beginning of a happy-ever-after marriage. On Pope Day, 1765, there were no riots on King Street. The once-battling gangs marched together in what the patriot press called "a military review." The scrappy workingmen of North and South Boston had become Sam Adams's "Mohawks," devoted to his cause and obedient to his orders.*

When the era of good feeling toward Great Britain set in, the archrebel refused to despair. "We cannot make events," he said philosophically. "Our business is wisely to improve them."

He had every reason to believe that sooner or later the blundering gentlemen in charge of His Majesty's government would give him improvable events—and in time they did.

---

* The street gangs of aristocrats who somewhat later spread terror in London called themselves "Mohocks," an altered spelling of the American term.

England's hopes of paying all royal officers in the colonies from the proceeds of the Townshend duties had vanished with the repeal of most of those taxes. In Massachusetts only the governor was receiving his salary from English sources. A cry of foul play filled the air of Boston when in the summer of 1772 Hutchinson announced that hereafter the five superior-court judges of the colony would receive their pay as he did, not from the General Court but from the duties collected by the British customs service.

Writing under the name of Valerius Poplicola, Sam Adams outdid himself. He reminded the readers of the *Boston Gazette* that Governor Hutchinson was being paid from moneys "extorted from the people in a manner, most odious, insulting, and oppressive." Now, he asked, "Are we still threatened with more? Is life, property, and everything dear and sacred to be . . . submitted to the decisions of PENSIONED JUDGES . . . ? Merciful God! . . . let not the hand of tyranny ravish our laws and seize the badge of freedom, nor avowed corruption and the murderous rage of lawless power be ever seen on the sacred seat of justice!"

The chill days of October had come when these bombastic words appeared. On the twenty-seventh the archrebel confessed for the first time that he would like to see all America rise against English law. "I wish," he told a close associate, "that we could arouse the continent."

Less than twenty-four hours later, at a Boston town meeting, he unveiled a proposition brilliantly designed to accomplish that objective.

The scheme that Adams proposed and that the town meeting adopted set up a local committee of correspondence. Its twenty-one members were instructed to persuade the other towns in Massachusetts to do the same. In addition, the Boston committee was to draw up a declaration of the rights of the colonists and publish them to the world at large. Within a few weeks nearly every town in Massachusetts had its own committee of correspondence, and the Boston committee's declaration of

American rights was appearing in newspapers throughout the colonies.

The archrebel had no intention of confining his committee of correspondence to Massachusetts. He sent a circular letter to the assemblies in the other provinces, urging them to promote similar organizations. Virginia was the first to act. Other colonies quickly followed. Before the middle of 1773 there were committees of correspondence everywhere. Linking colony to colony and town to town, this network of revolutionary bodies provided the patriots with a foundation for united action.

Sam Adams's "great political engine" (as John Adams called the committees of correspondence) materialized none too soon. In London the East India Company, one of England's most important enterprises, was in financial straits. Struggling to prop up the ailing mercantile giant, His Majesty's ministers were once more casting covetous eyes on their prosperous colonies across the Atlantic.

# 6

# Tea and Trouble

WITH ITS TRADING POSTS and dockyards strewn across the subcontinent of India, "the Governor and Company of Merchants of London, trading into the East Indies"—the East India Company—was more than a commercial venture. A joint stock company in form, it was an arm of the British government in reality. It was the agency through which the ministry at Westminster governed His Majesty's possessions in the Far East. The company's troubles were England's troubles. And in 1773 the company was broke.

It traded in innumerable products, but for half a century 90 percent of its income had come from the sale of black bohea and green hyson, two of the teas brewed from the cured leaves of the *Camellia sinensis* bush of China.

Prior to the passage of the Townshend Acts the American colonials had purchased most of the bohea, but the little tax placed on tea by those laws, which was still in effect, had cut sales to a disastrous degree. Seventeen million pounds of East India Company bohea now languished in warehouses along the Thames River in London, and the company was petitioning the government for a loan of 1½ million pounds.

Lord North agreed to the loan, but money by itself could not save the East India Company. Ways must be found of moving the bohea out of the crowded storage bins along the Thames.

For many nights the candles burned late at Whitehall, while important men in cutaway coats and pigtail wigs conferred, and clerks with curl papers in their hair and tapered quills in their hands scribbled. At length the Tea Act of 1773—a measure slyly designed to lure the Americans into once more purchasing East India Company bohea—went to Parliament.

Previously English law had required the East India Company to bring all of its tea to England and dispose of it there at public auction. British exporters dealing with the colonies bought the bohea. They sold it to American wholesalers, who in turn sold it to American retailers. To enable the company to offer its product at a low price in the colonies, the Tea Act eliminated most of the middlemen from this process. It did this by letting the company ship bohea directly from England to agents of its own choice in America.

Tucked away in the measure was the old Townshend duty, the requirement that the American importer pay a trifling duty—threepence—on every pound of English tea brought in. "Take that out!" a score of voices pounded at Lord North as he placed his new bill before the House of Commons. "The colonials will not buy the tea if the tax is on it."

North himself was worried about that little excise, but he was caught between Parliament and palace. King George insisted that the tea duty be retained as a symbol of England's right to tax her American subjects. Frederick North was no fool, no coward either; but as chief minister of England in a treacherous hour he suffered from a fatal flaw. He could not bring himself to argue with his royal master.* He knew well how to connive and bribe the British lawmakers, but George III could neither be connived nor bribed nor disengaged from any idea on which his obstinate mind had fastened. The Prime Minister connived and bribed in Parliament, and by late May the Tea Act of 1773—threepence duty included—had begun its journey to America.

The thunder it raised there was deafening. Nothing like it

---

* Toward the end of his days, ill and blind, Lord North confessed that going along with King George's colonial policies had been "the greatest mistake of my life."

had been heard since the Stamp Act crisis. Once again conservative colonial merchants became rebels.

Even in peace-loving Philadelphia the uproar was almost universal. In mid-October radical Whigs and ordinarily pro-British Quaker merchants jointly addressed eight thousand angry citizens in the statehouse yard.

The Whigs called the Tea Act an underhanded trick. They said that England's object in lowering the price of the dutied bohea was to entice Americans into buying it, thus vindicating Parliament's right "to heap taxes upon our unwary heads."

The merchants said the act portended the destruction of free enterprise in the New World. If England could grant one private company a monopoly on the sale of tea in America, what was to prevent it from giving other companies the exclusive privilege of purveying even more necessary items?

The Quaker City had ignored Sam Adams's plea that it set up a committee of correspondence. Now a storm of approval greeted a resolution calling for the election of such a body. More resolutions were quickly adopted. As its agents in Philadelphia the East India Company had named six of the city's leading merchants. One of the resolutions likened these appointees to the tax collectors of the Stamp Act era. It instructed the newly created committee of correspondence to demand that they relinquish their posts.

Within a few weeks all six had done so. It was already known that several vessels loaded with East India Company tea were en route to America. One of them, the *Polly*, was bound for Philadelphia. A second mass meeting ordered the committee of correspondence to make certain that the *Polly* did not disembark her taxable cargo.

It may be wondered why the Quaker City patriots did not simply allow the tea to land and let the townspeople refuse to buy it. The answer is that they were realists. All along a goodly number of Americans had been secretly purchasing the taxed tea, some of them brewing it in coffee pots to disguise its identity. At the lowered price soon to take effect, the bohea would sell briskly. There was only one way to wreck the British ministry's scheme. That was to see to it that not one leaf of the tea now crossing the ocean landed on American soil.

The red and gold of October faded into the brown of November, and in the Quaker City's stout brick-wall houses men waited for the arrival of the *Polly*, for the "tea party" that was being planned in her honor.

When the time came everything went as scheduled. Surrounded by thousands of screaming Philadelphians, the captain of the tea ship saw the folly of putting his freight ashore. Back to England went the *Polly*, her holds as full as when she had left there. On other American waterfronts similar "parties" followed. Only at Charleston did the tea land, and there the liberty boys immediately carted it off to a cellar where it remained under lock and key until 1776.

None of these cities, however, was the first to act. That privilege fell to Boston.

# 7

# Indian Caper

T HE RUMOR IN BOSTON in the late fall of 1773 was that England was sending to that city no fewer than four ships packed to their gunwales with East India Company tea. The rumor was correct, although one of the vessels, wrecked off Cape Cod, would never make it.

By November the New England seaport was in turmoil. A note of doom was throbbing through the diary of affable John Rowe, self-made possessor of one of Boston's largest import-export fortunes, owner of one of its busiest wharves, and pewholder at elegant Trinity Church.

By word and deed Merchant Rowe had earned his credentials as a Whig, but he was avowedly a conservative one. He was always ready to serve on any committee rounded up to send off another petition to crown and Parliament, but he could not bring himself to approve of the violence of Sam Adams's Mohawks.

Convinced that if the colonies "acted with dignity and firmness" England would in time do the right thing, Merchant Rowe was profoundly shocked as the details of the Tea Act of 1773 became known. As a tide of ill will washed over his beloved Boston, he found himself in the position of being a middle-of-the-roader in a town where there was no longer any middle of the road for a man to stand on. The hand that pushed the pen across the pages of his famous diary shook a little as he made note of the efforts of Sam Adams and his followers to exploit this latest "blunder" by the ministers of "His Most Gracious Majesty."

For a time, Rowe noted, the archrebel and his friends had worked through official channels. On November 4 a town meeting, called at their request, roared its approval of resolutions almost identical with those passed by the Philadelphia mass meetings. As in the Pennsylvania city, one of the resolutions demanded that the men scheduled to act as local agents for the East India Company resign their positions at once. Boston's Whigs were stronger and better organized than those in Philadelphia, but so were Boston's loyalists, under the leadership of Governor Hutchinson. In the face of stone-throwing mobs at their places of business and articles in the patriot press descanting on the persuasiveness of tar and feathers, the five Boston tea commissioners refused to resign.

On November 18 the town meeting reconvened. Again it asked the tea commissioners to give up their jobs. Again the agents held firm, whereupon the town meeting voted their attitude "daringly affrontive" and adjourned.

At this point the popular leaders gave up all pretense of working through the regular town bodies. Supported by the Sons of Liberty and the Caucus Club, Sam Adams's revolutionary committee of correspondence began to act on its own.

When on Sunday, November 27, the first of the tea ships, the *Dartmouth*, reached Boston, twenty-five liberty boys hastened to the Long Wharf to stand guard and make sure none of its taxable cargo came ashore. Within the week two more tea-bearing vessels, the ship *Eleanor* and the brig *Beaver*, were beating their way through the close-set islands rimming Massachusetts Bay.

By this time the liberty boys had discovered that the busy expanses of Long Wharf were hard to watch. They ordered all three of the tea ships to tie up at smaller Griffin's Wharf at the foot of Hutchinson Street.

For two days, at the end of the month, five thousand Whigs from the city and the adjoining countryside gathered at Old

South Church to pass resolutions and hear patriotic oratory. Following a practice begun during the Stamp Act days, this assemblage called itself "the Body of the People."

Merchant Rowe was there, not because he wanted to be but because he knew that his absence would subject his thriving import-export establishment to the wrath of Sam Adams's Mohawks. The "Body" named him to a committee, "much against my will but I dare not say a word." The unhappy merchant was not the only Bostonian to realize that "King Mob" had taken over. The five tea commissioners had already fled to redcoat-guarded Castle William in the harbor.

Under English customs regulations, the first of the tea ships to arrive, the *Dartmouth*, could remain at the docks only twenty days. During that period its owners must pay the duties on their cargo and unload it. Failing that, British soldiers would take off the tea and put it up for auction and payment of duties.

Principal owner of the *Dartmouth* was Francis Rotch, a local Quaker. Rotch informed the committee of correspondence that he and his fellow owners were willing to send their vessel back to England as it was. Rotch himself had already applied to the royal customs service for the necessary clearance papers.

The young Quaker made these disclosures during the first week of December. On the eleventh he was summoned before the committee of correspondence and asked why the *Dartmouth* was still at Griffin's Wharf. The unhappy shipowner could only throw up his hands. He revealed that he was getting nowhere with the customs service. The officials there sent him from office to office, giving him no satisfaction. He had even tried to see Hutchinson, but the governor was not in Boston. Like the tea commissioners, His Excellency had left town. He was at his country place in Milton, seven miles to the south.

The members of the committee urged Rotch to forget about clearance papers. They suggested that he have the *Dartmouth* make a run for it at night. That was out of the question, they were told. Governor Hutchinson had ordered John Montagu, admiral of the British fleet in the harbor, to alert his warships. Every outlet was under surveillance.

The twenty days were speeding by. On December 16 they would be up. Then Rotch and his associates would have to unload the *Dartmouth* or the military would do it for them.

On the fourteenth the town was carnival-like with newly-tacked-up notices fluttering in a chilly gale. The posters read:

> Friends! Brethren! Countrymen! The perfidious act of your reckless enemies to render ineffectual the late resolves of the body of the people, demands your assembling at the Old South Meeting House, precisely at ten o'clock this day, at which time the bells will ring.

They rang and the patriots assembled. More resolutions, more forensics. Then the Body of the People adjourned with the understanding that they would reconvene at the same place on the afternoon of the final day to do whatever had to be done.

On the morning of that day, Thursday, December 16, 1773, Quaker Rotch headed for Milton. His orders from the committee of correspondence were to be back early enough in the evening to let the Body of the People know how Governor Hutchinson had responded to his request for clearance papers.

In Boston the weather had changed. A springlike rain was falling. Sam Adams and his henchmen spent the afternoon at the home of Benjamin Edes, publisher with John Gill of the *Boston Gazette*. The purpose of this conclave was to perfect the already-agreed-upon plan of action to be followed if Governor Hutchinson turned down Quaker Rotch's plea.

By early afternoon seven thousand people had jammed into Old South's mahogany-railed pews. As darkness came, the rain ceased. Outside, a nearly full moon dropped a waxy haze on the damp roadbed of Milk Street, catching in its glow a knot of men loafing near the meetinghouse doors. All of them were dressed like Mohawk Indians. All carried tomahawks. Why the disguise? Sam Adams's idea no doubt. No mean psychologist, the archrebel may have reasoned that behind some paint and feathers even an ordinary man would feel up to extraordinary deeds.

Inside the candlelit meetinghouse a speaker droned on. He broke off when young Rotch appeared, breathless after his ride from Milton, to give his report. The governor had refused. There would be no clearance papers for the *Dartmouth,* or for the brig *Beaver,* or for the ship *Eleanor.*

Pandemonium! Sam Adams, getting to his feet on the platform, waved his arms. Patiently he waited for the uproar to subside. Then:

"This meeting," he said, "can do nothing more to save the country."

His words were a signal. From the men outside, in their comic garments, came a burst of war whoops. There were yells of "Boston harbor a teapot tonight!" Then, suddenly sobering, the Indianized patriots formed a line of two's and marched for the waterfront.

Half of Boston, it would seem, was expecting them. There were lights in every window along the way, throngs of spectators on both sides. At Long Lane, the Mohawks turned right into Hutchinson Street. Back at the church there had been no more than a score of them. Now their numbers were swelling as other groups, disguised like themselves, fed in from side streets to join them.

By the time Griffin's Wharf was reached, there were almost 150. There, at barked orders from their "chiefs," they divided into three groups, each group taking over one of the tea ships.

On the vessels everything went far too smoothly to push aside the conviction that the crown authorities were either unbelievably unaware of what was going on or deliberately had chosen to ignore it.

For weeks everybody in Boston had known that something big would happen on December 16. Yet on this critical night not one of the tea-ship captains was with his vessel.

There were British warships nearby. Why did they not close in? The only answer is found in a letter penned on the following day by Admiral Montagu to his superiors in London. Montagu wrote that the authorities "never called for my assistance; if they had I could have prevented . . . [the tea party] but must have endangered the lives of many innocent people by firing upon the town."

Swarming onto the decks of the three ships, the painted and feathered invaders summoned the mates in charge, demanded and got keys and lights. Swiftly and methodically they brought 342 tea chests up from the holds, axed them open, and spilled their contents into the harbor. Early-rising Bostonians would see a windrow of tea on the waters, extending all the way from Griffin's Wharf to the village of Nantasket, fifteen miles to the south.

The performance aboard the tea ships lasted three hours. It took place in a blaze of whale-oil light and in the face of the English.

Admiral Montagu was spending the night in town with a friend whose house stood at the head of Griffin's Wharf. From this near point the British sea dog watched the systematic destruction of the East India Company's property in silence. Only when the putative braves left the vessels to begin their trek home did he fling open a window of his host's house and give them a piece of his mind.

"Well, boys," he shouted, "you have had a fine, pleasant evening for your Indian caper—haven't you? But mind, you have got to pay the fiddler yet."

The Mohawks marched on in a roar of mocking laughter.

# 8

# The Unspoken Word

DURING THE ERA of good feeling John Adams had written "Goodbye, politics" in his diary and moved his family from Boston to the quiet of their farmhouse in nearby Braintree (now Quincy), Massachusetts. As a lawyer he still maintained an office in the city, but on the day of the "Indian caper" he was out of town. It was not until his return about noon of the day after that he heard about it.

John Adams was thirty-eight that winter. Recent illness had diminished temporarily the rotundity that confronts us in the old pictures of him. All the other familiar features were there, the full and impressive face, the iron mouth, and the fierce, censorious eyes.

Whatever John Adams's faults and virtues, blind consistency was not among them. Like so many of the great Americans of his day, he was simultaneously a rebel and a traditionalist, a dissenter and a lover of law and order. One of traditionalist John Adams's reasons for hurrying his family to Braintree had been to get them away from the disorders perpetrated by his cousin Sam Adams's street gangs. Now, on this winter afternoon of 1773, having received an account of the greatest disorder of them all, rebel John Adams swelled with patriotic ecstasy.

"This," he wrote of the Boston Tea Party, "is the most significant movement of them all . . . This destruction of the tea is so bold, so daring, so firm, intrepid and inflexible, and it must have so important consequences, and so lasting, that I cannot but consider it an epocha in history . . ."

57

Before he closed his diary that night, John Adams placed in it the question that would soon be on the tongues of all Americans.

"What measures," he wondered, "will the ministry take? Will they punish us? How?"

No one expected to hear the answer soon. London lay three thousand miles away. Caught in the toils of the Atlantic, the best of the little wooden sailing vessels of the eighteenth century, in the best of seasons, took at least six weeks to cross it.

Most of February 1774 had gone before the news reached the English capital. An earthquake could not have raised more alarm in the wainscoted chambers of Whitehall.

*Ten thousand pounds' worth of English tea utterly destroyed!*

This was almost more than any law-abiding, right-thinking, property-loving Englishman could face over his morning cup of black bohea or green hyson.

Not that acts of destruction by insurgent colonials were new. Englishmen had not forgotten the smashing of Governor Hutchinson's house, or the burning of a British customs-service schooner in Narragansett Sound, or the seizure of another revenue cutter on the Delaware River by a gang of cutlass-wielding ruffians. But these and similar eruptions could be attributed to momentary mass frenzy or to a greed for money, emotions not unknown to the breasts of Britishers.

The Boston Tea Party occupied a different category of crime altogether. Here was a deliberate act, minutely planned and executed by men so thoroughly rehearsed that at the last moment, having dumped the tea, they had taken the time to sweep the decks, leaving the *Dartmouth,* the *Eleanor,* and the *Beaver* as tidy as they had found them.

No one in London was more distressed by the news than His Majesty. George III was easily upset. There were times when the problems of imperial government plunged him into protracted bouts of melancholia. During these seizures he would sit for hours at his desk, utterly idle, his tall and as he grew older alarmingly gross figure bent slightly forward, his chin on one hand, his big, blue, distended and temporarily unseeing eyes fixed on the paneled walls.

King George III was neither the stupid oaf nor the unmitigated cad placed before us in some accounts of the American Revolution. The third member of his German family, the House of Hanover, to wear the English crown, the first to be born on English soil, he was a competent administrator, a shrewd political operator, more of a statesman than most of his ministers, and a friend of human liberty as that term was understood in the England of his day.

He was thirteen when he became heir to the English throne following the death of his father, the Prince of Wales. He was twenty-two when, on October 25, 1760, George II died, and Prince George became King George III.

Both of his Hanoverian predecessors had shown more interest in the affairs of the microscopic German principality of Hanover, where they ruled with the title of Elector, than in those of powerful Britain. Great-grandfather George I had not even bothered to master the English language. George II had left most of the running of England to his ministers.

Trained by a mother who told him, "Be a king, George," and by a Scottish tutor steeped in the lore of political intrigue, George III deviated vigorously from the behavior pattern of his royal forebears.

The earlier Georges had let Parliament choose the Prime Minister and his cabinet. George III selected his own ministers. He also tried to guide their activities—a difficult goal but one that he achieved in 1770 when in Frederick Lord North he found a chief minister willing if not always happy to follow his orders.

The earlier Georges had made only intermittent efforts to influence Parliament. George III yearly set aside 52,000 pounds for buying votes in that august assembly.

His opponents read an ominous significance into his determination to exercise what he called "personal rule." They said he was not content merely to take an active part in the governance of the empire. His ultimate objective was to subvert the British constitution by diminishing the powers of Parliament and increasing those of the crown.

Imperious the King was, autocratic and stubborn; but as a modern British writer, Eric Robson, has wittily observed, if George III saw in the American rebellion an opportunity to weaken Parliament and strengthen the throne, he chose to fight on the wrong side.

In 1774 the American patriots were not openly angry at the King. Their quarrel was with Parliament. They made this plain in their numerous petitions to the crown. Repeatedly they assured His Majesty of their allegiance to the office he held. Had the King been truly fighting the British lawmakers, it would have behooved him not to oppose but to cooperate with his American subjects. When he finally decided that the time had come to stamp out the spirit of insurrection across the sea, his aim was not to enlarge his own privileges but to uphold those of Parliament.

"This legislative war"—thus he described the hostilities when they came; and long after the "American War," as London called it, had become unpopular with the English people, His Majesty ploddingly pursued it until convinced that the Parliament for which it was being waged had lost heart.

A charge brought against the King in his time and later was that he welcomed battle with the colonies. Critics said his scheme was first to suppress liberty in America and then to use his victorious armies to do the same in England. A dubious theory at best: during the opening years of the great quarrel the King showed no desire for war. He grumbled about the laws repealing the Stamp Act and the Townshend duties, but when one of his ministers proposed that punitive measures be taken against Massachusetts and New York, he said no.

In a letter to the minister, he described himself as opposed to

any act "calculated to increase the unhappy feudes that sub-
sist . . ." He thought it wiser to try to "asswage" the erring
colonials.

Such was the King's state of mind in 1769. It seems to have
remained substantially unchanged until February 1774, when
word of the Boston Tea Party struck London like a hurricane
and George III concluded that the time for "asswagement" had
passed.

"The die is now cast," he told Lord North. "The colonies must
either submit or triumph."

Few men in Parliament disagreed with him. In that winter of
1774 the British lawmakers were riding a wave of righteous
indignation, out of which so many of mankind's blood baths
have been launched.

On March 31 the King signed a law that ordered the harbor
of Boston closed to all commerce. It was to stay closed until the
Yankees paid for the tea they had destroyed, repented of their
wicked conduct, and yielded to parliamentary rule.

This measure, the Boston Port Bill, was only the first flick of
the cat-o'-nine-tails that Britain's lawmakers were now determined to lay on American backs. Others followed, a string of
measures reducing the powers of the Massachusetts legislature
and increasing those of the royal governor.

The British spoke of these blows at the Bay Colony as "coer-
cive acts." The Americans called them "intolerable acts."

Since 1772 the commander of His Majesty's forces in the New
World, General Gage, had been on leave in England. On Gage's
advice the King ordered four regiments to be sent to Boston to
enforce the intolerable acts. Gage went with them. Until the
Bay Colony capitulated, the general was to function as its military governor. Governor Hutchinson meanwhile was to enjoy a
rest in England.

Rumors of what Parliament was doing were filtering into
Boston in April. On May 10 the ship *Harmony* out of London
brought an official copy of the Boston Port Bill. On the thir-

teenth a town meeting endorsed a resolution asking the local merchants to unite in what Sam Adams called "a solemn league and covenant."

During the Stamp Act and Townshend crises, the merchants had limited themselves to non-importation agreements. The archrebel now urged them to establish a total boycott. Under this arrangement they would pledge themselves not only to buy no goods from England but also to sell her none as well.

Boston's merchants responded with their usual caution. They stood ready to participate in a total boycott only if the merchants of the other American seaports would act with them— but the merchants elsewhere were not yet ready to go that far.

From New York, from Philadelphia, from Williamsburg came a counter suggestion. Instead of setting up a trade boycott with no machinery to enforce it, let all of the colonies once again send delegates to a general meeting to be known as the Continental Congress. If the members of this gathering solemnly pledged their constituents to suspend all commerce with England, well and good.

The idea of a continental congress was not new. Whig contributors to the press had been advocating it for months. Some suggested that the Congress be given the powers of a national government, that it take steps to divorce America from Britain and establish "an American Empire."

A *continental* congress—an American *empire!* The inhabitants of the thirteen little colonies along the narrow eastern shelf of North America were beginning to think in large terms. Too large for Sam Adams. The archrebel was not immediately receptive to the idea of a continental congress. Perhaps he saw in the proposal the nucleus of the sort of strong central government he admittedly abhorred.

Whatever his fears, he shrugged them aside for practical reasons. His heart was set on a total boycott, and he soon realized that there would be none until all of the colonies could be induced to support it. Only an intercolonial gathering, a continental congress, could achieve that end.

By the close of the first week of August, the place of the forthcoming meeting, Philadelphia, and the date for its opening session, September 5, had been settled; and in most of the colonies the election of delegates had been completed or was under way.

Only in four colonies were the patriots able to take this action through their legislatures. Where the royal or proprietory governors had the power to dissolve the legislature, most of them managed to do so before the lawmakers could act. Barred from using regular channels, the Whigs improvised other methods. Virginia named her seven delegates—George Washington and Patrick Henry among them—at a popular convention in Williamsburg. In Tory-ridden New York the patriots resorted to local meetings. According to a loyalist source, the nominating convention in Kings County consisted of Simon Boerum and his secretary. Boerum was unanimously elected.

The intolerable acts moved the capital of Massachusetts from Boston to Salem, and Governor Gage established his headquarters in that vicinity. When he called the House of Representatives into session, he instructed the members to set up a program for paying for the destroyed tea. Instead they elected delegates to the Continental Congress.

Before doing so they locked the doors of their meeting room. As the voting began, however, a loyalist member pleaded a "call of nature" and got out of the chamber long enough to tell the governor what was happening. Gage drew up a proclamation, dissolving the House. He ordered Thomas Flucker, long-time secretary of the colony, to speed it to the chamber.

Flucker sped in vain. While he read the proclamation on the wrong side of the locked doors, the lawmakers completed their work. Rapidly they elected a five-man delegation to the Continental Congress that included what someone later called "the brace of Adamses," Sam and his cousin John.

One of the Massachusetts delegates, James Bowdoin, was unable to serve. Tradition says it was he who supplied the munificent coach-and-four that on the hot morning of August 10 carried the other four delegates through cheering crowds along the streets of Boston, to begin their journey to Philadelphia.

On a dusty morning nineteen days later, the travelers reached the little town of Frankford, five miles north of Philadelphia. There they found that a group of Whigs had ridden up from the city to greet them. The Philadelphia patriots had not made the journey merely to say welcome; they had come to describe the touchy political situation in the City of Brotherly Love.

Pennsylvania was a crucial colony. Without her cooperation no effective stand could be taken against Great Britain, and Pennsylvania's seven-man delegation to Congress was headed by loyalist Joseph Galloway. Most of Galloway's fellow delegates were thought to be "lukewarm Whigs" at best, and Philadelphians generally regarded Sam Adams as a troublemaker. The patriot leaders of that city were nervous about his coming. They were fearful that he would alienate the less-than-bold Pennsylvania delegates by demanding that the Congress move too fast.

Among the band of Philadelphia Whigs at Frankford was bright and talkative young Dr. Benjamin Rush. For the rest of the journey Rush rode in a carriage with the "brace of Adamses." Perhaps it was he who solemnly cautioned them that once in the "theatre of action . . . you must not utter the word independence."

They didn't. Forewarned, the Bostonians kept their voices low. Happily for them, some of the delegates from the aristocratic South—Richard Henry Lee of Virginia and Gadsden of South Carolina,* among others—were as radical as the New Englanders and glad to do the shouting for them.

At the time of the Massachusetts delegation's arrival in the

---

* In his book *E. Pluribus Unum* historian Forrest McDonald describes Gadsden as a conservative, but the South Carolinian's actions before and at the First Continental Congress were definitely those of a radical.

Quaker City, only a week remained before the scheduled opening of the Congress on Monday, September 5. For John Adams it was a week of socializing and politicking. To the incoming delegates the people of Philadelphia opened their homes, and especially their dining rooms, with a profligacy that had the plump Boston attorney filling his diary with descriptions of one "sinful feast" after another.

"Curds and creams, Jellies, Sweetmeats of various sorts, twenty sorts of Tarts, fools, Triffles, floating Islands, Sillabuds &c, &c," he drooled over one of these gustatorial marathons. He wrote his wife Abigail that his Quaker hosts were trying to kill him with kindness. In view of their distaste for his Yankee radicalism, perhaps they were.

On his second day in town he mounted the two-hundred-foot bell steeple of Christ Church on North Second Street. From here one could see all of Philadelphia, a pretty, tree-shaded little town divided by broad Market Street into two almost-equal wings.

Its founder, William Penn, had envisaged the city as a perfect gridiron. According to the instructions to his surveyor general, it was to be a mile wide along the Delaware waterfront and to extend to the shores of the smaller Schuylkill River two and fifteen-hundredth miles to the west.

But Penn failed to reckon with the magnetism of the Delaware. Instead of pushing west, the settlers had thrust north and south, rapidly creating two suburbs, the Northern Liberties and Southwark. It was cooler in these areas along the big river during the tropical summers. Industry gravitated to the shores of a waterway that before the city was half a century old had become one of the liveliest commercial arteries in the world. For two miles, from the big shipyards on the outskirts of the Northern Liberties down almost to the end of Southwark, wharves and storehouses, smithies, foundries, anchor forges, rum distilleries, cooperages, sail lofts, and ropewalks had sprung into being.

By 1774 Philadelphia had become, not the neat oblong of its

founder's dream, but a shallow triangle, its apex at the corner of Seventh and Market Streets where the open spaces called the Commons began, its base along the majestic Delaware.

In the early 1770's France's aging literary genius Voltaire had expressed a wish to end his days in the Quaker City. Very likely, as was suggested by a Frenchman acquainted with both Voltaire and Philadelphia, the great philosopher would have ended them there soon enough—"of ennui." Still, the distractions of eighteenth-century Philadelphia, if not those of Paris or London, were not unsubstantial.

For the thirsty there were no less than 120 licensed taverns. For the cultured there were the scientific demonstrations at the College and Academy of Philadelphia that would someday be the University of Pennsylvania, and the lectures sponsored by the American Philosophical Society. For the sports-minded there were the annual races on Race Street; for the patrons of vice the drinking dives and bawdy houses along the waterfront alleys of "Helltown"; and for the rich the fortnightly gatherings in the hall of a club called the Assembly, where the performance of the quadrille was taken so seriously that when a lady missed her turn the dancing master reminded her that she was not there for pleasure.

John Adams examined it all. Philadelphia, he concluded, had but one fault. "With all its Trade and Wealth and Regularity," he wrote, "it is not Boston."

For both the Adams radicals and the Galloway conservatives the week preceding the opening of the Congress was one of incessant get-togethers for the purpose of plotting measures to be proposed and strategies to be followed.

Radicals and conservatives alike looked forward to the first decision the Congress would have to make as a test of their relative strengths. Two meeting places had been proposed. One was the chamber used by the provincial legislature in the state-house, five blocks west of the Delaware on Chestnut Street. The other was Carpenter's Hall, a two-story cruciform structure a block and a half closer to the river. The room in the statehouse was the logical place, but in 1774 Joe Galloway was still Speaker of the Pennsylvania Assembly. He alone had the privilege of inviting the congressmen to use the Assembly chamber; and, as Silas Deane of the Connecticut delegation wrote home, because "*he* offers, the other party oppose."

During that hectic week the question of how to handle another upcoming decision was a subject of earnest talk in both political camps. Someone would have to keep the congressional minutes. The leaders on each side realized that it would be helpful to have in this post a man sympathetic to their interests.

When on Thursday the brace of Adamses spent considerable time with two Philadelphia Whigs, Thomas Mifflin and Charles Thomson, they were not paying courtesy calls. They were scouting for a satisfactory candidate for the secretaryship. John Adams made his own preference clear when he concluded that Charles Thomson was "the Sam Adams of Philadelphia."

Galloway was not idle. He was pushing Silas Deane for the secretaryship, hopeful of breaching the solid radicalism of New England by luring that opportunistic Connecticut Yankee into the conservative fold.

When the break with England came, people would say that strong-minded Joseph Galloway had chosen the British side out of a desire to augment an already extensive fortune. In truth, his loyalist stand lost him much of his fortune and was a logical outgrowth of positions he had taken throughout his long political life.

The Stamp Act had struck him as unwise, but the violence of colonial reaction to it appalled him. Taking to the press, he reminded his readers that Britain's towering debt was the result of spending large sums of money to prevent "Indian barbarities" on the American frontier. He argued that as the power of making war to defend British subjects lay with the crown, the colonials should permit themselves to be taxed to help His Majesty do so. He regarded the forthcoming Congress with disfavor. He had agreed to serve in it only on condition that he write the instructions for his province's delegates. These ordered the Pennsylvanians to support only those measures aimed at closing the rift with the mother country.

As the opening session of Congress drew near, the activities of the conservative leader were those of a man confident that common sense—meaning his own views—would triumph. On Saturday he wrote a loyalist friend that he thought most of the delegates would "behave with Temper and Moderation." He was not fooled, however, by the "modest conduct" of the Bostonians. He observed that they were throwing out "hints, which, like straws and feathers, tell us from which Point of the Compass the Wind comes."

As Galloway would learn on Monday, the wind was not blowing his way. The First Continental Congress chose to meet in Carpenter's Hall, and the election of Charles Thomson to the secretaryship was carried without serious opposition.

The radicals were delighted with these small victories, and on Tuesday circumstances further strengthened their position. That day brought a report that in Massachusetts General Gage had sent his redcoats to Cambridge and Charlestown to seize military supplies belonging to the Bay Colony. The story went that the inhabitants of the two towns had resisted Gage's regulars, that six Americans had been killed, that Boston was under bombardment.

The reports were false. No shots had been fired in Massachusetts, no lives lost; but by the time the facts were known in the Quaker City, the fear of what could have happened in Boston—and by extension to every other American seaport—had produced its effect. When a few days later the people of Philadelphia entertained the delegates to the Congress at a banquet, John Adams was thrilled at the change in local attitudes. He wrote his wife that the "admiration for the people of Boston and Massachusetts which were expressed . . . were enough to melt a heart of stone."

To Joseph Galloway these evidences of growing influence on the part of the "violent party" were distressing. His fears leaped when on the day of the banquet Paul Revere of Boston galloped into town. Riding express for the Boston committee of correspondence, the silversmith brought with him a copy of a document known as the Suffolk Resolves.

Forbidden by Gage to hold meetings in Boston the patriots of that city had gathered in Suffolk County. There, under the leadership of Dr. Joseph Warren, they had drafted a list of grievances against Great Britain. They accused the mother country of "infractions of those rights to which we are justly entitled." They announced that "no obedience is due from this province" to the intolerable acts. When at Carpenter's Hall the delegates voted approval of the Suffolk Resolves, Galloway asserted that Congress had declared war on England.

In a despairing effort to turn the tide, the conservative leader proposed "a plan of Union with Great Britain." He suggested the establishment of an American legislature or "Grand Council," to be selected by the colonial assemblies. The Grand Council would be a branch of the English Parliament. Bills dealing with strictly American affairs would become law only after receiving the approval of both bodies.

Mystery wraps this development. What became of Galloway's "plan of Union"? It was entered on the minutes of the Congress with an order requiring it to be considered later, but no such consideration occurred. Shortly before the close of the session all mention of the plan was stricken from the record. The talk in the Philadelphia taverns was that the one ballot on Galloway's proposition showed only a small majority opposed to it. Alarmed by this situation, Sam Adams contrived to have all mention of the plan erased from the congressional minutes. Some said that the archrebel put through this action at a time when all of Galloway's supporters were absent from the meeting room.

In October the delegates sent three documents to London in

an effort to give the English people and their rulers a picture of conditions in the colonies. In a petition to His Majesty they listed American complaints and implored redress. Having gotten these exercises in diplomacy out of the way, they moved on to other matters.

On October 20 they ceremoniously signed their most important measure. On the surface it was merely Sam Adams's total boycott. In effect it was infinitely more. Incorporated in the measure were the Articles of Association. Taken together, these recommendations constituted the framework of America's first national government, crude precursor to the Articles of Confederation of 1781 and the Federal Constitution of 1787.

Five of the Articles of Association laid down the economic ground rules. For the time being there were to be no imports from the mother country, no exports to her, no consumption of English goods. Congress lacked the power to enforce a single phrase of the Association, but in Article XI its makers confidently proposed to surmount this weakness by providing that:

> . . . a committee be chosen in every county, city or town . . . to observe the conduct of all persons touching this association; and when it shall be made to appear . . . that any person within the limits of their appointment has violated this association, that [the committeemen] do forthwith cause the truth of the case to be published in the gazette [the main local newspaper]; to the end, that all such foes to the rights of British-America may be . . . universally contemned as the enemies of American liberty; and thenceforth we respectively will break off all dealing with him or her.

Sam Adams's committees of correspondence had given the colonies a base for cohesive action. The committees envisaged by the Association gave them the machinery essential to the conduct of a war.

The response to Article XI was instantaneous. Bodies set up

to enforce the Association, usually known as committees of safety, sprang up everywhere.

It was an amazing phenomenon, this swift emergence of government by committee throughout the thirteen colonies. Historian John R. Alden has aptly described it as resting "not on Blackstone's law but on People's law."

Naturally there were abuses. Publicity and social ostracism were the committees' chief instruments of persuasion. These could be brutal weapons in the hands of vengeful or ignorant men, working beyond the reach of courts and suddenly empowered to make the laws and execute them too.

Unscrupulous men invaded the moral and even the mental life of the people, arbitrarily condemning as Tories individuals to whom they were indebted or with whom they had a score to settle. In sections of the country suspected loyalists lost their homes to flames or endured the searing embrace of tar and feathers.

"Which is better," cried an agonized Boston loyalist, ". . . to be ruled by one tyrant three thousand miles away or by three thousand tyrants not a mile away?"

Grim though these incidents were, the American Revolution shows none of the wholesale liquidations of human beings practiced by the supporters of twentieth-century ideologies. Nowhere were the acts of injustice systematic. Nowhere were they sufficiently comprehensive to justify the assumption, advanced by Americans of a later generation, that the United States was born in a holocaust of violence.

The laws of the British Parliament were flouted, yes; but the era, far from being a lawless one, was marked by a popular determination to give the effect of law to the mere recommendations of Congress. Imbedded in one of that body's resolutions was the understanding that if King George complied with the petitions sent to England, the First Continental Congress would be the last Congress. If not, a second one would convene in the spring.

At least one member was certain that a second session would be necessary. At a supper attended by trusted friends, John Adams said that he "had no expectation of a redress of grievances." He predicted that war was near.

On October 26, 1774, the first Congress adjourned. Two days later, in a pouring rain, the indefatigable diary keeper headed for his home in Massachusetts, where something very close to war was already in effect.

# 9

## His Majesty's Lenient General

K ING GEORGE'S SELECTION of Thomas Gage to subdue rebellious
Massachusetts was dictated by that officer's background.
Few Englishmen knew the colonies as well. Gage had lived in
America for more than half of his thirty-five years as a soldier.
He had married an American woman. All but one of their
eleven children had begun life on American soil. During the
French and Indian War he had become friends with a young
Virginian whom he would always speak of as "Mister" Wash-
ington.

In 1774, when Gage took over as military governor of Massachusetts, he was in his fifty-fourth year, tall, broad-shouldered,
and softly handsome. Bostonians commented on his resemblance
to, of all people, Sam Adams. The old portraits bear them out.
One sees the same sheeplike face and senses the same hidden
diffidence. In the case of Sam Adams the mildness was only
skin deep. It was the whole of Thomas Gage.

King George called him "my lenient general." Prudent, pa-
tient, honest, benign, and unimaginative, he was the last man in
the world to execute intolerable acts.

In urging Parliament to pass those measures, the King's ministers admitted that the fires of insurrection were burning in many
parts of America. As England had neither enough men nor
enough money to smother all of them, its only course was to
concentrate on the biggest of them.

That one was in Massachusetts. "Crush that province," His
Majesty's ministers argued, "and all the others, impressed by

British strength, will fall into line." Like many predictions then being aired at Whitehall, this one was inaccurate. Instead of frightening and dividing the American patriots, the intolerable acts angered and united them.

Even as General Gage crossed the ocean to assume his new duties, militia units were being activated in colony after colony. In Philadelphia the members of an exclusive fox-hunting club converted themselves into a cavalry troop. In Rhode Island a Quaker meeting read out of the Society of Friends a young blacksmith named Nathanael Greene, whose sin consisted of helping set up an armed body called the Kentish Guards.

In the Bay Colony itself militiamen were drilling on the green of every village. Each town had its special company of minutemen, pledged at the tap of a muster drum or the peal of a church bell to grab their muskets and report to their captains. Patriot leaders were collecting powder, cannon, guns, and other military supplies, and secreting them here and there about the commonwealth.

Boston was a caldron of unrest. The law banning all commerce from its harbor struck at the jugular vein of its economic life. A person standing on one of the countryside hills that looked down on the little seaport could see at a glance why this was so.

There were still open spaces in the center of town, but along the city's watery fringe—especially on the north, east, and south—there were no free areas. Here warehouses and produce markets, shipbuilding yards and sail lofts, chandlery shops and sailors' groggeries huddled so close as to give the impression of being piled one on top of the other. On this bulging waterfront, teethed with wooden wharves from one end to the other, nearly all of Boston's inhabitants depended for their daily bread.

Geographically the city was only a sliver of today's Boston. Much of the land that supports the modern metropolis would be created later, chiefly by lopping off the tops of its major hills and throwing them into the Back Bay, as people called the wide estuary of the Charles River where it flowed into the Atlantic

Ocean. Colonial Boston occupied a hilly, pear-shaped peninsula, only seven hundred acres in all. Linking it tenuously to the mainland at the south or Dorchester end was Boston Neck, a mile-long stretch of mud lapped on the east by the tides of the Atlantic and on the west by the brackish waters of the bay. Boston Neck was less than a mile across at its widest, barely sixty yards at one point.

Within the city the largest open space was the Common, lying along Back Bay. Above it, to the north, rose Beacon Hill, higher then than now, its fine brick and stone houses set in elm-shaded yards. Two more high hills—Copp's in the far northeast and Fort in the lower southeast—and a dozen church spires completed the "skyline."

By day it was a city of sound. Farmers coming in to trade their flour meal and milk cheese for newly arrived West Indian molasses and English foot stoves complained of being "deaf-ened" by the grind of carriage wheels on cobblestones, the thump of handlooms, and the screech of wooden machinery. The bells in the church spires were forever ringing. They rang to open the market and to close it, to summon the people to worship on Sunday and to prayer meeting on week nights.

The nearer one got to the waterfront, the greater the uproar. The more appalling was the contrast in that sector, therefore, when on June 1, 1774, in accordance with parliamentary decree, the port closed and the once-busy harbor became a still life.

Everybody in Boston and for miles around knew for whom the church bells tolled that day. They tolled for thousands of suddenly idled craftsmen, warehouse clerks, and dockside me-chanics. For the next several months these men would mill about the city streets, exchanging insults with British officers and picking fights with scarlet-coated guard units.

In August, alarmed by the turmoil in the city, Gage moved his headquarters from Salem to Province House in the center of Boston.

Boston was full of Tories. From among these people the general assembled a band of able spies. He instructed them to ascertain the extent of the military preparations in the Massachusetts countryside. When their reports began coming in, he could only hope that they were exaggerated.

On the first day of September he sent 250 redcoats to Cambridge and Charlestown with orders to commandeer powder that the Bay Colony authorities had stored at those places. It was the exaggerated reports of this excursion that the Continental Congress in Philadelphia would soon hear—and act upon. Gage's soldiers got the powder, but the uproar that ensued convinced the general that his spies' reports were correct.

Early the next morning some twenty thousand armed farmers appeared on the shores of the Charles River across from the city. Later that day a royal official, riding through Cambridge, escaped a pursuing mob screaming "Tory son of a bitch!" only by abandoning his carriage and dashing for Boston on his servant's horse.

After dissolving the provincial lawmakers, Gage forbade them to convene again. They convened nonetheless. Following an election that the general tried in vain to stop, the legislators gave their assembly a new name—the Provincial Congress—and began holding meetings at Concord and other villages. In most of Massachusetts they continued to exercise their customary functions. In addition they named a committee of public safety and three general officers to command the Massachusetts militia.

Before his departure from England, General Gage had assured King George that he could restore order in the Bay Colony with four regiments. If in March Gage actually believed four regiments would suffice, he was thinking along quite different lines by the end of the summer.

In letters to his superiors in London he called his situation "desperate." He had already requested additional troops from the other English garrisons in North America. He would soon have about 3,500 regulars on hand. He wrote home that with this force he could hold Boston, but that he could do nothing about the "armed and infuriated populace" in the rural regions on the far side of the Charles River. He pointed out to the British ministers that unless England acted quickly and "with overwhelming force" she would have a long and costly war on her hands. He begged for reinforcements.

"If you think ten thousand men sufficient," he wrote William Wildman (Viscount) Barrington, the British Secretary at War, "send twenty."

An informative aspect of Gage's letters home was the frequency with which he asked permission to arrest some of the patriot leaders and send them to England for trial on charges of treason. A law authorizing this procedure had been on the statute books since the days of King Henry VIII, but for months after Gage's arrival in Massachusetts the legal experts in London argued over whether it was applicable to New England. Not until the spring of 1775 did Gage receive authority to invoke the old treason law. By that time the only important patriot leader still in Boston was young Dr. Joseph Warren, member of the committee of safety and president of the Provincial Congress. All the others had fled beyond the reach of British arms.

The simmering rebellion in the rural areas troubled General Gage only slightly more than the recurring crises within the city itself. Today when we think of a militarily occupied town our minds go to Prague in Czechoslovakia or to Budapest in Hungary. We think of Russian soldiers equipped with tanks and flame throwers in total control of a helpless citizenry.

That was not Boston in the winter of 1774–5. Bay Colony law obliged every able-bodied man, "ministers and half-wits excepted," to own "a firelock, bayonet, & pretty considerable quantity of ammunition" for use in the event of Indian raid or other invasion. Some chroniclers of the second occupation of Boston marvel at the British general's restraint. It was not wholly the product of his kind heart. Gage knew the people he was dealing with. At one point the patriot leaders had all they could do to discourage five hundred armed liberty boys from assaulting the general's headquarters.

Gage's spies were no busier and only a little more competent than their rebel counterparts. Once a month, in a big barren room on the second floor of the Green Dragon Tavern, thirty mechanics-turned-informers assembled to receive their instructions from silversmith Paul Revere, patriot spy master of Boston.

Revere's mechanics did not confine themselves to collecting intelligence. At night they patrolled the city in pairs. With these alert citizens abroad, it behooved a redcoat walking guard to have eyes in the back of his head. In the diary kept by one of Gage's younger officers, Dublin-born Lieutenant Frederick Mackenzie, we read of almost daily court-martials for soldiers goaded into fracases by Paul Revere's night strollers.

On the fifth of April Lieutenant Mackenzie was writing in his journal, "Snowed 'till 12 this day." On the ninth, "The weather begins now to grow . . . pleasant." At Province House General Gage fretted. Almost five months had passed since his last bid for help had gone to London.

Finally it came, the answer he was waiting for, a secret dispatch from the Earl of Dartmouth, who had succeeded Lord Hillsborough as Secretary of State for the Colonies.

Gage read it with more pain than pleasure. The King's ministers promised him reinforcements in due time. Meanwhile, they saw no reason why Gage should not use the troops he had to strike a decisive blow, some action that would show the rebels that His Majesty's government meant business.

A soldier for many years, Gage knew an order when he saw one. He considered the possibilities. According to his spies the rebels had hidden large amounts of military supplies at Worcester and at Concord. Worcester was forty-four miles to the west. Concord was only half that far. Perhaps a detachment could grab the stores there and return before the patriots realized what was happening.

For months Gage had strained to avoid any incident that

would allow future generations to say that the British had started the war. Now he had no choice but to take that risk.

Carefully he developed his plans. He would create a task force consisting of his grenadiers and light infantrymen. In the eighteenth century these soldiers were considered the "flower" of the English army, each regiment having attached to it one company of grenadiers and one of light infantry.

The grenadiers were so called because in addition to the arms toted by every redcoat, a firelock and a bayonet or sword, they sometimes also carried a pouch filled with fire bombs or grenades and slung from a bandoleer. According to *The Gentleman's Compleat Military Dictionary*, published in Boston in 1759, the grenadiers were "generally the tallest and briskest fellows, and always the first upon attack." Gage's grenadiers carried no grenades, but they wore the high and pointed headgear that made these special troops look even bigger and fiercer than they were. The light infantry were men of more active build, lightly armed, and trained to work along the flanks of an army.

Gage's plan was to separate these picked troops from their regular units and place them under Lieutenant Colonel Francis Smith, a seasoned officer known for his caution. Smith's second in command would be Major John Pitcairn of the marines, a more vigorous warrior than Smith but equally self-controlled.

In his orders to Smith, Gage emphasized that the soldiers were not to "plunder the inhabitants or hurt private property." Not a word did his instructions contain about seizing patriot leaders, an action certain to ignite American ire. He did everything possible to keep his preparations a secret—a difficult task in a town where every other man was his enemy and every other enemy an amateur spy.

Such was the situation in Boston when on the morning of April 15, 1775, another diary-keeping British officer, Ensign John Barker, read the general orders for the day and snorted in disbelief.

Irish-born Ensign Barker was not a man to take every word

he read at face value, even when that word came from the "Old Woman," as he and his fellow officers called Thomas Gage. The general's orders specified that until further notice all of the grenadier and light infantry were "to be off duties" to learn "new evolutions." As those troops had already mastered enough "evolutions," Ensign Barker could only conclude that Gage's directives were "by way of a blind."

Something far more important than the learning of new drills and formations was in the wind.

# 10

# A Little Action near Boston

G AGE'S GENERAL ORDERS were known to the Boston patriots as soon as they were known to Ensign Barker, and the rebels drew the same conclusions from them. Within less than twenty-four hours, they had a pretty accurate idea of what the general's plans were and of when he intended to act on them.

By early Sunday, April 16, Paul Revere's spy-mechanics were carrying bits of information to the red-brick house on fashionable Hanover Street where Dr. Joseph Warren lived. Late the night before the British had removed the small boats from their troop transports. They were now mooring them in Back Bay near the shores of the Common. This activity could mean that they were going to repair the craft. It could also indicate that they were planning to ferry troops across the bay to Lechmere's Point near the road winding northwest from Cambridge to Lexington and Concord.

Some time Sunday Dr. Warren sent Revere on one of his lesser rides. His destination, Lexington; his purpose, to inform Sam Adams and John Hancock, lodging there at the home of the Reverend Jonas Clark, that the British troops would soon be coming through that village en route to Concord five miles beyond.

There were two ways a man on horseback could come and go from Boston. One was over the Neck to Dorchester. The other was on the ferry that traveled the Charles River between North

Boston and the village of Charlestown on the southern shores of the Charlestown peninsula.

Revere came home by way of Charlestown, stopping there to confer with Colonel William Conant of the provincial militia and other friends. He told them that the redcoats would probably be leaving Boston some time after dark on Tuesday, the eighteenth. The city would be heavily guarded that night. Revere might not be able to get out. In that case one of the Charlestown patriots must take horse and alert the people living along the Lexington-Concord road. When the time came, a signal would appear in the steeple of North Church (officially Christ Church, Episcopal) on Beacon Hill—one lantern if the British left by Boston Neck, two if they used Back Bay.*

On Tuesday morning General Gage dispatched small patrols into the country with instructions to post themselves along the routes to Concord. They were to arrest any travelers suspected of carrying messages westward. Occasionally, in recent months, the general had sent officers disguised as workmen into the country. These informers had supplied him with maps showing the location of the rebels' supplies at Concord.

During the daylight hours of Tuesday, the weather was on the warm side, but the night came on crisp, promising a frost later on. As soon as Dr. Warren was certain that the British were preparing to leave town by way of the bay, he summoned William Dawes, Jr., an energetic young man who, like Revere, rode express for the committee of safety. Warren was worried. Sam Adams and John Hancock were still in the home of

---

* Readers familiar with Henry Wadsworth Longfellow's poem, "The Innkeeper's Story" or "Paul Revere's Ride" in his *Tales of a Wayside Inn* will notice some discrepancies between that account of Revere's activities on the night of Lexington-Concord and this one. Longfellow's spirited story glitters with inaccuracies. The poet, for example, tells us that Revere was "on the opposite shore" when the signals flared in the steeple of Old North. Actually he was still in Boston and apparently took a hand in displaying the lanterns. Longfellow carries his hero all the way to "Concord town," but Paul Revere failed to reach that village.

Reverend Clark at Lexington. They must be warned. He asked Dawes to get out of town by any means he could find.

Dawes had struck up an acquaintance with a guard at the British fortifications on Boston Neck. That circumstance plus a "liquid bribe" got him across. Gaining the mainland at Dorchester, he turned his steed northward, heading for the main road to Lexington by way of the bridge over the Charles River at Cambridge.

An hour or so later Revere was at Dr. Warren's house. Warren feared that Dawes might be unable to reach Lexington. Revere too must leave town.

"I left Dr. Warren," Revere would write later, "called upon a friend, and desired him to make the signals [the lanterns in the steeple of Old North]. I then went Home, took my Boots & Surtout, & went to the North part of the Town, where I had kept a Boat; two friends rowed me across Charles River."

It was as the three men pushed off that Revere noticed that a moon was rising. Its bright rays were no pleasure to him. To reach Charlestown his craft had to pass under the stern of the sixty-four-gun British warship, the *Somerset*. Their oars muffled by a flannel petticoat that the silversmith had borrowed from a Boston lady at the last moment, the nervous boatmen slithered across in safety.

Colonel Conant had seen the lanterns and was waiting on the Charlestown shore. With his assistance, a "very good horse" was borrowed from Deacon John Larkin, and Paul Revere was on his way.

He was in Lexington shortly after midnight. His first task there was to arouse Captain John Parker, commander of the local militia. Forty-five-year-old Parker moved as fast as his considerable poundage permitted. Soon the drum was booming and the minutemen were straggling onto the green, blinking the sleep from their eyes, asking questions, shivering a little in the nippy night air.

Parker lined them up in two uneven rows. In this formation

they remained for an hour or so, until the militia captain concluded that the alarm was false and dismissed them with orders to stay on the alert.

The Reverend Jonas Clark's house was on the outskirts of the village. Captain Parker had placed militiamen there to protect the pastor's distinguished guests. When Revere appeared the sergeant challenged him in a whisper. He said the inhabitants of the house were abed. They wanted no noise.

"Noise!" bellowed Revere. "You'll have noise enough soon! The redcoats are coming!"

From within the farmhouse came a familiar voice. It was John Hancock shouting, "Come in, come in, Revere. We are not afraid of *you!*"

There had been rumors of trouble earlier. No one in the house had slept. Hancock and Sam Adams were not the Reverend Clark's only guests. Also on hand were the wealthy merchant's old aunt, Mrs. Lydia Hancock, and his pretty fiancée, Dorothy Quincy.

On learning that the militia were mustering, Hancock waved aside the suggestion that he flee with Adams. He had no intention of leaving, he declared. He would stay and fight with the minutemen on the green.

No doubt Aunt Lydia and Miss Quincy were as impressed as the young merchant intended them to be. The archrebel was not. The arm he looped around his impetuous disciple's shoulder quivered a little—Sam Adams suffered from palsy. He pointed out that he and Hancock were "not for the field of battle." They were "for the cabinet," he added. This was a reminder that both of them were delegates to the Second Continental Congress, scheduled to open in Philadelphia less than a month hence. Eventually "King John" would permit himself to be spirited to the safety of a house farther from the Lexington-Concord road, but he and the archrebel were still quarreling when Revere departed, eager to get to Concord and raise the militia there.

By this time William Dawes had reached Lexington. The two

couriers rode out of town together, to be joined en route by Dr. Samuel Prescott. A resident of Concord, the young doctor had spent the evening with his girl in Lexington. He was a "high son of liberty," according to Revere. He knew everyone living between Lexington and Concord, knew in which of the houses militiamen resided.

He and Dawes were knocking on doors when Revere, riding ahead, spotted a couple of the British officers who had been sent out from Boston during the day to scout the region and were now coming from the direction of Concord. In a loud voice, Revere called to his companions to come "quick and help me captivate them." But the two Britishers turned out to be six, four other troopers swiftly materializing from the shadows.

In the ensuing melee Dawes managed to get away, fleeing toward Lexington. The troopers prodded their remaining captives into a pasture and began questioning them. Suddenly Dr. Prescott whirled his mount to the left, eluded his pursuers by jumping a stone wall, and streaked for Concord to spread the alarm there.

Revere broke away at the same time, only to find that the woods toward which he was dashing were alive with still more soldiers. Forced to dismount, he was the recipient of a round of stout English cursing, cut short when the senior officer, a Major Mitchell, informed the silversmith that he was interested only in nabbing British deserters. Taking Deacon Larkin's horse, the patrol moved on, leaving Revere to foot it back to Lexington.

In the pasture, surrounded by his captors, the silversmith had indulged in a little military fibbing. He had told Major Mitchell that when Gage's task force reached Lexington it would find "a large force" of at least five hundred men awaiting it. The actual number would be only a fraction of that. He told Mitchell that the boats carrying the British troops across Back Bay had sunk. That too was a fiction. Another of Revere's statements—that the departure of the redcoats from Boston had suffered a critical delay—happened to be correct.

The troubles of the British had begun early in the evening on the Boston side of Back Bay. The orders were for the redcoats to embark at ten o'clock. From eight on they were to proceed to the "Place of Rendezvous" at the foot of the Common "in small parties." As they assembled—some seven hundred in all—confusion arose following the discovery that there were not enough boats. Two crossings were required, a time-consuming operation. One member of the expedition was disgusted. "Ill plan'd and ill executed," was Ensign Barker's judgment on the British march to Concord.

It was two in the morning before the task force stepped onto the main road. By then, according to the grumbling ensign, "the Country People had got intelligence & time to assemble." There were sounds in the night everywhere: church bells ringing, men shouting, alarm guns barking. At the village of Menotomy (now West Cambridge) every house was lighted, every window a frame for curious eyes.

In an effort to speed the expedition, Colonel Smith formed his light infantry, six companies, into an advance column with orders to seize anyone encountered along the way. The main body continued to march in the center of the road. Pushing rapidly ahead, the officer in charge of the infantry units divided his men into two files. Each moved along the roadside in the gloom of the trees.

An hour or two earlier, in Lexington, Captain Parker had sent out four scouts to look for the enemy. One by one, three of them fell into the hands of the British advance column. The fourth, a boy named Thaddeus Bowman, escaped capture.

Traveling across the fields, off the road, Bowman remained unaware of the approaching British until his horse, sensing them, suddenly balked. Put on the *qui vive*, the boy looked harder—and saw what he had been sent out to see: not the infantry files hugging the dark roadsides but the main British column in the brightly moonlit distance. Wheeling his mount sharply, young Bowman galloped for Lexington, shrilling his news.

The men of the advance column, fast nearing the village,

heard the roll of the muster drum on the green there. They heard, too, a scattering of shots somewhere in the fields to their right. Warning shots? Or were these armed rustics actually firing on His Majesty's forces?

A hundred yards to the rear Colonel Smith and his second in command, Major Pitcairn, were also wondering. Smith ordered Pitcairn forward, to take charge of the advance unit.

The British had no cavalry. Either they had commandeered horses along the line of march or they had ferried a few across Back Bay. Pitcairn was mounted. Fated to die of wounds during the Battle of Bunker Hill, this virile marine officer was a man of above-average character, rough in manner but fair-minded and considerate. The charming miniature of him at the Lexington Historical Society is an amusing commentary on the craft of the portraitist. It is difficult to associate that Dresden-doll face with the hardy major or to think of those cupid-bow lips as a passageway for his blunt and often profane language.

Reaching the head of the advance column, Pitcairn was in time to greet Major Mitchell and his patrol, the unit that a short time before had captured, questioned, and then released Paul Revere. The silversmith's exercise in counterintelligence had worked. Mitchell passed on Revere's concocted tale that "a large force" of armed militiamen was waiting on the Lexington green.

Playing it safe, Pitcairn stopped his troops long enough to permit them to load and fix bayonets. This was a complicated procedure. Slightly more than five feet long overall, the standard British musket—called the Brown Bess because both walnut stock and metal barrel were brown—could be loaded only by placing the butt on the ground with the muzzle high. The soldier then tore open with his teeth one of the sixty paper cartridges he carried, poured the powder into the muzzle, and dropped the ball on top of it. Crumbling the paper, he ram-rodded it in as a wad. Then he lifted the frizzen or lid from his firing pan and tapped the barrel with the heel of his hand to force a puff of powder through the touchhole and into the pan.

Even a seasoned soldier needed fifteen seconds to fire and

reload. He aimed at nothing. The Brown Bess had no back sight. Were the slightest breeze blowing the soldier did not even look in the direction he was shooting. He turned his head away as he squeezed the "tricker" lest a flareback through the touchhole deprive him of his eyebrows or worse.

The uncertain light of dawn was setting in as Pitcairn and his troops came abreast of the Lexington meetinghouse at the narrow end of the green. Facing them on the far side were two ragged rows of armed farmers, some eighty men at the most.

Pitcairn called on the "damned rebels" to disperse. The American line wavered. Captain Parker seems first to have commanded the minutemen to hold. Then, realizing the futility of his situation, he told them to withdraw. They did, some with more alacrity than others.

Then there was a shot.

From a Brown Bess or from an American squirrel gun?

In his official report Pitcairn insisted that some of the retreating rebels turned back long enough to release "Four or Five Shott." Only then, according to the British officer, did the redcoats begin "a scattered Fire." The major was an honest man. No doubt this is what he thought happened. The minutemen and other American eyewitnesses thought otherwise. In depositions taken within a few days, over ninety of them affirmed that the first shot of the war came from a British musket.

Ensign Barker's story was that when the first shot was heard, the British regulars ran amuck, firing wildly, wielding their bayonets mercilessly, and momentarily ignoring the repeated orders of their commanding officer to stop. Not until Colonel Smith came up with the main British column were the berserk redcoats brought under control.

Obviously there was ample shooting on the British side, some on the American side. When it was over, eight Americans lay dead, nine wounded. Major Pitcairn's horse received two slight nicks in the flanks, and one redcoat would nurse a grazed and bloodied leg all the way to Concord.

At that town the patriots, alerted during the night, had

moved some of their military supplies to new hiding places. The British found and destroyed a substantial amount, although their disposal of much of it was the work of men unnerved by the unanticipated resistance they had encountered. General Gage had suggested that the troops pocket whatever musket balls turned up and scatter them about after they left the village. Instead, acting in haste, they dropped some five hundred balls into a millpond, whence on the following day the natives fished them out.

The militia leader at Concord, sixty-eight-year-old Colonel James Barrett, had a force of 250 militia. At midmorning, at the North Bridge over the Concord River, Barrett and his minutemen boldly attacked a British detachment of six companies. The British fired first—one volley; the Americans replied, and the redcoats broke in disorder and ran, rejoining their companies in the center of the village. At this point the rebels, no match for the total enemy component, retired to the hills.

It was when the British left Concord to begin their return march that their real troubles began. During the preceding hours the alarm had spread. Militia units from forty Massachusetts towns had poured into Middlesex County, well over three thousand men in all.

As the redcoats slogged homeward, they were the target of angry farmers, many of them shooting from behind the stone walls that are still the fences of New England.

"Before we had gone half a mile," Ensign Barker would write, "we were fired on from all sides, but mostly from the rear, where People had hid themselves in houses, till we passed and then fired; the Country was an amazing strong one, full of Hills, Woods . . . etc. . . . all lined with people who kept an incessant fire upon us, as we did too upon them but not with the same advantage, for they were so concealed there was hardly any seeing them; in this way we marched . . . their numbers increasing, ours reducing by deaths, wounds and fatigue, our ammunition near expended."

Hours earlier Colonel Smith, disturbed by the tumult of the

countryside, had rushed a messenger to Boston requesting a relief force. Again there were delays in the city. Smith and his embattled troopers had retraced their steps almost to Lexington before the reinforcements came, not quite a thousand men under Colonel Hugh Lord Percy.

His lordship had brought along two cannons. Emplaced first at one point and then at another, the six-pounders had only a slightly deterring effect. As the now-enlarged British column moved on, the firing on its flanks and rear continued.

Lieutenant Mackenzie had come with the reinforcements. "Several of the Troops," he wrote, ". . . were so enraged at the suffering from an unseen Enemy, that they forced open many of the houses from which the fire proceeded, and put to death all those found in them." A minuteman from Groton, young Amos Farnsworth, would recall stepping into one of these houses to find himself in a room "where Blud was half over shoes."

On the western outskirts of Cambridge the British officers conferred. Leaving Boston by the Neck, Percy had brought his men up the mainland by way of the Charles River bridge. By now it could be assumed that the patriots had destroyed the bridge. Instead of proceeding south from Cambridge, the British turned left. Moving rapidly, they headed for another neck, the marshy isthmus joining the mainland to the Charlestown peninsula. The rebels would know better than to follow them there, as the British would have the advantage of the peninsula's high hills.

Lieutenant Mackenzie would never forget the dash for Charlestown Neck, how patriot bands, following "pretty close," kept "calling out 'King Hancock forever!'"; how one of the last Americans to shoot at the fleeing troopers was a husky black man who was wounded in the return fire of the British.

It was seven in the evening before the redcoats gained the safety of the Charlestown heights, dawn of the next day before all of them, succored by boats rushed across the river, were in Boston.

At Province House Thomas Gage listened impassively to his

officers' preliminary reports. When a few days later he sat down to write his own report for London, he could only trust that his superiors would remember how often he had pleaded for help. Stolidly he set forth the statistics: 73 British soldiers killed, 174 wounded; as against 40 Americans known killed and 39 wounded. Soldierly pride impelled him to make light of the affair. In his opening remarks he described it as a "little action near Boston."

He knew better. He knew that it was little only in the sense that the acorn, seed of the oak, is little. The family quarrel had become an armed rebellion.

# PART TWO

## THE WAR

# 11

## A Gentleman from Virginia

WORD OF THE "tragikal carnage" at Lexington and Concord moved through the colonies as fast as young Israel Bissel, a Massachusetts postrider, could carry it.

In the best of summer weather the stagecoach out of Boston needed six days for the run to New York. Starting near Boston, at Watertown, Bissel made it in five days and a few hours, having halted at numerous places so that local patriot leaders could copy his message from the Bay Colony committee of safety.

By noon of Sunday, April 23, he was in New York; by five o'clock the next afternoon, in Philadelphia, where at a mass meeting on the following day thousands of citizens endorsed resolutions calling for the raising by that town of three volunteer battalions to be known as the Associators.

From the Quaker City Bissel streaked to Annapolis to deliver his message to the Maryland Provincial Congress, in session there. Other men rushed copies westward. Before the end of the month the news was in north-central Kentucky, where a group of pioneers, some of them just building their houses, cheered and named their new settlement "Lexington."

As the news traveled southward from Annapolis, the patriots of the lower colonies bestirred themselves. In the capitals of Georgia and the Carolinas the liberty boys raised armies, commissioned warships, seized the military supplies belonging to their provinces, organized provincial congresses, and took over the reins of government.

When the news reached Williamsburg on April 28, the Virginia Whigs were already in action. Earlier that month the royal governor, gruff and impulsive John Murray Lord Dunmore, had removed the military stores of the colony, twenty barrels of gunpowder, from the magazine in Williamsburg to a British warship in the James River. Accused by the people of stealing "their powder," the governor said he had heard rumors of a slave uprising. He had shifted the supplies to place them beyond the reach of the blacks.

No one believed him. The patriot leaders said his lordship's real objective was to leave the colony "defenseless" against Great Britain.

At Hanover Patrick Henry deserted his law office to put himself at the front of a citizen army and march for Williamsburg. Ahead of him ran an ultimatum to the governor: Put the military stores back or face armed resistance. His lordship gave in to the extent of agreeing to pay for the powder, and Henry returned in triumph to Hanover. There he made ready to travel to Philadelphia to take his seat as one of his colony's seven delegates to the Second Continental Congress.

On the dogwood-dappled banks of the Potomac River, in the manor house of Mount Vernon plantation, another Virginia delegate pondered events.

In that troubled spring George Washington was forty-three. Carrying some 280 pounds on a six-foot-two-inch frame, he presented an impressive appearance, notwithstanding the narrowness of his chest and shoulders and the faint markings left on his blond features by a near-fatal attack of smallpox in his youth. We have the word of his contemporaries that the face which eyes us so blandly from the dollar bill was in fact exceedingly changeable—occasionally distorted by a lifelong effort to control a violent temper, always lively when its owner's feelings were engaged, frequently softened by a bright and amiable smile.

By 1775 the Virginia squire had been a force in the affairs of the Old Dominion for over two decades. While still in his early twenties his marked abilities had won him the patronage of two of the colony's most powerful figures—Scottish-born Robert Dinwiddie, the then royal governor, and Colonel William Fairfax, prominent planter.

Courtly, charming, aggressive, and ambitious, young Washington made the most of the opportunities these influential men threw in his path. He fought capably in the French and Indian War, part of the time as the commanding officer of the Virginia army. He sat for years in the House of Burgesses. In the early 1750's he became the master of Mount Vernon plantation. Toward the end of that decade he further improved his fortunes through marriage to the wealthy widow Martha Dandridge Custis.

His financial situation was similar to that of most of the Southern planters. He was rich in land and slaves but poor in pocket. He seldom had enough cash to meet his mortgage payments and his bills, and like the other members of his class in Virginia he was keenly aware that a major source of this embarrassment lay three thousand miles away. England was his one big customer. As such it dominated the transactions involved. It paid him relatively little for his wheat and tobacco. It charged fancy prices for the manufactured goods he could procure only from it. It is easy to understand why in 1765 the Stamp Act struck Washington as one discomfort too many. Thereafter he supported every patriot move.

In common with most Virginia gentlemen he had a passion for real estate, and a rather complex development lends color to the British charge that he was "avaritious" in this respect.

Desperate for soldiers at the onset of the French and Indian War, Governor Dinwiddie set aside 200,000 acres of crown land along the Ohio River for distribution among those who volunteered in the Virginia army. The clear intent of Dinwiddie's proclamation was that at least most if not all of these lands were to go to enlisted men. But when, after many delays, the grants materialized, several officers contrived to lay their hands on sizable shares, and Colonel Washington got the biggest share of all.

The patents to these lands became effective in 1772 and 1773—or so Washington thought. He blazed with chagrin when in the spring of 1775 Governor Dunmore announced that because of technical illegalities connected with their acquisition, none of the colonel's Ohio claims was valid. Washington's letter of protest to the governor was politely worded. His lordship's answer was not. In a chill, spare note, Dunmore informed the master of Mount Vernon that the patents to his western properties were "null and void"—a pronouncement that in no way lessened George Washington's devotion to the patriot cause. Grim were his thoughts on the morning of May 4, 1775, as he got into his chariot to begin the journey to Philadelphia, having packed in his trunk the militia uniform—red jacket trimmed with blue cuffs and lapels, and blue breeches—that he would wear during the opening sessions of the Second Continental Congress.*

Far to the north another delegate to the forthcoming Congress, John Adams of Massachusetts, was in a state of mind bordering on delirium. When the news of Lexington-Concord reached him at his Braintree farmhouse, he told his wife that here was an event he had been half hoping for and half dreading all along. What more proof, he asked Abigail, did any American need that the day for polite petitions to crown and Parliament had passed. It was time now to talk of independence—of war, if need be.

Quivering with pride that his countrymen had chased the "flower of His Majesty's army" all across Middlesex County,

---

* Tradition puts Congressman Washington in the blue and buff uniform he later donned as commander in chief, but in his great biography Douglas Southall Freeman (volume 3; footnote, page 426) cites circumstantial evidence to the contrary. The buff and blue seems to have been introduced by the Light Infantry Company of the First Battalion of the Philadelphia Associators. Washington found it becoming and later used it.

Adams hastened from home to look at the situation in Cambridge, where the fat senior officer of the Massachusetts militia, General Artemas Ward, had established his headquarters. The troops bivouacked around the general were no longer the "Massachusetts army." They had become the "New England army," their ranks swollen by units from Connecticut, Rhode Island, and New Hampshire. Already thousands of them had encamped in a thin, fourteen-mile arc around Boston, imprisoning General Gage and his forces behind that city's liquid boundaries.

The excitement of it all was too much for John Adams's never-robust health. He was scarcely home again when he fell ill and had to take to his bed.

The doctor diagnosed a "fever." He spoke of "alarming symptoms." To the stricken patriot the medical findings were a death sentence. The opening date of the Congress, May 10, was close at hand. History in the grand manner would certainly be made at that session. As the fever lingered and the "alarming symptoms" refused to leave, John Adams was stabbed with the agonizing possibility that he might not be there to help make it.

Finally word came that the other Massachusetts delegates had taken off for Philadelphia without him. The disgruntled invalid could be persuaded to remain where he was only two more days. Then, against the advice of the doctor, he was on his feet, getting ready to head south in the family sulky.

Abigail saw him off in the pale light of a spring dawn, monotonously abjuring him to drive slowly and to take his medicines. He drove so fast that he caught up with the other Bay Colony deputies at Hartford. From there on the events of the journey were just the medicines John Adams needed.

At New York the provincial militia turned out to escort the delegates down Broadway. Adams noted with satisfaction that "not a single Tory dared show his face" among the hurrahing crowds. On the outskirts of Philadelphia the travelers—their party enlarged now by Connecticut, New York, and New Jersey deputies—were greeted by hundreds of citizens and citizen-soldiers.

At the journey's end John Adams's "alarming symptoms" recurred; but neither a scratchy throat nor inflamed eyes could dim his pleasure at finding that the City of Brotherly Love had become a "field of Mars."

Philadelphia's newly formed battalions were marching and executing the manual of arms in every open space. Even some of the Quakers were in uniform.

Congress this time was meeting in the Assembly room on the first floor of the statehouse. In this Georgian chamber with its white-paneled walls and twin fireplaces, curving rows of delicate chairs faced the low dais where sat portly Peyton Randolph of Virginia—elected president for a second term—and ascetic Charles Thomson, reappointed to the secretaryship he would hold throughout the life of the Continental Congress.

Looking around, John Adams saw many familiar faces and some new ones. In his eyes the most welcome new face belonged to Dr. Lyman Hall of Georgia. Little Georgia had sent no delegates to the First Continental Congress. Dr. Hall came with the blessing of only one parish (county), but his presence meant that at last all thirteen colonies were at least physically represented.

One of the new delegates bore a name well known to everyone. His sixty-nine years resting easily on his hulking shoulders, Benjamin Franklin had come home after years of service in London as agent for several colonies, unofficial ambassador for all of them.

Boston's son by birth, Philadelphia's pride by adoption, the white-haired patriarch radiated calm and common sense. A man well aware of his great worth—and marvelously adept at hiding that awareness—Ben Franklin spoke seldom during the debate on any measure but influenced every measure in those informal confabs off the floor where the real decisions of a legislative body are hammered out.

One of the old faces was in evidence only fleetingly. Returned to his seat against his will, Tory Galloway resigned at the close of the second meeting.

Emboldened by the martial atmosphere around him, John Adams started the proceedings with a call to arms. As he saw it, the Americans had "unsheathed the sword" at Lexington and Concord. They must not now "pusillanimously" return it to the scabbard. He proposed that the colonies forget their royal charters and set up their own governments.

As Adams reached the peroration of his remarks, he realized that he had said too much too soon. On the faces around him he saw puzzled expressions. Even Cousin Sam was frowning as though to say, "Not so fast, John, not so fast." The proposal that the colonies form new governments was set aside, and John confessed in a letter to "Dear Abigail" that he had made a mistake. He likened the colonies to a "convoy at sea." The faster ships were going to have to hold back until the slower ones caught up. The delegates realized that the Americans must now put themselves in a posture of defense. Many, however, still longed for a reconciliation with Mother England.

In the days that followed they set up a committee charged with preparing what would be America's last petition to the King for a redress of grievances. They named George Washington and others to another committee charged with drawing up plans for a "Grand American Army." John Adams wrote Abigail that his colleagues were "oscillating between love and hate." One minute they pleaded for peace, the next they prepared for war.

On the eighteenth, incredible news arrived. Far away in the upper reaches of New York Ethan Allen of the New Hampshire Grants (now Vermont) and Connecticut-born Colonel Benedict Arnold had twisted the tail of the British lion.

Allen, backed by his Green Mountain Boys, and Arnold, leading a parcel of militia, had captured Ticonderoga, a star-shaped, bluestone fort garrisoned by a few British regulars. The story went that the redcoats capitulated without a shot when Allen called on them to do so "in the name of the Great Jehovah and the Continental Congress."

The Almighty may have sanctioned this startling development, but no one in Congress had. The news was no sooner on hand than a dozen delegates were on their feet. Some gloated, some deplored. A few insisted that Ticonderoga be returned to England at once along with a note of apology to His Majesty—a suggestion that would have sent John Adams back to his sick bed had anything come of it. The revelation that the fort was loaded with cannon, a scarce item in American arsenals, had a soothing effect even on those who shivered at the thought of how Great Britain might react to this unprovoked seizure of His Majesty's property.

Late May brought a blistering sun that put the delegates to the trouble of deciding whether to open the windows and endure the horse flies from a nearby livery stable or close them and suffocate.

On the thirtieth they approved of sixty-four articles of war drafted by Washington and his fellow committeemen. Now the United Colonies of North America, as they were starting to call themselves, had the rules for an army. All they lacked was the army.

There were conflicting ideas among the delegates as to how that body should be summoned into being. The Massachusetts committee of safety requested Congress to "adopt" the New England army dug in around Boston, but there were objections to this procedure. Most of them came from the Pennsylvania, New Jersey, and New York delegates. The feeling among these gentlemen was that the New England colonies should not be allowed to dominate the situation lest they foist their "demokratical ways" and iron "Presbyterianism" on the others. Instead of taking over the Yankee troops, the delegates endorsed a resolution that "six companies of expert riflemen . . . be immediately raised . . ." These units, the nucleus of what would later be the Continental Army, were to "march and join the army near Boston, to be there employed . . . under the command of the chief officer in that army."

The delegates' emphasis on "companies of expert riflemen" tells us that they shared the popular feeling that in the rifle, as developed on the Kentucky frontier, America had a new and irresistible instrument of war.

For two centuries gunsmiths had known that they could increase the accuracy and range of a musket by cutting spiral grooves in the bore, thus giving a spinning motion to the bullet. But European armies had not adopted the rifle because it took even longer to load than the smoothbore musket. America's ingenious backwoodsmen overcame this difficulty by placing the ball in a greased patch of linen or leather before driving it in with a ramrod. The result was the world's first precision gun. Whereas the smoothbore was inaccurate beyond one hundred yards, the rifle could hit a target as large as a man at up to three hundred yards.

Having called the rifle companies into existence, the delegates turned to a touchy matter. They must now select a commander in chief for their new grand army. New England had borne the brunt of the quarrel with Britain. It stood to reason that the "chief officer" of her forces, Artemas Ward, should receive the honor. But at forty-eight Ward was heavy and sickly.

Had he been younger, vigorous, and the veteran of a dozen wars, John Adams and his cohorts would have passed him over. The Massachusetts delegates realized that the American union was paper-thin. The loss of just one of the more important of the wavering colonies—of Pennsylvania or New Jersey or New York—could tear it. The choice of a New Englander to lead the army could easily crack the union. On the other hand, the appointment of a man from one of the more southerly provinces would most certainly cement it.

Not his own area then but the union was on John Adams's mind when on a stiflingly warm June afternoon he rose to nominate the man he and his colleagues had selected after many ardent parleys.

Adams began by saying that he was about to recommend a man dedicated to the cause and "of independent fortune." At this point John Hancock—temporarily presiding in the place of Peyton Randolph—sat a little straighter in the presidential chair. The wealthy young merchant had let it be known that he would not be averse to shouldering the burdens of high command. Never mind that his military experience had been limited to Boston Common. Anyone who had ever seen him lead his nattily attired cadets across that rolling green could confirm that he guided his prancing horse with aplomb.

But Adams was not thinking of Hancock. The name he had in mind belonged to a "*gentleman from Virginia* who is among us here . . ." At the word "Virginia," Hancock slumped, and George Washington hurried into an adjoining room, overcome with embarrassment.

The debate on Adams's nomination ran on for two hot and airless days. Several delegates, by no means all of them from New England, reiterated vehemently that the commanding officer should come from that region. Several said that Adams had chosen the wrong Virginian. Another and far-more-qualified one was available.

Their reference was to Charles Lee. Exactly sixteen days Washington's junior, England-born and classically educated, Lee was famous for his military acumen. He was equally well known for his quick temper, his sloppy dress, and his unbelievable appearance. His dark and fleshy face was a catastrophe, "fascinatingly ugly," as someone said: large round eyes; a long, springing, aquiline nose, incongruously delicate in its coarse setting. His jutting chin gave the impression that his head was on the verge of leaving a body of skeletal thinness.

Born near the walled city of Chester in northwest England, the son of people who were gentry on both sides, Lee had practically grown up under arms. He received his first commission in the British Army in his fourteenth year. Coming to America with his regiment in 1755, he fought in the French and Indian War and fell in love with "charming Philadelphia." Its women, he said, were "extremely pretty and . . . passionately fond of red coats, which is for us a most fortunate piece of absurdity." The Indians intrigued him. Off and on he lived among them, temporarily marrying the daughter of a chief who bore him twins, a boy and a girl.

When after his return to England his regiment broke up and all chance of military advancement disappeared, he offered his services to Poland. He was a major general in the army of that country when in 1773 he came back to America to make his home on a Virginia plantation. Already he had concluded that the provincial cause was just. Soon after his return to the colonies he announced that, if the need arose, he would gladly command American troops.

Those who favored him over Washington dilated upon Lee's long and varied experience under fire. Eventually, however, their arguments fell before a point stressed by John Adams. Washington was native-born, Lee was not. Too much was at stake to entrust the job to a man whose origins lay in the mother country.

Adams waited impatiently for the arguments to cease. He had long ago discovered that wordiness was inevitable in an assembly in which every member considered himself "a great man, an orator, a critic, a statesman." He wrote Abigail that were it "moved and seconded that three and two make five, we should be entertained with logic and rhetoric, law, history, politics, and mathematics, and then—we should pass the resolution unanimously in the affirmative."

Which was precisely what happened to his nomination. At length the delegates talked themselves out. On the morning of June 15, 1775, John Hancock—still presiding—lowered his gavel portentously. It was "the order of Congress," he said, "to inform George Washington, Esq. of the unanimous vote in choosing him to be General and Commander-in-Chief of the forces raised and to be raised in defense of American liberty. The Congress hopes the gentleman will accept."

He did, touchingly. The master of Mount Vernon did not

account himself one of the orators of the assembly. He read his brief acceptance speech from a paper taken from the pocket of his uniform. He was aware of his inadequacies, he said, but he would "exert every Power I possess . . . for the Support of the glorious Cause . . ."

Washington's orders were to proceed to Cambridge, and before his departure the Congress hastily completed the framework of the army he would take over there.

The articles of war left to the various colonies the naming of the regimental and company officers—colonels, majors, captains, and below. The Congress now drew up a slate of general officers. This operation, like the selection of the commander in chief, was riddled with political implications. If the new army were to be fully supported, the distribution of its principal leaders, the major generals and brigadiers, must be wide enough geographically to give every segment of the country a voice in its high councils.

With only a minimum of oratory, the name of Artemas Ward went on the list as senior major general. As New England had been denied the big prize, it seemed only fair to let her have two of the second prizes. Happily the intensely patriotic province of Connecticut had an authentic military hero in burly, hard-chinned Israel Putnam.

At fifty-seven Putnam was a legendary figure. Colonial mothers outlined to their sons the kind of men they wanted them to be by relating how "Old Put," attacked by an enormous wolf, had overwhelmed the beast with his bare hands. Many tales were told of his exploits in the French and Indian War and in the battles against the great Ottawa chieftain Pontiac, during the Indian uprising that had succeeded that conflict. The delegates in Philadelphia inscribed his name on their roster of major generals with higher hopes than Old Put, a brave and honest man but slow-minded and unimaginative, would be able to fulfill.

Turning from New England to the middle colonies, the delegates found in Philip Schuyler, chief squire or "patroon" of the upper Hudson River valley, a man acceptable to the half a dozen aristocratic families who dominated the affairs of conservative New York.

The South presented no problem. The delegates wrote the name of Charles Lee immediately under that of Ward, making the well-born eccentric the third-ranking officer in the Continental forces. When Lee demanded $30,000 to compensate him for the loss of his British pension, they paid it promptly, convinced that they were getting a bargain.

The problem of designating the major generals out of the way, the delegates issued commissions to eight brigadiers. Of the names proposed for these positions, only one—that of Nathanael Greene of Rhode Island—raised serious misgivings. It was said on the Rhode Islander's behalf that he had been one of the first officers of his colony to lead troops to the support of Massachusetts following the skirmishes at Lexington and Concord. On the debit side were physical disabilities. Greene walked with a limp, owing to a stiff knee contracted from standing too long in one position before the forge of his father's anchorsmith shop. He was a recurrent sufferer from asthma, and the anxious delegates had no way of knowing that he would be one of the ablest officers in the American Army.

It was one thing to give birth to a grand army on paper. It was another to finance it. Where were the representatives of a nonexistent nation to get the money? They could try to borrow it, but from whom? No American patriot had the resources that the creation of a Continental force required. Until the Americans decided whether they were going to wage war or sue for peace, little likelihood existed that they could negotiate loans in Europe—eager as were France and some of the other Old World governments to assist any enemy of Great Britain.

In the summer of 1775 the delegates did the only thing they could. They turned on the printing presses, thus opening the floodgates to a torrent of "continental dollars" that would fall in value so swiftly that within a few years the barbers of Philadelphia would be using them to paper the walls of their shops.

On June 22 the delegates *"Resolved,* That a sum not exceeding two million of Spanish milled dollars be emitted by the Congress in bills of credit, for the defence of America." And on the following day, with a needle-sharp drizzle draining from a burned-looking sky, George Washington set forth on his ride to destiny.

"I have this morning," John Adams wrote Abigail, "been out of town to accompany our generals, Washington, Lee and Schuyler, a little way on their journey to the American camp before Boston. The three generals were all mounted on horseback . . . All the delegates from Massachusetts, with their servants and carriages, attended; many others of the delegates from Congress; a large troop of light horse in their uniforms; many officers of the militia besides, in theirs; music playing, &c, &c. Such is the pride and pomp of War. I . . . worn out with scribbling for my bread and my liberty, low in spirits and weak in health, must leave others to wear the laurels which I have sown; others to eat the bread I have earned . . ."

Poor Adams! Left behind to deal with the grubby details of civilian administration while Washington and his aides cantered northward to revel in "the pride and pomp of War."

A war that had already begun.

Twenty miles north of the city, Washington and his cavalcade encountered a sweating express rider speeding important news to Philadelphia. On the highlands of the Charlestown peninsula above Boston, the first full-scale engagement of the Revolution—the Battle of Bunker Hill—had taken place.

# 12

# "Fire and sword, a dreadful prospect"

According to dainty Ann Hulton, sister of one of the British commissioners of customs in Boston, that town was "unfit for civilized habitation" in the late spring of 1775. To a friend in England she wrote that no sooner had His Majesty's "brave soldiers" returned from Concord than "the Country pourd down its Thousands, and at this time, from the entrance of Boston Neck at Roxbury round by Cambridge to Charlestown the city is surrounded by at least 20,000 Men . . . We are threatened . . . with fire and sword, a dreadful prospect . . ."

In telling "Dear Mrs. Lightbody" of distant Liverpool that Boston might be attacked at any moment, Miss Hulton was overestimating the resources of the enemy. The Americans had men enough to contain the city, but they were hopelessly deficient in ammunition and weapons. In the lines commanded by Nathanael Greene at Jamaica Plain and in the square of Harvard College at Cambridge, men drilled with empty guns or wooden staves on their shoulders.

But Miss Hulton spoke truly when she informed Mrs. Lightbody that Boston, "cut off from all communication with the Country," faced famine and disease. Supplies could come only from the sea, and that would become an increasingly insecure source as America's first "navy" took form—a gaggle of New England privateers happy to seize supply ships from under the very bows of British men-of-war.

In blockaded Boston, within a few months, beef would be selling at an unprecedented eighteen English pence a pound.

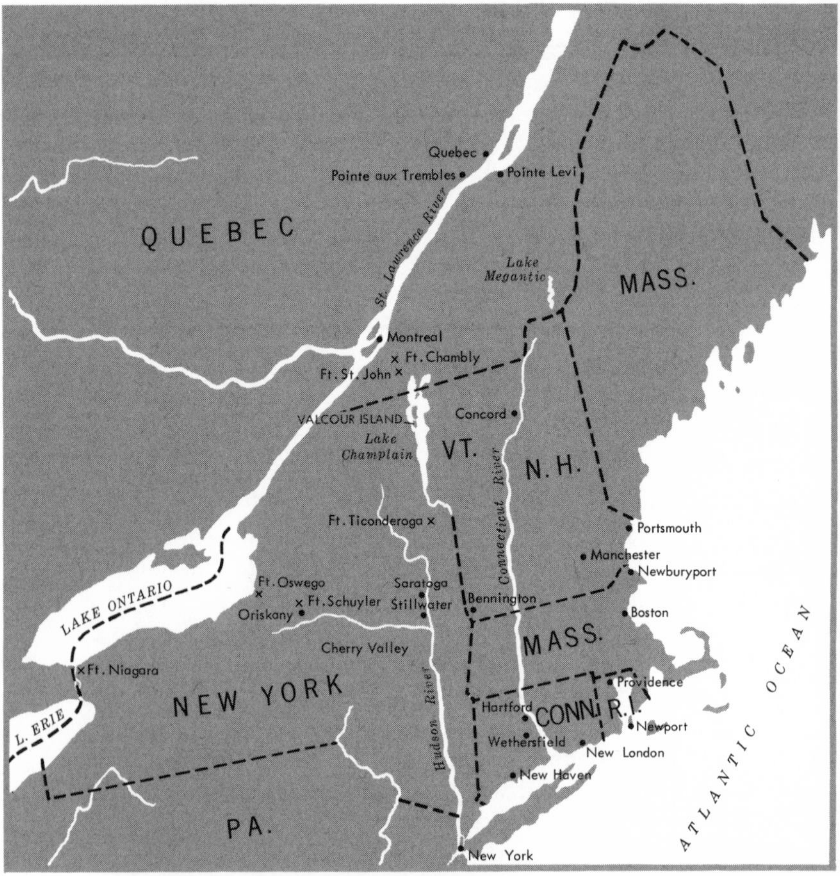

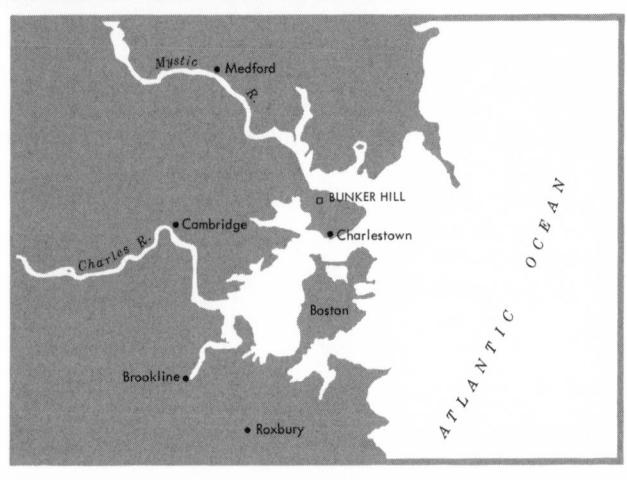

QUEBEC

Quebec
Pointe aux Trembles • • Pointe Levi

Lake
Megantic

MASS.

× Ft. Chambly
Montreal
Ft. St. John ×

Lake
Champlain

VALCOUR ISLAND

Concord •

VT.

N.H.

St. Lawrence River

Connecticut River

Ft. Ticonderoga ×

Portsmouth
Manchester •
Newburyport

Ft. Oswego
×
LAKE ONTARIO × Ft. Schuyler
Oriskany •

Saratoga •
Stillwater •

Bennington •

Boston •

× Ft. Niagara

Cherry Valley •

MASS.

L. ERIE

NEW YORK

Hartford •
Wethersfield •

CONN.

Providence •
R.I.

Newport •
New London •

PA.

Hudson River

New Haven •

New York •

ATLANTIC OCEAN

Mystic R.
• Medford

□ BUNKER HILL

Charles R.
• Cambridge

• Charlestown

Boston

Brookline •

• Roxbury

ATLANTIC OCEAN

The coming of winter would bring new hardships. Before the British left town, every fence in Boston and most of the outbuildings would be gone. Even some of the wooden churches would disappear, ripped apart to supply fuel for heating homes and preparing food.

For distressed Ann Hulton a little hope flashed in the gloom when on May 25 a ship of the line brought into Boston harbor three high-ranking British officers, along with word that the troop reinforcements Gage had been begging for would be on hand in a few days.

Senior officer of the wildly welcomed trio was tall, dark, heavy-featured Major General Sir William Howe. A good soldier, Billy Howe was at his best on the battlefield. Off it he was just a big, bluff, easygoing man, fond of liquor and women. At one time he had declared himself sympathetic to the colonials. He had said he would never fight against them. Later many people explained his lackluster performance in America by contending that he never did fight them—not, at any rate, wholeheartedly.

The two major generals who accompanied Howe to Boston in 1775 were strikingly unlike.

John "Gentleman Johnny" Burgoyne was flashy, debonair, and outgoing. His soldiers adored him. He treated them as if they were human beings, a practice that most eighteenth-century British officers regarded as unwise if not immoral. Burgoyne's talents were not limited to the battlefield. He was the author of a comedy that only recently had delighted the theatergoers of London.

Sir Henry Clinton* had the stealthy eyes and pinched expression of an extreme introvert. He once described himself as "a shy bitch." Shy he was, a man desperate for friends but so distrustful of other men that he could seldom accept the friendship they offered. His mind teemed with what were often

---

* He did not actually become "Sir" Henry until a few months later. Nor did "Sir" William Howe.

excellent military ideas. He might have made a name for himself as a strategist had not his inner uncertainties again and again caused him to execute his plans improperly or not at all.

The arrival of the three major generals was known on the American side of the Charles River almost as soon as it occurred. General Gage had permitted most of the patriots of Boston to leave the city. Those who stayed had become adept at getting messages through the lines. The soldiers manning the American positions around the city enjoyed a chuckle on learning that the three generals had crossed the ocean on a vessel called *Cerberus*. In Greek mythology Cerberus was the three-headed dog who guarded the gates of hell. Around the camp-fires jeweling the western banks of the Charles during the soft summer nights the Yankees chanted:

> Burgoyne, Clinton and Howe:
> Bow, wow, wow!

In Boston the British generals conferred. What steps should they take to protect the city against the nearby prominences that commanded it? On the mainland, to the southeast, stood Dorchester Heights. On Charlestown peninsula, to the north, rose two high hills: Bunker Hill, near the isthmus joining the peninsula to the mainland, and Breed's Hill, a few hundred yards to the southeast. From all of these points the town lay open to bombardment.

Fatefully ignoring Dorchester Heights, the British leaders sketched plans for taking over Charlestown peninsula. They set June 18 as the date for carrying them out.

On the thirteenth their intentions were known in the headquarters of General Artemas Ward in Cambridge. On the sixteenth Ward ordered twelve hundred men to march the four miles to the peninsula and fortify Bunker Hill. Israel Putnam, having rushed to Cambridge from his Connecticut home immediately on hearing about Lexington-Concord, went along as a volunteer.

Young Corporal Amos Farnsworth of Groton—a member of the expedition—noted proudly in his journal that the officer in charge, William Prescott, was the colonel of "our own regiment." At Cambridge, "agreeable to orders," Farnsworth wrote, "our Regiment Preadid [paraded] . . . was Drawn up and herd Prayers, and about Dusk . . . our men marched to Bunker-Hill and begun their intrenchment. And Careed it on with the utmost Viger all Night."

Separated from the main body to help set up "centers" (outposts) in Charlestown village, the Groton corporal failed to notice that the entrenchments were not dug on Bunker Hill. Prescott and his fellow officers concluded that Bunker was too far from the city for their four small fieldpieces to be effective. They pressed on to Breed's Hill. This 67-foot mound behind the village was close to Boston. It was even closer to the British frigate *Lively,* standing in the Charles.

On Breed's circular summit, shortly after midnight, the men began throwing up a roughly oblong earthen bastion, reinforced with twisted branches, 160 feet long and 80 feet wide. When at sunrise an astonished British sailor spotted this structure from the deck of the *Lively,* it was almost finished.

Boston was awakened that Saturday morning by a bombardment from the British warships and from the batteries in the city itself that would spew Breed's Hill with grape and chain shot until well into the afternoon.

At Province House the British warlords argued. Sir Henry Clinton proposed meeting the emergency in the classic manner. Go in behind the newly erected fort, he urged; land troops on the neck of Charlestown peninsula, support them with a crossfire from British vessels in both the Charles and in the smaller estuary, the Mystic River, which formed the peninsula's northern boundary.

To this sensible proposal Admiral Samuel Graves objected. Although Graves had been in command of the fleet at Boston for more than a year, he had not yet got around to testing the Mystic River. He knew nothing of its shoals and mudflats.

The decision was for Howe to ferry 2,400 redcoats across the Charles. He was to land them at Morton's Hill on the eastern-most tip of the roughly triangular peninsula. From there the redcoats were to walk up to the fort into all the fire the enemy could offer and simply grab the place.

Boston wilted under a sun that would send the thermometer into the nineties for the first time that summer. The British regulars assembling on the Long Wharf and at the North Battery sweated under their woolen coats and 100-pound field packs. Drums rattled and fifes skirled as they stepped into the rowboats that would carry them over the Charles.

They were a special breed, these wiry, muscular little men of Great Britain's eighteenth-century army. They came, with rare exceptions, from the dregs of England's society: from the slums of its seaports, the alleys of its mill towns, the dank cells of its prisons. Not all came of their own volition. His Majesty's need for soldiers always exceeded the supply. Illegal press gangs, roving England's dingy waterfronts, regularly shanghaied men too destitute to protest and sold them to the military.

Once in the army the English private remained there for life. He got threepence a day, paid for his food and equipment, for everything he needed except his uniform, his quarters, and the repairs to his weapon.

The bravery he exhibited during the Revolution cannot be attributed solely to the savage discipline under which he fought. British Tommy and Massachusetts Yankee had a common denominator. Each believed he was fighting for the right. "Poor Bloody Tommy" wasn't knowledgeable about the great affairs of his time and place. He was aware, however, that at the close of the French and Indian War Great Britain could have had one of the richest French islands in the West Indies. It had chosen instead to take Canada, to protect its American subjects against their old enemies there.

Most of the soldiers who went across the Charles River with General Howe that hot Saturday in 1775 were eager to take on a "contumacious set of scoundrels" whose defiance of "the best and kindest government in the world" struck them as "rank ingratitude."

To be sure, a few of them were not of this mind. Soon after the British began their landing on the peninsula, five redcoats broke away. Off they ran to Breed's Hill to join the enemy. All were caught within minutes, two executed on the spot.

Throughout the war desertions would be a problem for both sides. By daybreak the close to twelve hundred men originally on Breed's Hill had shrunk to nine hundred. By noon another four hundred had stolen away.

All morning the exhausted Americans remaining on the hill strained to complete their fort and to protect their left flank with knee-high breastworks across the lowlands along the Mystic River. At dawn Israel Putnam had hastened to Cambridge to beg General Ward for men and provisions. Already frightened at his daring in dispatching three regiments to the highly vulnerable peninsula, Ward refused to spare another man from the encampments within his immediate vicinity. He did call for wagons and supplies—wagons that were never found or if found were never loaded and moved. Only reluctantly did he dispatch a plea for help to Medford, where Colonel John Stark and his New Hampshire militia had stationed themselves. Stark led two hundred troops to the peninsula. These soldiers, along with a few from other companies, were the only reinforcements the men at the fort would receive.

Early in the afternoon the president of the Provincial Congress, Dr. Joseph Warren, made his way to the Charlestown area. A widower and the father of four small children, the handsome physician had recently closed his Boston practice to devote all of his time to the Whig cause. Offered the relatively safe post of physician-general in the Massachusetts army, he had turned it down, had accepted instead a commission as a provincial major general.

En route to the peninsula he met an old friend who begged

him to stay away from the fort on Breed's Hill. The friend predicted that before evening every man there would be "killed or captured." Warren remembered a Latin epigram from his grammar-school days. *"Dulce et decorum est pro patria mori,"* he quoted. "It is sweet and fitting to die for one's country."

Leaving his horse at Bunker Hill, Warren walked the half mile to the banks of the Mystic where Israel Putnam, back from Cambridge, was directing the completion of the riverside defenses. Old Put saluted and asked for orders. Warren said he had not come to take command but to serve wherever an extra hand was needed. Putnam sent him up to the fort where the appearance of the president of the Provincial Congress bolstered the spirits of its weary occupants.

About three o'clock the British cannonading ceased. A leaden silence wrapped Breed's Hill as the British regulars, moving in precise lines, emerged from the tall grass at the foot of the long eastern slope to begin their climb.

From the summit, cracking the stillness, came a few shots. Only a few. Within seconds American officers were darting along the parapets of the fort, kicking up the guns in their men's hands, reminding them that powder was scarce, to wait until the British were close.

Twice the redcoats marched up the hill. Twice a blast of musketry from the fort at the last minute sliced off their forward ranks like a knife.

As the survivors reeled back down the hill for a second time, Dr. Warren ran from group to group within the fort. "Lick them once more, boys," he entreated, "and . . . we can drink tea in peace for the rest of our lives." At this point American casualties were small, two dead, twenty-four wounded; but Dr. Warren's cheering words could not obliterate an unpleasant reality.

The only gunpowder left was in the cannons. Hastily torn from its containers and distributed, it gave the men only three rounds apiece.

In the hummocky pasture at the bottom of the hill, General

Howe was regrouping his men. At last he was letting them drop their heavy packs. His command now was "Fix bayonets!"

From behind their hilltop curtain of earth and brush the Americans watched these preparations. Those who had served with the British in the Old French Wars knew what they meant. To compensate for the limited accuracy of the "Brown Bess," the British had raised to a high art the maneuver of finishing off an attack with a bayonet charge. The men huddling behind the fort and husbanding their failing stock of ammunition realized what they were in for as once more General Howe's regulars came stolidly up the hill.

This time there was no stopping them.

Amos Farnsworth had hurried up from Charlestown during the day. He was inside the fort when the British began hurtling the parapets. There was bloody hand-to-hand fighting before the defenders gave up. Tumbling down the western slope of Breed's Hill with the others, Farnsworth was struck twice in the back.

Probably not one of the retreating Americans realized that Dr. Warren was not with them. He lay just behind the fort, a brown dent in his left temple where the fatal ball had struck.

Beside him lay Caesar Bason, one of the eight blacks fighting with the Americans that afternoon. The conduct of another black patriot, Salem Poor, would prompt fourteen Massachusetts officers to commend him to Congress as "a brave and gallant" soldier who "in the late Battle at Charlestown behaved like an experienced officer." Unlike Bason, Poor had survived, would serve at White Plains and at Valley Forge.

By five o'clock the misnamed Battle of Bunker Hill was over. During the afternoon the British had set Charlestown village afire to destroy the American outposts there. That night in the reddish glow of its embers they sadly collected their dead, their wounded, and their prisoners.

Sir Henry Clinton urged General Howe to go after the fleeing Americans. Howe refused. It was an understandable reaction in view of what the day's work had cost him: 270 of his troops killed, 828 wounded—a total of 1,098 of the approximately 2,400 Britishers engaged. American casualties were about 140 men killed, 270 wounded. Another thirty men were prisoners.

Militarily the slaughter changed nothing. The British were still in Boston, unable to get out. The Americans were still around the city, unable to get in.

Psychologically the effects were profound. As rapidly as the news of Bunker Hill spread through the colonies, lively tongues transmuted defeat into triumph. "Look what our untrained farmers did at Charlestown," the Whigs bragged. "For two hours they held off four times as many seasoned British regulars!" For the first time the conviction spread that if this were really war, the Americans could win it. At Cambridge, Amos Farnsworth came away from divine services thrilled to have heard from the minister that he and his fellow soldiers were the "new Children of Israel," soon to enter into the Promised Land.

In Philadelphia, Congress, still oscillating between love and hate, veered sharply in the direction of the latter. Lord North had sent across the Atlantic a "plan of conciliation." It would not be the last olive branch to come from his lordship. Neither would it be the last to wither on reaching American soil. His Majesty's chief minister offered to lift all British taxes, except those on commercial imports, in any colony that agreed to tax itself for the benefit of the crown.

Congress turned down the proposal. To a man the members endorsed the sentiments of a tall, tawny-haired delegate from Virginia. The burden of Lord North's offer, said Thomas Jefferson, was that England would quit oppressing the colonies on condition that they oppress themselves.

On July 6 the Congress adopted an address explaining why the Americans had created a Continental Army. They called this document the *Declaration of the Causes of taking up Arms* and forwarded it to Cambridge to be read to the soldiers there. What the troops around Boston heard was an American declaration of war.

Composed by John Dickinson of Philadelphia, the address said in part:

> . . . The arms we have been compelled by the enemy to assume . . . we will . . . employ for the preservation of our liberties; being with one mind resolved to dye Free-men rather than live Slaves.

# 13

# "Nothing heppeng extroderly"

S UNDAY, JULY 2, 1775, was a dreary day in Cambridge, Massa-chusetts. All morning a steady rain echoed in the yard of Harvard College. It sluiced down the gambrel roof of the big house across the street where General Artemas Ward had made his headquarters. It splashed from the sloping eaves of the smaller Wadsworth house—home of the college president—which Ward had commandeered for the momentarily expected commander in chief. At noon the rain stopped, but the afternoon skies were slate gray. As the dripping summer night set in, a soldier summed up the day succinctly.

"Nothing heppeng extroderly," wrote James Stevens in his personal record book.

In point of fact, an incident of some consequence had occurred. General Washington had arrived. General Schuyler was no longer with him. The Hudson River patroon had stopped off at New York City to take command in that area. Later he would move upriver to organize at Albany, New York, the first headquarters of the Northern Department of the Continental Army.

An engraving, appearing sixty-two years later, pictures Washington taking over his command at Cambridge in a grand ceremony of welcome on the Common. In actuality the ceremony took place in the sedate living room of the Wadsworth house. It consisted of an exchange of handshakes between the incoming officers and those previously on the ground.

Flanking Artemas Ward during the ceremony were some of

the other generals already on duty at Cambridge. Israel Putnam had come running, eager to imprison George Washington's hand in his powerful paw. William Heath of Roxbury was there. "Our General," as Heath calls himself in his enlightening memoirs, had been the only general officer in the field on the day of Lexington-Concord. It was he who had rushed a force to the bridge over the Charles River, thus blocking one of the two escape routes open to the retreating Britishers. During the next eight years the corpulent, bald-headed Bay Colony farmer would serve his country well in his plodding and unheroic way.

By three o'clock in the afternoon the ceremony was over and Washington was in the saddle again, inspecting the encampments on Cambridge Common and along the river.

Although Washington's military experience had been far from extensive, other aspects of his background would prove helpful to him in his new job. At Mount Vernon he had initiated a raft of enterprises. He had developed a systematic wood-cutting operation, erected sawmills and flour mills, and converted his fruits into salable brandy. He had experimented with the growing and treatment of hemp. These and other ventures, all involving the management of men, were useful training for an army commander.

A stumbling speaker, he had never shone on the floor of the House of Burgesses. As a committeeman, however, he had tended diligently to a multitude of humdrum tasks. He had helped with the drawing up of county boundaries, the setting of standards for the weight and quality of tobacco, the provision of relief for upcountry-Virginia debtors. Dealing constantly with the Continental Congress during the years ahead, he would be thankful for this legislative experience.

Above all, it had taught him respect for the civilian mind. The rage for domination that creates a Napoleon or a Hitler would find no soil for growth within George Washington. En route from Philadelphia to Cambridge, he had remarked that "when we assumed the soldier, we did not lay aside the civilian." He meant it. Twice during the Revolutionary War Congress would give him dictatorial powers. Each time he would gladly abandon them when the emergency ended.

One thing his limited combat experience had taught him: freedom for America could never be won by an army in which every man was free to do as he pleased. He was appalled at the lack of discipline he found at Cambridge, at the practice of many New England military units of conducting their affairs as if they were an extension of the Boston town meeting. Having elected their officers themselves, the soldiers obeyed them or not as their moods dictated.

The results were noticeable. Most of the areas where the men had thrown up their sailcloth tents and turf huts looked more like garbage dumps than military compounds. Uneaten rations rotted in the sun. Verminous shacks alternated with thoughtlessly located "vaults," as latrines were styled in those days.

Further confusion arose when the "companies of expert riflemen" decreed by the Congress began marching in. From the Pennsylvania, Virginia, and Carolina back countries the riflemen came, fourteen hundred in all—strong, upright, seamy-faced men, proud of their long-barreled weapons and unhampered by any modesty about their ability to use them. Ringed tails dangling from their fur hats, the frontiersmen had come to Cambridge to do mighty deeds. A great restlessness shook them when they discovered that before the American Army could perform deeds of any sort it must first organize and equip itself.

Bored with digging ditches and cleaning latrines, the riflemen squabbled and gambled. They thirsted for military action, but for many months there was little of that. Washington worked always with one eye on the Charles River, wondering when the British would come over. But the redcoats never came.

Occasionally they raided one of the islands in Massachusetts Bay, looking for grain and livestock. Occasionally the rebels went after them and chased them home again. At intervals the British artillery batteries in Boston laid down a barrage along the flats of the Charles. No one on the American side paid much attention to this activity. The inability of the British to hit anything was a standing joke.

There were exceptions to the prevailing disorder. Natty in cocked hats, abbreviated blue jackets, and loose white trousers, the Marblehead, Massachusetts, fishermen belonging to Colonel John Glover's infantry regiment saw no threat to their manhood in saluting officers and hopping to carry out orders. Impending in Parliament was another "intolerable act," one that would deny these hard-handed men of the sea access to the cod-filled North Atlantic waters where for generations they had earned their living.

John Glover and his troops brought to Cambridge a genuine grievance against the mother country. They brought also an awareness, born aboard wave-tossed fishing boats, that in moments of high danger the habit of obedience can spell the difference between life and death.

Washington's blue eyes sparkled when he saw these soldiers. They sparkled again when he inspected the campsite where the regiments from Rhode Island had planted themselves. One look at these rows of clean tents and marquees told him that in Nathanael Greene he had a general who would bear watching.

A small engineering unit at Roxbury also caught his attention. Its officer, a 280-pound volunteer named Henry Knox, had already shown himself valiant in romance. His pretty wife was the daughter of Thomas Flucker, loyalist secretary of the Bay Colony. When the Fluckers had barred their house to patriot Knox, he and Lucy had blithely eloped. For years Knox had run Boston's popular London Book-Store. He told the commander in chief that he had spent his spare time reading military tomes. He said he was fond of "fiddling around" with artillery—a statement that no doubt brought a sigh from Washington, along with the hope that one of these days the Continental Army would have something more than a few light mortars and swivels for big, baby-faced Knox to fiddle with.

Artillery was not the only lack. Some of the companies at Cambridge had uniforms of a sort. Most did not. Washington wrote the Continental Congress "that a Number of hunting Shirts, not less than 10,000, would in a great Degree remove this Difficulty . . ." In other letters he cited the absence of guns, ammunition, food—of just about everything that an army requires.

The Congress did what it could. Delegate Benjamin Franklin suggested that bows and arrows be issued. If some of his colleagues were amused, they did not let on. No one laughed at America's most famous citizen, the man who had proved what other scientists had merely guessed, that lightning is electricity, and who had invented the rod that kept it from destroying a man's home. At Franklin's suggestion they voted to arm some units with pikes and spears. In several encounters these primitive weapons would be employed with good effect. Actually bows and arrows, too, would sometimes be used, especially in the South.

At Cambridge Washington and his staff worked around the clock. From the Wadsworth house and later from the more commodious Vassal house on Brattle Street flowed a stream of orders: Drunkenness, profanity, and stealing must cease. Officers must wear cockades or ribbons to distinguish themselves from their men. The men must obey their superiors. Stronger and deeper fortifications must be dug on every hill and along the river. "Lewd women" must be barred from the camp.

The New Englanders grumbled. Some purported to see "a streak of Toryism" in their stern commander, but little by little something about Washington won them over. By the end of August the Reverend William Gordon, the Massachusetts minister who would turn out the first history of the Revolution, was writing that the conditions of the camp "have become greatly . . . better . . . Every officer and private begins to know his place and his duty."

Many of the problems Washington faced at Cambridge would be with him throughout the war. Short-term enlistments running for eight months or less, for one. The colonial legislatures—soon to be the state legislatures—insisted on retaining this practice where their militia were concerned. Only belatedly did the Congress call for eighty-eight battalions of Continentals "to serve during the present war," and at no time was this request honored in full. Again and again, often at critical moments, regiments melted away as terms of service ended and men hurried home to harvest crops or revive neglected businesses.

For the Continental Army the Congress set what for the times was a high pay schedule. A private got six and two thirds dollars or forty shillings a month. Officers' monthly rates ranged from thirteen and two thirds dollars for a lieutenant, through twenty dollars for a captain, to 125 dollars for a brigadier and 165 dollars for a major general. Unhappily the money was not always available. There were countless desertions, even mutinies, by soldiers whose wages were long in arrears.

As the summer of 1775 began its slow turn into the red and gold of autumn, Washington counted about sixteen thousand "effectives" on hand. Only once in the years ahead would his army be larger. Most of the time it would be far smaller.

The commander in chief could not devote all of his time to the minutiae involved in giving form to chaos. He must think hard about the larger aspects of the war, about the big plans, the strategy. On these topics he corresponded regularly with the Continental Congress. For a time he was host to members of America's first congressional junket—a three-man committee on what-to-do-about-the-war consisting of Benjamin Harrison of Virginia, Thomas Lynch of South Carolina, and Ben Franklin.

On all essential points commander in chief and Congress were in agreement. The strength of England was her navy. Sooner or later she would try to invade the American continent by way of the many navigable rivers stabbing deeply inland from the Atlantic coast. New York City must be watched. The larger of her two rivers gave access to the Hudson River valley, a great slash in the land whose occupation by the enemy would separate New England from the rest of America. Charleston, too, must be watched. The big rivers flowing into her generous bay, the Cooper and the Ashley, made that prosperous seaport the gateway to the South.

To the north lay British-held Canada, with many streams and lakes dangling from her southern border—a perfect jumping-off place for an invading army.

Here was a problem dripping with history. Even after New France became a British possession, the Americans continued to distrust her mostly French and mostly Catholic citizens. Still alive in their minds were the troubles that New France and her redskin associates had once created, and in 1774 Parliament had opened old wounds with the passage of the Quebec Act.

That measure established a constitution for His Majesty's "fourteenth colony" in North America. Protestant New England winced at those sections of it that recognized the Catholic Church in Canada and allowed it special privileges. Democratic New England deplored the failure of the Quebec Act to give the Canadians an elected law-making body, putting all of the political power of the province in the hands of a royally appointed governor and council. Virginians viewed with distaste those clauses of the measure that placed parts of the Illinois country and the Ohio River valley under Canadian control. Speculation in the lands of those regions was a cherished occupation in the Old Dominion. Virginia's ambitious planters made little money out of their schemes for exploiting the West, but men's dreams of wealth influence their attitudes as much as wealth itself.

The Quebec Act gave the people of Canada exactly what the Americans were asking, a government congenial to their customs and interests. It was a statesmanlike document, but the citizens of the other thirteen colonies did not so regard it. The last thing they wanted on their northern borders was a society built on French ideas and friendly to the Church of Rome.

In the fall of 1774 the Continental Congress was denouncing the fourteenth colony as a "breeding ground of autocracy." Only a few months later the Congress was singing a gentler tune. Reports reaching the Quaker City indicated that the inhabitants of Canada (her small landholders) were discontented under British rule. Time would prove these reports exaggerated. The inhabitants were not enthusiastic about British rule, but they were even less enthusiastic about an American congress dominated by Protestants, whose disapproval of their religion was common knowledge. Only a few of them stood ready to assist the patriots in their battle with the mother country. Most of them were neutral, and would remain so during the war.

Ignorant of the true situation in Canada, the men meeting in the statehouse in Philadelphia concluded in the summer of 1775 that if American soldiers could seize Montreal and Quebec, the people of the fourteenth colony would rise against Great Britain.

By the end of August the Congress had completed its plans. We can only wonder if General Washington smiled a little ruefully at the thought of sending portions of his artilleryless, uniformless, almost gunless forces northward to attack the Canadian strongholds along the St. Lawrence River. If the daring inanity of it all occurred to him, he made no known mention of it. One of his biographers has speculated that he welcomed the idea of invading Canada because it would give his restless troops something to do—a frame of mind which may explain why he lost no time in dispatching them northward.

Off they went, seemingly unaware of how untimely their departure was. The fall of 1775 had already come when they left. By the time they reached their destination the numbing Canadian winter would be on hand.

# 14

## Glorious Failure

THE PLANS for taking Canada called for a two-pronged attack. Under Brigadier General Richard Montgomery of New York, a small American force was to move by way of Lake Champlain and the Richelieu River to the island city of Montreal in the St. Lawrence. Simultaneously Colonel Benedict Arnold and eleven hundred men were to smash through the forests of Maine to Quebec. There, hopefully, the two groups would be able to combine for an assault on that formidable bastion.

On the first day of September Montgomery and his detachment began their trek from Fort Ticonderoga. Five days later Arnold's force left Cambridge on the first lap of a six-hundred-mile journey about which British General Sir Henry Clinton later remarked that "for . . . the fortitude and perseverance with which the hardships . . . of it were surmounted, will ever rank high among military exploits."

Certainly it will never be forgotten as long as men can read. Dr. Isaac Senter of Rhode Island, Private John Joseph Henry of the Pennsylvania riflemen, Major Return Jonathan Meigs of Connecticut—the pictures that leap from the accounts kept by these and the other soldier-journalists who marched to Quebec with Benedict Arnold are painfully vivid.

"Marched" is too feeble a word to describe the expedition. For weeks the men battled the currents of swift rivers or felt their way along the sedgy channels of treacherous swamps in

128

tublike wooden boats called bateaux. For other weeks they toted these awkward vessels—each weighing four hundred pounds empty—across rock-strewn land or through the under-brush of thick woods that one diarist described as "a direful howling wilderness."

A driving rain pelted them as they left the Kennebec River in the mountains of upper Maine to move west to the Dead River. The first frosts struck suddenly. Dying weeds yellowed steel-bright waters as they traversed a network of lakes and morasses en route to the Chaudière, a wildly churning stream that rises in the hills above Lake Megantic, to dash 190 miles due north to the St. Lawrence.

Three discouraged companies turned back. As the others labored on, food dwindled. Before so large a force even the small animals of the woods fled from guns that could have relieved the hunger of their owners. On October 24 some of the troops were "almost destitute of any eatable, except a few *candles*." These, Dr. Senter wrote, were "used for supper and breakfast by boiling them in water." On November 1 Major Meigs saw troops "who had no provisions . . . One or two dogs were killed which the distressed soldiers ate with good appetite."

Even in a galaxy of heroes, some men stood out, none more so than Captain Daniel Morgan of Virginia, leader of the rifle companies.

At thirty-nine Daniel Morgan's brawny body and agile mind were a match for almost any difficulty Mother Nature or human nature might put in his way. During the French and Indian War he had served with the British. On one occasion a head-strong nature had got him into trouble. His broad back still recorded a fierce flogging; his lusty laugh still sounded when he remembered how the British had miscounted, stopping one short of the forty lashes stipulated as his punishment.

He was himself a disciplinarian. There were times when his "severity" made John Joseph Henry "shudder." Henry admitted,

however, that there were other times when the expedition liter-
ally moved on Daniel Morgan's spirit.

Knowing that Morgan would keep his men on the go, Benedict Arnold forged ahead of the column. Collecting provisions
from the French and Indian settlements along the northerly
banks of the Chaudière, he hurried them back to his followers.
In early November he was able to send back good news.
Montreal was in American hands. On the eighth Arnold and the
advance units of his expedition were at Pointe Levi on the St.
Lawrence, immediately across from Quebec. By the night of the
thirteenth most of the marchers had crossed the river. Before
the end of the month they were encamped at Pointe aux Trembles (now Neuville), twenty-nine miles above Quebec.

A surprisingly large percentage of them had survived, about
675 of the original eleven hundred. To be sure they were an
army of skeletons in rags—"naked men," Arnold called them in
a message to Montreal, imploring General Montgomery to rush
reinforcements and supplies. The general came down the river
himself, bringing enough troops to put the total American Army
at slightly more than eight hundred combatants.

Enough to storm the walls of fortress Quebec on its scowling
cliff three hundred feet above the St. Lawrence? Montgomery,
in a letter to a New York friend, was optimistic. His force was
small but, according to deserters from the Canadian capital,
those behind Quebec's walls were "not great." They consisted
mostly of untried provincial troops and citizen volunteers.

The Americans moved on the last night of the year, in a
blinding snowstorm that they hoped would work to their benefit. The plans called for two small units to make feint attacks at
different gates in the walls of the Upper Town. The main
columns were to approach the fortress from the Lower Town,
lying along the narrow shelf of land between the foot of the cliff
and the river.

Arnold, with about half of the men, moved in from the east or
St. Charles River side; Montgomery, with a smaller number,
from the west or Cape Diamond side. Although the assault

plans have been severely criticized, they might have worked had it not been for a series of mishaps and one crucial accident.

The feints on the Upper Town were too small to be convincing. At the vital moment the defenders of Quebec were concentrated at the very points in the outer ramparts toward which Montgomery and Arnold were heading.

Huge blocks of ice along the shores of the river gave Montgomery and his troops only a narrow defile through which to drag their heavy scaling ladders. Even so, according to an American officer on the scene, the armed Canadians awaiting them at an old cottage converted into a blockhouse were uneasy. As the curtain of snow parted to expose the approaching Americans, the mostly civilian defenders took fright. Concluding that "all was over," they were abandoning their posts when a drunken sailor among them touched a lighted linstock to the breech of one of their four primed and loaded cannons.

The grapeshot screaming into the milky light of the dawn killed General Montgomery and his principal aides. Unnerved, the next in command, Quartermaster Donald Campbell, ordered a retreat. Too bad for the Americans, according to the officer-diarist. Had Campbell "advanced . . . he would have met little opposition, as the citizens had thrown down their arms."

On the opposite side of the Lower Town, a different story unraveled. Here both defenders and attackers were determined. When Arnold fell, wounded by "an incessant fire of musketry from the walls," Captain Daniel Morgan took over. It was not a matter of rank, for there were colonels and majors with the American force; it was a matter of endangered men following a born leader.

At daybreak a battery of two cannons and their crews fell before the invaders. Efforts to lean ladders against the cliff and climb to the fortress itself were unavailing. Still Morgan and his followers pushed on, heading for a barricade at the end of a narrow lane in the Lower Town. Too late the Americans discovered that the snow had left most of their firelocks useless.

Men ducked into stone houses to wipe and reload, hurried out again to answer the fire coming from the barricade or raining down from upstairs windows.

There was a period during which the patriots could have retreated, but Morgan held on, expecting at any moment to be joined by Montgomery and his troops. Striking the now-drifting snow, the bright northern sun blinded the men's eyes. Increasingly the blood of the slain and wounded crimsoned the white roadbed. At ten o'clock, surrounded on all sides, Captain Morgan surrendered.

So ended the March to Quebec—a glorious failure. Of the American assaulting force, more than half were out of action for the time being, some forever. Forty-eight were dead, thirty-four wounded, 372—Morgan among them—prisoners of war. Worst of all, Montgomery was gone. "Of a genteel, easy, graceful, manly address," as Major Meigs described him, this English-born officer had enjoyed the "love, esteem and confidence of the whole army."

His loss created a void that the fierce energies of his successor, Colonel Arnold (soon to be Brigadier General Arnold) could not wholly fill. Carried from the field, a ball lodged in his left heel, Arnold found himself in command of the tag ends of an army that during the remaining winter months would hang dispiritedly about the outskirts of Quebec, waiting for reinforcements and struggling with the ravages of smallpox.

# 15

# *Boston Regained*

IN THE THIRTEEN COLONIES, during most of 1775, feeling against Great Britain was so strong that the Congress could have raised an army of 150,000 men had it had the means to support them.

In England the situation was different. There the indignation generated by the Boston Tea Party was wearing away. Most Englishmen agreed with His Majesty that the Americans were "a sad nest" of "ungrateful wretches" who should be taught a lesson. But a war? No. Since the close of the last conflict with France in 1763, the English people had been reveling in the unaccustomed pleasures of peace. Never had the theaters and concert halls of London been better patronized, the levees better attended, the drawing rooms of the upper class more glittering. Never had the English people felt less inclined to fight with anyone. Some of them were not only averse to war in general, but to this one in particular. Most merchants and industrialists saw in the conflict only an interruption in their profitable trade with the Americans.

But Parliament was not consulting the English citizenry. It was taking its orders from Prime Minister North and he was taking his from the King.

In the House of Lords the first Earl of Chatham pleaded in vain for a bill that would recognize the Continental Congress, give the colonies dominion status, and grant the Americans everything they wished short of separation from the empire.

Ghostly in the white-flannel bandages wrapping his stricken

limbs, the Great Commoner, now sixty-seven and visibly dying, was a fountain of wrath. "I rejoice that America has resisted!" he shouted; and one dark winter afternoon, as he walked from the shabby chamber where the red-robed peers assembled, he turned back at the door for a final warning. He did not believe England could win a war against America. He prophesied that the results would be so dire that the very men sitting in this room would be stripped of their positions and reduced "to that state of insignificance for which God and nature designed you!"

In the House of Commons the brilliant Whig leader Edmund Burke deplored the course his country was taking. Sadly he observed that "a great empire and little minds go ill together." All who listened knew who the "little minds" were in Burke's opinion.

Heading his list was the Prime Minister himself. About two months younger than George Washington, Frederick Lord North was an amiable and honest man with a flare for making people like him and do as he wished. Those who commented on his striking resemblance to King George flattered neither man. An associate pictured North as having "large legs, walks heavily, manners clumsy, very large features, thick lips, wide mouth, high forehead, large nose, eyes not lively." England abounded with jokes about his lordship's homeliness. Half of them originated with North himself. "Happen what will," a friend remarked, "the Noble Lord is ready with his joke."

He was not ready to pilot his country through her quarrel with the colonies. The "Noble Lord" suffered from what is perhaps the greatest affliction a man in high position can have. He was modest. Throughout his long career as England's government head, he was always willing to abandon his own ideas whenever they failed to conform to those emanating from what he considered to be the superior mind of his royal master.

Also on Burke's roster of "little minds" was Lord George Germain, who had succeeded Dartmouth as Secretary of State for the Colonies. Perhaps the German soldiers who served in America with the redcoats had the colonial secretary in mind when they asserted that the story of Britain's defeat could be summed up in the Biblical injunction, "Pride goeth before . . . a fall." No Englishman ground out the phrase "American peasants" with more gusto than Germain; none endorsed more openly the statement, often heard in London's better clubs, that one could do business with the colonials but that an English gentleman would no sooner consider mingling with them socially than he would think of marrying his mistress.

During a life that began in 1716, Germain had three different identities. The third son of the Duke of Dorset, he was Lord George Sackville until 1770. At that point he received a fortune from Lady Betty Germain on condition that he adopt her family name. He did so until 1783, when the King elevated him to the House of Lords as First Viscount Sackville, his title at the time of his death two years later.

He grew up on an estate called Knole, where the main house had 52 staircases and 365 rooms. By the age of fourteen he had mastered all of the skills required of a young lord—drinking, gambling, and swearing. He chose the army as his career and showed bravery on the battlefield. He had risen to major general when in 1759, during a critical engagement in Germany at Minden, he failed to carry out the repeated orders of his superior, was court-martialed, and was drummed out of the service.

The pride that went before his personal fall did not desert him in disgrace. He held on to his seat in the House of Commons. He walked with his large head high among men who had sworn to have no "social intercourse with the Coward of Minden." As the quarrel with America waxed warm, he espied an opportunity to recoup his lost prestige. He reasoned that the King would want around him men who shared the royal view of the situation.

Coming and going from his London haunts, he let it be known that in his opinion crown and Parliament had the right to rule America by force of arms. His ardor did not go unnoticed. On November 10, 1775, George III offered him the colonial secretaryship. By this act the King placed in the hands of arrogant George Germain the overall conduct of a war that His Majesty had recently made official by proclaiming the thirteen American colonies to be in a state of rebellion. One of Germain's biographers flatly describes him as the man responsible for Great Britain's defeat. With all of his faults, the colonial secretary was incapable of losing a great war all by himself, but no one can deny the diligence with which he labored to that end. His orders to his generals in America were often vague, sometimes contradictory. He had never set foot in the New World, but ignorance of its climate and terrain did not deter him on occasion from telling his officers there where they should fight their battles, what equipment they should employ, what tactics they should follow.

Whether helping his country or hindering it, Germain was always diligent. From the moment he took charge, the British Isles hummed with the clangor of military preparation. England's peacetime army was well run and well trained. It was unequal, however, to the task of simultaneously protecting the homeland and crushing a rebellion overseas.

Press gangs combed the city slums and midland industrial areas, picking up thieves and tosspots and petty scoundrels; but even in England the number of derelicts was limited. Recruiting officers sallied forth, calling for volunteers and dangling before them purses of gold and promises of land in the New World. On the whole the response was poor. Even had the cause been popular, few would have enlisted. Voluntary citizen participation in war is a democratic concept, and there was no democracy in eighteenth-century Europe. Most of its wars were fusses between crowned heads. The average civilian prudently regarded them as professional affairs to be carried on by professional fighters.

For the King of England it was a routine matter to hire mercenary soldiers wherever he could. Russia turned him down, but the rulers of the little German principalities along the Rhine were always in need of cash. A large number of the thirty thousand mercenaries employed belonged to the duchies of Hesse-Cassel and Hesse-Hanau. In America all of them were known as Hessians.

The news that King George had declared war and was hiring "foreign mercenaries to torture and kill" his transatlantic subjects reached the colonies in October. It sent the pitch of patriotism to new heights. Holding its third session in Philadelphia with every colony officially represented at last, Congress called for thirty thousand volunteers and established a navy. At Cambridge the commander in chief had already put six armed schooners into action. Commanded by Commodore John Manley, "Washington's Navy" had captured thirty-five British vessels when in late October it was merged into the Continental Navy breathed into life by Congress.

Infuriated by the depredations of Washington's seagoing guerrillas, the British admiral at Boston, Samuel Graves, sent two sloops of war northward to "burn and destroy" American coastal settlements.

The British captains put in first at Gloucester, Massachusetts, decided that fishing port would be difficult to level, and moved on to Falmouth, now Portland, Maine. There they gave the inhabitants only two hours to get out. Then they burned the town. Quickly permeating the colonies, the news of this exercise in petulance fueled the flames of patriotism.

In Virginia the feisty royal governor, Lord Dunmore, fueled them further by undertaking to win the war for His Majesty in one swift stroke. Commandeering the British vessels lying off Virginia, Dunmore assembled an army consisting of loyalist volunteers and a few English soldiers and sailors. From his waterborne headquarters he called on the border Indians to attack from the west while he moved in from the east. When this plea was ignored he tried another tactic. He invited Virginia's blacks into his army. In a proclamation that horrified the white South, he promised freedom to any slaves who joined him.

For months his lordship and his so-called "Ethiopian army"

hovered along the shores of the province, intercepting colonial trading vessels and raiding coastal plantations. The patriots responded by sending out a thousand militia under Colonel William Woodford.

In December, at a little bridge over the Elizabeth River near Norfolk, the two armies clashed. In a move reminiscent of Sir William Howe's disastrous marches up Breed's Hill, Dunmore ordered his men to cross the narrow span six abreast. Within half an hour sixty of them were dead and his lordship was in retreat. After this disaster, Dunmore made only one more military move—an attempt to capture Norfolk that the Virginia patriots frustrated by burning the little city to the ground before his lordship could seize it.

His "war" would never be forgotten. In this attempt by the British to enlist some of America's 400,000 black slaves, twenty-four-year-old James Madison of Virginia detected an "astute attack" on "our Achilles Heel." His reference was to the existence in all of the colonies of the institution of human bondage.

The fears of a "black uprising," inspired by Lord Dunmore's War, did not stop at the borders of the Old Dominion. On December 14 Philadelphia's *Pennsylvania Evening Post* described an encounter on one of the city's footpaths between a "well-dressed gentlewoman" and a "saucy Sable." When the lady requested the Negro to stand against a wall so that she might pass, he defied her. "Stay you d——d white bitch," the newspaper quoted him as saying, "till Lord Dunmore and his black regiment come, and then we will see who is to take to the wall."

Colonial policy had always been to exclude Negroes from militia service, but more often than not a need for soldiers had dictated a contrary practice. Many blacks had fought in the French and Indian War. As the dispute with Parliament neared breaking point, Negroes volunteered for the New England militia. All were accepted.

A black man was among the patriots killed at Lexington-

Concord. Several blacks fought in those skirmishes and on Breed's Hill. At least fifteen marched to Quebec with Benedict Arnold.

In the late fall of 1775 Southern delegates to Congress were complaining that the Continental Army had become "a refuge for runaway slaves." They insisted that the blacks already enrolled be dismissed and that future volunteers be turned down. The Congress at first rejected these proposals. Then the delegates reversed themselves to the extent of barring future enlistments. On this matter they would alter their position several times during the war. Meanwhile, in the face of changing official edicts, blacks continued to join both their local militia and the Continental Army. Nor were Lord Dunmore's "Ethiopians" the last to serve with the enemy. In New Jersey a young Long Island black, Benjamin Whitcuff, while spying for the British Army, came within a minute of dying on an American gallows.

In Cambridge, as the fall of 1775 sharpened into winter, General Washington waited for news from Canada and continued his anxious watch on the enemy in besieged Boston. Inwardly he fretted at the refusal of the British to cross the Charles so that his keen-eyed riflemen could get at them. Outwardly he preserved the air of calm that would be an inspiration to many tired soldiers on many battlefields.

October brought word that General Gage had returned to England. William Howe had succeeded him as supreme commander of His Majesty's forces in British America. To Washington's disappointment, Howe proved as unwilling to risk a sortie to the mainland as his predecessor had been.

The Congress had authorized an attack on the city. Washington longed to take action at once, but he realized that without adequate artillery the attempt could not succeed.

Artillery! On a brisk November morning the commander in chief summoned Henry Knox to Vassal House. When the

Boston bookseller came out, he was no longer a volunteer engineer. He was Washington's chief of artillery with the rank of colonel.

Orders in his pocket directed him to proceed to American-held Ticonderoga on Lake Champlain. He was to select the best of the captured guns there and bring them to Cambridge. We know not who suggested this mission, only that neither Washington nor Knox had the dimmest idea of how it was to be carried out. When cheerful Henry Knox left Cambridge, he realized that his commanding officer was counting on him to do the impossible.

He did it—with the help of horses, sleighs, and teamsters provided by General Schuyler from his newly established headquarters at Albany. Writing from near Albany in mid-December, Knox informed Washington that "within 16 or 17 days" he would be presenting him with "a noble train of artillery"—fifty-nine cannons ranging from fat little mortars to a two-and-three-quarter-ton twenty-four-pounder that his teamsters had nicknamed "Old Sow." Knox underrated the difficulties ahead. The "16 or 17 days" had gone before the sleds carrying the heavy guns reached the shores of the Hudson River.

Crossing the frozen stream was a tortuous maneuver. The heavier cannons had to be sent over one at a time with the team that pulled the sleigh moving far ahead at the end of a long rope and accompanied by a man with a sharp ax whose orders were to cut the horses loose should the gun break through. Two of them did.

The last big test came at the Berkshires, the laborious haul up the western face of the mountains, the even more difficult descent on the other side. It was late January 1776 before the guns were in the vicinity of Cambridge.

With ample artillery on hand, Washington was in a fever of impatience. He advocated storming the city at once. His generals demurred. They pointed out that the departure of short-term enlistees at year's end had shrunk his army to little more than nine thousand men—too few for a frontal attack on the strongly entrenched British. A better scheme, in their opinion, would be to put some of the bigger cannons on Dorchester Heights. From that rocky elevation they could threaten the city with destruction and force Howe to depart.

Reluctantly Washington agreed, but even his aides' more conservative proposal offered a problem. It would be folly to emplant guns on the heights without first fortifying the area, and the winter ground was too hard for digging.

A Massachusetts kinsman of General Putnam had the answer to that. Lieutenant Colonel Rufus Putnam proposed that instead of building a fort *in* the earth, the rebels build one *on* it. He suggested that all of the necessary parts of the structure be constructed at Roxbury, not far from the heights. First, he said, erect a number of "chandeliers." Stuff these heavy timber frames with fascines (bundles of logs), gabions (baskets full of earth), and baled hay. Cut down the fruit trees near Roxbury and fashion an abatis (an arrangement of sharpened stakes) to protect the front and flanks of the fort. Carry all of these elements to the heights and assemble them there.

By the second day of March the work on Rufus Putnam's prefabricated fortress was well advanced. That night two batteries of cannons, set up miles north of Roxbury, opened fire in an effort to mislead the British into believing that the Americans were planning to attack from that sector. Two nights later, with the northern batteries still booming away, the hard climb to the heights began at Roxbury.

Three hundred and sixty oxcarts toted the chandeliers and the sharpened stakes. Trundling behind them came "Old Sow" and nineteen more of the fieldpieces that Henry Knox had dragged east from Ticonderoga.

In the morning the people of Boston awakened to find two formidable redoubts staring down at them from Dorchester Heights.

Admiral Graves had returned to England. Rear Admiral Molyneux Shuldham, his successor, handed Sir William Howe an ultimatum. The admiral could not leave his ships in Boston harbor with enemy guns standing directly over them. The general must either evacuate the city immediately or push the Americans out of their miraculously created stronghold.

Howe ordered two detachments to move by water to the peninsula where Dorchester Heights stood. Neither group got there. During the night a storm struck. A rain-drenched rebel lieutenant standing his lonely post under an apple tree on Dorchester Heights cursed the thunder and the lightning and declared it the "worst night" he had ever seen.

His discomforts were minor compared with those of General Howe's men bobbing in their little boats on the shredded waters of the bay. The British commander had no choice but to call them back and issue orders to evacuate the city.

A few weeks later he was gone and Boston was in American hands again. Many fine houses stood vacant, for a thousand Tories had gone with Howe. It was a dark hour for these people. Behind them remained nearly everything they possessed. Some were leaving the only homes they had ever known. Even their going into exile was a misery. "Thirty-six besides myself in a single cabin," one of them wrote. "Men, women and children; parents, masters, and mistresses, obliged to pig together on the floor, there being no berths."

Howe's immediate destination was Halifax, but Washington was convinced—rightly—that eventually he would concentrate his forces at New York. Early in April the American commander paid his last visit to Cambridge, to receive an honorary degree from the grateful faculty of Harvard College. Then, taking the bulk of his army along, he set out for the busy seaport at the mouth of the Hudson River.

# 16

# The War Spreads

IN THE OPENING MONTHS of 1776 New York was not the only spot in America that the British were planning to visit. Many schemes for invading the colonies were taking form in the wainscotted offices of Lord Germain in London.

One of them was in response to a letter from Josiah Martin, the royal governor of North Carolina. Like the other crown officials below the Potomac, Martin was in exile. The North Carolina Whigs had seized power, and the governor had taken refuge on the *Cruizer*, a British sloop of war lying in the mouth of the Cape Fear River below Wilmington. Stocky, horse-faced Josiah Martin was an ebullient man with a mind as lively as a jumping jack. His long letter to the British ministry was at once a plea for help, a sermon on the "depraved and wicked conduct" of the local rebels, and a treatise on local history.

The significance of that history ran all through the governor's densely scrawled paragraphs. In common with the other colonies south of the Potomac, North Carolina was really two worlds in one. Geography had decreed the division.

The "Tidewater"—the broad coastal plain along the Atlantic—had spawned one kind of culture. The "upcountry" beyond—the great central plateau or Piedmont and the mountains forming its western border—had engendered a far different one.

Tidewater North Carolina was rich. Upcountry was poor. Tidewater was a land of rice and indigo plantations worked by armies of slaves. Upcountry was a warren of small farms, each tillable by "a man, a mule and a nigger," provided all three worked from dawn to dusk. In the three lower colonies, the Carolinas and Georgia, the Tidewater planters controlled the legislature, made the laws, fixed the taxes, and dominated the courts. In these areas, consequently, west distrusted east and vice versa.

In North Carolina the strain between the two sections came close to being civil war. Under Governor William Tryon, Josiah Martin's predecessor, the upcountry people had risen in revolt. Coining a defiant name for themselves, "the Regulators," they had set out to take the law into their own hands. Alarmed by the ensuing violence, Tryon activated the colonial militia and marched west.

On the banks of the Alamance River the inevitable collision occurred. A quick and sanguinary encounter, it ended with some of the Regulators dangling from improvised gallows and the rest in ragged flight.

Soon after the battle on the Alamance, hard-bitten William Tryon moved north to become the governor of New York. Josiah Martin, taking his place, instituted reforms designed to placate the upcountry citizens. As the fires of civil war faded before those ignited by the quarrel with England, Martin made haste to take advantage of the popularity his reforms had earned him. Traveling from town to town, he persuaded many of the upcountry inhabitants to take an oath of allegiance to the King. Thousands of them swore that if war came they would fight for England.

In his long letter to the British ministry the governor confessed that some of the upcountry farmers would think nothing of going back on their word. He was sure, however, of one of the largest groups—the rugged Scottish Highlanders who had settled along the upper reaches of the Cape Fear River. To these devout Presbyterian Covenanters, an oath was sacred. Whatever their real sentiments (and Martin suspected some of being Whigs at heart), they would keep their promise. Let the ministry send an army of British regulars to Wilmington and the governor would see to it that a "vast army of Highlanders" was there to meet them.

Optimism spurted from Josiah Martin's busily moving quill. He predicted that the allied force he proposed—his kilted loyalists and England's redcoats—would readily overthrow the rebel government and return North Carolina to royal rule.

Martin addressed his letter to Lord Hillsborough, but by the time it reached London, Lord Germain was colonial secretary. He approved of Martin's ideas, and in the opening weeks of 1776 a British fleet under Sir Peter Parker was on its way from Ireland, and Sir Henry Clinton and a smaller fleet were coming down from Boston. At Cross Creek (now Fayetteville, North Carolina) Colonels Donald MacDonald and Donald McLeod planted the King's standard and summoned the clans. The Highlanders rallied. It was not quite the "vast army" Josiah Martin had envisaged. Still, it was a goodly gathering, some eighteen hundred sturdy farmers in all.

Kilts fluttered and bagpipes squealed as they began the march to Wilmington, 125 miles to the southeast. A dim and frosty dawn brought them to the northern end of a bridge across Moores Creek, a swampy stream eighteen miles from their destination. Awaiting them in the rank bulrushes of the opposite shore was a rebel band under Colonels Richard Caswell and John Lillington.

The bonnie Caledonians had the advantage in numbers, but the patriots had made preparation. They had thrown up embankments on their side of the creek. They had ripped the planks from the bridge and layered the girders with oil. The slowly rising sun of February 27 lighted a poignant exhibition of bravery and foolishness. Without even bothering to reconnoiter the terrain, the clansmen charged, slithering and stumbling on the greased stringers of the bridge.

Three minutes later, according to a New York newspaper, the Battle of Moores Creek was over. Eight hundred and fifty

Highlanders were prisoners of war. The rest—three men to a horse in some cases—were fleeing for their upcountry homes.

It was a memorable moment for the North Carolina Whigs. In a lightning stroke they had crushed a loyalist uprising that could have sliced the three southernmost colonies from the union, perhaps forever.

When a few weeks later Sir Henry Clinton reached the mouth of the Cape Fear, no kilted warriors were there to greet him, only Governor Josiah Martin with his doleful report. The British general could only wait for Admiral Sir Peter Parker and ponder the vexing question of what to do now. By the time the admiral arrived, Sir Henry had found the answer. The sun of late May polished the slowly unfurling sails of eleven warships and thirty troop transports as the British armada stood out to sea and turned south.

George Washington's intelligence service was amply capable of keeping track of Sir Henry's peregrinations. The departure of the British general from Boston on January 20 had been duly noted at Cambridge and the commander in chief had dispatched Charles Lee to New York in case Sir Henry had designs on that area. When after a brief stopover in New York waters Sir Henry moved on, Congress acted. A Southern Department of the Continental Army was formed and Lee was placed in charge of it.

In Virginia the new commandant stumbled into luck. Intercepted letters exposed the intentions of the enemy. A British attack on the only city below the Potomac—Charleston, South Carolina*—was imminent. Having rushed warnings to the endangered seaport, Lee moved south at the front of nineteen hundred Virginia and North Carolina troops.

The Charleston that greeted him was a dainty and gracious little town. Visiting Britons called it the "London of the New World" and wrote home that the Charlestonians lived in as

---

* Still, at this time, called "Charles Town," in honor of an English king. The name was changed after independence.

"high a stile" as English squires. In truth, the high living was limited to a small portion of the population. Nearly half of the city's fourteen thousand inhabitants were black slaves.

Charleston's singular architecture took its tone from the long, hot, miasmic summers. The Georgian townhouses of proud planters and wealthy merchants presented only their blind gable ends to the street. Their fronts lay along the side, generally facing south, away from the midday sun (which in summer shines at that hour from the north) and open to the prevailing evening breeze. Broad piazzas, dripping with bougainvillea and wisteria, looked down on gardens lush with tropical blooms.

Broad Street, running east to west, and Meeting Street, south to north, more or less quartered the town. The thinly towering steeple of the Anglican Church of St. Michael's on Meeting Street provided it with a delicate focal point.

Its busy docks poked into one of the finest bays in North America. During the Old French Wars the citizens had set up a line of gun batteries across the waterfront. During the ensuing years of peace, commerce had taken over. Warehouses and sail lofts had sprung up in front of the guns, blocking their field of fire. When Charles Lee arrived on June 5, these buildings were being leveled and thrown into the offshore waters.

The whole town was in a frenzy of activity, for the British ships had arrived. Their massed sails could be seen, bobbing in the sunlight beyond the shoal waters at the entrance to the harbor two miles to the east. In the city itself soldiers and workmen were hauling cannons, stacking sandbags, felling trees. Wandering among them, generous with suggestions and encouragement, was John Rutledge, president of the Provincial Congress, in effect governor of South Carolina.

The arrival of General Lee had no material bearing on the chain of command. To the Charlestonians his slovenly ways and brash speech were half amusing and half annoying—and they continued to take their orders from the men they knew: from solemn-faced Governor Rutledge. From Colonel Christopher

Gadsden, who had left his seat in the Continental Congress to come to the assistance of his town. From Colonel William Moultrie, long-time militia leader and Indian fighter.

Gadsden and five hundred troops established themselves at Fort Johnson on James Island, overlooking the southern entrance to the bay. Athwart the northern entrance lay a slab of orangey mud called Sullivan's Island. Here the Charlestonians had started to build a small star-shaped bastion. Named Fort Sullivan, it was constructed of palmetto logs backed by heaped sand. Moultrie and 450 men were now straining to complete it.

General Lee jabbed at Fort Sullivan's soft logs and softer sand and pronounced the structure "hopelessly ramshackle." Hastening back to the mainland, he so informed Governor Rutledge. He said the unfinished bastion must be abandoned. The governor refused to alter his plans. "Genl Lee," he wrote Colonel Moultrie, "wishes you to evacuate the Fort, you will not do so without an order from me. I will cut off my right hand sooner than write it."

In the red and sultry dawn of June 28, the British attacked. Nine warships, averaging fifty guns apiece, bore down on the southern shores of Sullivan's Island. Flame and thunder spewed from a hundred gun ports. Sharp musket fire answered from the fort.

General Lee, watching from the mainland, enjoyed a pleasant surprise. The still-unfinished bastion was not so ramshackle after all. The hardwood usually used in such structures would have cracked almost at once under the British bombardment. The soft palmetto logs resisted. Like sponge they received the enemy balls; like sponge they held them. Few projectiles penetrated the fort itself. Those that did created little damage.

In his unhurried way Colonel Moultrie kept his men at it, seeing to it that they fired fast—but not too fast. Ammunition was the big problem. For a short period there was none in the fort, but a swift and able reinforcement action by Governor Rutledge resolved that problem.

The Britons manning their slowly moving vessels were amazed at the effectiveness of the American fire. An officer of the lead ship, the H.M.S. *Bristol*, wrote in terror: "No slaughter house could present so bad a sight with blood and entrails lying about, as our ship." Admiral Sir Peter Parker drove his sailors relentlessly. When an American cartridge found its way to Sir Peter himself, it tore away his breeches, leaving the admiral only lightly scratched but unforgettably embarrassed.

Not until noon did the British discover that they were pounding the only strong portion of the fort. A hastily initiated effort to place their vessels where they could command the unfinished western wall raised serious navigational problems. For a time the *Bristol* swung broadside to the island, exposing the full sweep of her decks to a devastating American barrage. Two other ships collided.

As darkness gathered, the breathlessly watching Charlestonians on the mainland beheld a sight even the most sanguine had not dared to anticipate: nine bullet-shattered British warships limping sadly out to sea. They would remain there, close to the harbor opening, until August 21; but they would attack no more.

The ending might have been different had the entire British plan worked—but the land half of it never even got started.

Days earlier, ships had carried Sir Henry Clinton and 2,500 troops to Long Island, immediately north of Sullivan. The narrow channel of water separating the islands was known as the Breach. Intelligence reports differed as to its depth. Some put it at only eighteen inches, others at seven feet. Not until the British general had disembarked his men and begun a tardy reconnaissance did he discover that both reports were correct. In parts the Breach was shallow, in other parts quite deep. It could not be forded, and sharp rocks under the shallow parts made crossing it by rowboat impossible.

The few redcoats who struggled over were immediately driven off or seized when they reached the opposite shore. So much for Sir Henry's plans for throwing a wave of soldiers against the northern end of Fort Sullivan while His Majesty's warships pummeled it from the south.

Nightfall of June 28 found the bulk of the British land troops still taking their ease on the myrtle-mantled strands of Long Island. To their everlasting chagrin, Sir Henry Clinton and his men had sat out the Battle of Sulivan's Island.

# 17

# "We hold these truths . . ."

AND CONGRESS—head of the rebellion even as the fighting men were its heart—what was Congress doing during these feverish opening months of 1776? The Congress was buzzing, bristling with plans.

It met now in a changed atmosphere. The word "independence" was no longer one to be whispered in Philadelphia or better yet left unspoken. The word had rung out there as reverberatingly as a discharge of cannon. The ninth day of the year had seen the appearance in Quaker City bookstores of Tom Paine's pamphlet *Common Sense* with its militant plea that—

. . . since nothing but blows will do, for God's sake, let us come to a final separation [from Great Britain], and not leave the next generation to be cutting throats, under the violated unmeaning names of parent and child. . . .

Propagandist Paine had his own notions of natural law. It was not consistent with the reality of things, he proclaimed, for the tail to wag the dog.

. . . there is something very absurd [he wrote] in supposing a continent to be perpetually governed by an island. In no instance hath nature made the satellite larger than its primary planet; and as England and America, with respect to each other, reverse the common order of nature, it is evident that they belong to different systems: England to Europe—America to itself.

Nearly everything that *Common Sense* had to say had been said before. But never had it been said so compellingly. Learned John Adams could sneer that its stocky author with his bitter face and luminous blue eyes was a "disastrous meteor." None could deny the meteor its brilliance.

In 1776 Tom Paine was a newcomer to the American cause. He was an Englishman by birth, the product of a lower-class home troubled by the gloom of a Quaker father and the meddlesomeness of an Anglican mother. He began his adult life as a corset maker. Unsuccessful at this trade, he moved on to a lackluster career as a tax collector. At intervals he taught school and studied Newtonian physics.

In a biographical novel the Marxist writer Howard Fast pictures Paine as a revolutionary firebrand sizzling to the New World in 1774 to ignite the flames of rebellion there. In point of fact, thirty-seven-year-old Paine came to America like thousands of immigrants before him in the hope of finding an outlet for talents England had spurned. He himself was not sure what those talents were. He was as delightedly surprised as his readers to find in himself a flair for propaganda unexcelled by any penman of his era.

Armed with letters of introduction from Ben Franklin, then still in London, Paine quickly found work in Philadelphia—first as a tutor for gentlemen's sons, later as a journalist. One biographer describes him as a "highly impressionable man." His writings tended to reflect the "sentiments of the people with whom he was most recently in contact." Fortunately for the American cause, he fell in with some of Philadelphia's most ardent Whigs, Dr. Benjamin Rush among them.

Rush was a troubled man when he and Paine met in 1775. It seemed to the young doctor that the lingering hope of many Whigs for a reconciliation with England was an illusion. Someone should call on the Americans to break with the mother country. He himself had prepared a paper to that effect, but he was hesitant about making it public.

Philadelphia was a heavily Tory town and Rush was just getting started in it as a doctor. To put himself on record as an advocate of independence could damage his career. On the other hand a journalist, free to ply his trade anywhere, could safely do so. Rush suggested that Paine write the paper.

Paine did, with shattering results. From the muscular prose of his *Common Sense* one strikingly new thought emerged. For years even the warmest Whigs had taken the position that their quarrel was not with the crown. In their view His Majesty stood above the fray. The British ministry and Parliament—and they alone—were responsible for the ills under which the colonies groaned.

Nonsense, said Paine. His Majesty was the very fountainhead of America's troubles. Paine could cite chapter and verse. In England he had known men who were privy to His Majesty's thoughts. George III was no kindly father of his far-flung subjects. He was "a hardened, sullen-tempered Pharaoh . . . the royal brute of Britain." Let all myths fall, let the facts prevail. Thus spoke Thomas Paine in January 1776.

America listened. Within three months after the publication of *Common Sense,* 120,000 copies had been sold. The figure would eventually rise to half a million. Not since the days of Dickinson's *Farmer's Letters* had print on paper gone so arrow-like to American hearts. Thousands of colonials were dubious about risking their lives for the abstract legal rights set forth by Dickinson. Those same thousands were ready at once to take up arms against a personal villain, "the royal brute of Britain." Their hearts vibrated at Paine's call for a crusade against monarchy itself.

The appearance of *Common Sense* was timely. On its heels came the suppression of the loyalist uprising in North Carolina, the repulse of the British fleet at Charleston. Everywhere Whigs concluded that if the colonies left the empire all the might of Great Britain could not force them to return.

The spirit of independence bubbling throughout the country

was quickly felt in the Assembly room in the statehouse at Philadelphia. For the second time John Adams urged Congress to ask every colony to set up its own government. This time there was no opposition to the proposal.

North Carolina had already instructed her delegates in Philadelphia to *concur* in any resolution for independence that might be offered. On May 15 Virginia went further. She instructed her delegates to offer one. On June 7 the leader of her group in the Congress, dapper Richard Henry Lee, presented the fateful proposition:

> *Resolved,* That these United Colonies are, and of a right ought to be, free and independent States, that they are absolved from all allegiance to the British Crown, and that all political connection between them and the State of Great Britain is, and ought to be, totally dissolved.

> That it is expedient forthwith to take the most effectual measures for forming foreign alliances.

> That a plan of confederation [a national government] be prepared and transmitted to the respective Colonies for their consideration and approbation.

Days of earnest discussion followed. John Dickinson spoke for the opposition. The brilliant Philadelphia lawyer predicted that a declaration of independence by the colonies would bring down on them the full vengeance of England. In the absence of such a declaration, he argued, the war could be got over faster. "Great Britain," he said, "after one or more unsuccessful Campaigns may be induced . . . to redress all grievances."

He noted that Richard Henry Lee's resolution called for the establishment of a national government, for the writing of the constitution that would later be known as the Articles of Confederation. Dickinson pointed out that the members of the committee appointed to draft the articles were arguing violently among themselves. It would take months, maybe years, for them to reach agreement. Wait until that was accomplished, he urged. Wait until a national government acceptable to all colonies was established. *Then* declare independence.

"To depart now from the protection we have in British rule," Dickinson asserted, "would be like Destroying a House in winter before We have got into another."

Impressive arguments. John Adams and others tried to answer them. They pointed out that should the war prove long and trying, the spirit of the people would flag unless early in the conflict the goal for which they were fighting—independence—was clearly agreed upon and officially proclaimed. Then, too, America must have assistance from England's enemies in Europe. France was already secretly helping, but this was an unsatisfactory arrangement, subject to the whims of the French government. Only a treaty of alliance could solidify it. Colonies could not execute treaties with foreign governments. An independent America could.*

John Dickinson admitted that the tide was not running his way, that the resolution would succeed. In truth, there were days when it seemed that it might fail. Its proponents toiled around the clock. Those delegates who did not yet have permission from their colonial authorities to vote for independence were prevailed upon to get it. One delegation—that of radical Massachusetts—went ahead and voted for independence without permission.** At last, on the muggy afternoon of July 2, the final roll call was heard, the motion carried.

* In May 1944—168 years later—David Ben-Gurion used these same arguments to persuade the other members of his governing council in then British-held Palestine to vote for the establishment of an independent Jewish state—Israel—in that area. Some of the council members wanted the Proclamation of Statehood to specify the boundaries of Israel. Ben-Gurion argued against this on the grounds that in issuing the Declaration of Independence the Americans had taken care not to set any limits to their new republic, thus leaving themselves free to expand in the years to come.
** Authorization for the Massachusetts delegation to vote for independence arrived one day after the taking of the final vote.

Wondrous day! John Adams wrote not one but two letters to Dear Abigail. After all, it is not every day that a nation is born.

This "second day of July, 1776," he told Mrs. Adams, "will be the most memorable epoch in the history of America. I am apt to believe that it will be celebrated by succeeding generations as the great Anniversary Festival . . . commemorated . . . by solemn acts of devotion to God Almighty . . . solemnized with pomp, and parade, with shows, games, sports, bonfires, and illuminations . . ."

But future Americans would not deliver their orations and light their bonfires on this, their country's birthday. They would do so instead on the fourth—the date that in 1776 saw the culmination of a moving episode.

Early in the course of the great debate over independence, those who favored it had won a small but prophetic victory. They persuaded the Congress to authorize a committee whose job it would be to explain to the world why the American people wished to leave the British empire.

The Congress named five men to the committee: Franklin, John Adams, Robert R. Livingston of New York, Roger Sherman of Connecticut, and Thomas Jefferson. We know not how it came about that the actual writing of the document fell to Jefferson. One story has it that the committee appointed a subcommittee to do the work. Its members were Adams and Jefferson. Adams was the older and Jefferson deferentially suggested that *he* do the writing.

"I will not," said Adams.

"Why will you not?"

"Reasons enough," replied Adams. "First, you are a Virginian and Virginia ought to appear at the head of this business. Second, I am obnoxious, suspected and unpopular; you are very much otherwise. Third, you can write ten times better than I can."

Jefferson agreed to "do as well as I can."

It was a difficult task. He realized that all Congress was

looking, as it were, over his shoulder. He knew that for generations to come men would seek in this document an understanding of an enormous event. He added words, deleted words,
shifted phrases around.

Occasionally the full committee met to examine what he had
written. The beginning of the second paragraph struck Franklin
as overwrought with verbiage. In a document of this sort no
glut of words should stand between reader and meaning.
Instead of writing, "We hold these truths to be sacred &
undeniable," he said, why not write, "We hold these truths to be
self-evident"? A good suggestion, thought Jefferson. The change
was made.

John Adams objected to calling the King of England a
"tyrant." It was all right for a mere journalist like Tom Paine to
indulge in name-calling. The language of "a state paper" should
be more elevated. Jefferson wondered if Adams could suggest
an elevated synonym for "tyrant." Adams thought hard, but in
vain. George III remained a "Prince, whose character is . . .
marked by every act which may define a Tyrant . . ."

On June 28 Jefferson's paper went to Congress, to lie on the
table until Richard Henry Lee's resolution was approved and
the independence that the paper had been written to justify
became accomplished fact. This happened on the second of
July, and on the next day Congress considered Jefferson's effort
word for word.

The magnificent opening paragraphs won almost instantaneous approval. Other portions underwent numerous but minor
alterations. Jefferson had accused the King of encouraging slavery, that "assemblage of horrors" in America. Adams had warned
that some of the delegates, especially those from the South,
would want this statement eliminated. They did; it was. Save
for this change, the Declaration of Independence—adopted by
Congress on the following day—was essentially the tract that
Jefferson had composed.

The modern eye skims over the long lists of crimes it attrib-
utes to George III. We know now that the King was not solely

responsible for any of them and that many of the accusations were exaggerated. The great passages, the essential ones, still arrest the eye and exalt the mind:

> We hold these truths to be self-evident, that all men are created equal, that they are endowed by their Creator with certain un-alienable Rights, that among these are Life, Liberty and the Pursuit of Happiness.—That to secure these rights, Governments are instituted among Men, deriving their just Powers from the consent of the Governed, that whenever any Form of Government becomes destructive of these Ends, it is the Right of the People to alter or to abolish it . . .

On the day of its adoption only two signatures went on the new nation's first state paper, those of John Hancock, president of Congress, and Charles Thomson, secretary. A few days later two orders connected with it emerged from Congress. One called for the Declaration to be engrossed on parchment. The other appointed a committee to arrange for the designing of a seal for the United States of America.

These formalities took time. It was August 2 before the official copy of the Declaration of Independence, stamped with the newly designed seal, was ready to receive the signatures of the members of Congress. Those not present that day signed later, the last of them on November 4. Voting as a unit, the Pennsylvania delegation had approved of the Declaration. No one could have faulted John Dickinson had he signed it. Honorable to the end, he refrained from doing so.

Well in advance of the formal signing, couriers had rushed printed copies to all sections of the country. At six o'clock on the evening of July 9, the commanding officers of the units serving under George Washington in New York formed their men into large squares. Fifes whistled and drums rumbled as brigade majors made ready to read the great proclamation to their troops. In camps scattered from the northern end of Manhattan Island to the hills of Brooklyn, the identical words rang out:

When in the Course of human Events, it becomes necessary for one People to dissolve the Political Bands which have connected them with another . . .

That night Washington's soldiers celebrated. They tore down the gilded leaden statue of King George III in Bowling Green, rid New York of other emblems of royal authority. These enterprises, according to a local newspaper, were carried out with "vigor" but with the "utmost decorum."

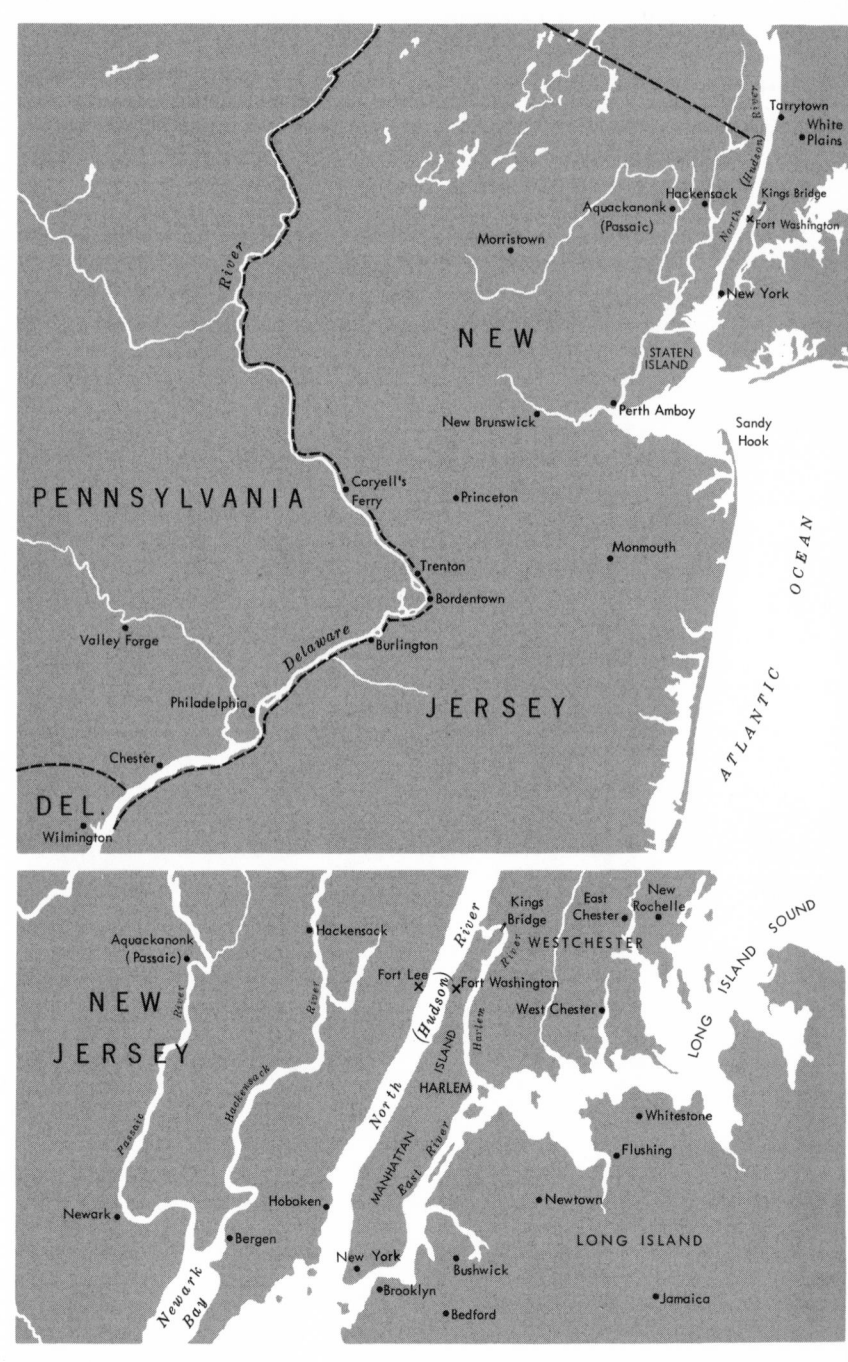

# 18

## New York Lost

T HE TROOPS ASSEMBLED at New York that summer needed
all the "vigor" and "decorum" they could muster. The
long-expected British attack on America's second largest city
was building up.

Sir William Howe had remained at Halifax only long enough
to disembark his loyalist refugees, refit his ships, take on supplies. Then he and his army had pointed south, heading for
Sandy Hook, New Jersey, where the Atlantic Ocean feeds into
the lower bay of New York.

From England came Sir William's older brother, Admiral
Lord Richard Howe, in command of the largest armada ever to
cross the Atlantic as of that date. Up from Charleston sailed
Admiral Sir Peter Parker, bringing Sir Henry Clinton and his
troops, Virginia's Lord Dunmore and his small army, and
Charles the Earl of Cornwallis, the able English general whose
revolutionary career would terminate at a little Virginia tobacco
port called Yorktown.

By early August the upper bay of New York—its harbor—
was white with the sails of fifty-two British warships and 426
transports. At night Staten Island, the hilly land mass separating
the lower bay from the upper one, glittered with campfires as
32,000 British Tommies and German Hessians shivered under
thin blankets during the frequent summer rains and cursed the
mosquitoes.

At Washington's New York headquarters the commander in
chief ruminated on the difficulties of his position. He had no

seapower to throw against the heavily armored vessels off the docks of New York. He counted twenty thousand effectives among his forces. It was the largest army he would ever command, but it was not the best. His men were green. Discipline was as much of a problem as it had been during his early days at Cambridge. When two British men-of-war entered the North River (the lower Hudson) and began cannonading the city, his orders to man the shore batteries were largely ignored. Drunkenness was prevalent among those artillerists who did report. Their fire made no impression on the sturdy oak of the invading warships.

The town that Washington had been called on to hold could have been tucked into a corner of today's metropolis. It occupied only the lower tip of the thirteen-mile-long island later known as Manhattan. North of where City Hall now stands lay mostly open country with here and there a lonely farm or backwoods village.

Militarily, Washington's chances of defending the seaport were slim. Politically, he had no choice but to defend it. The loss of New York would be a staggering blow to a nation so young that it measured its existence in weeks.

When would the British attack? Deserters from enemy vessels said soon. Meaning tomorrow or a month from tomorrow? Where would they strike? The possible places were so numerous as to make adequate fortification of all of them an impossibility.

At the northern end of the island, Kings Bridge, a small wooden span over the Harlem River, provided the only link between Manhattan and lower Westchester County on the mainland. On neighboring Long Island, across the East River to the south, loomed Brooklyn Heights.

A strike by the British at Kings Bridge could imprison the American forces on Manhattan. Enemy cannons implanted on Brooklyn Heights could do to New York City what the American field guns on Dorchester Heights had done to Boston.

Eighteenth-century military textbooks spoke of the doom awaiting the general who divided his forces, but terrain, not textbooks, guided Washington's preparations. Up Manhattan went General Heath and one thousand troops with instructions to encamp on both sides of the Harlem River at Kings Bridge. Across the East River went nine thousand soldiers, to complete the chain of forts already started on Brooklyn Heights, to guard the Long Island shore where it bulged westward into the slender channel of water—the Narrows—that divided it from British-held Staten Island.

Both of the rivers flanking the city itself received attention, especially the Hudson, as its broad waters constituted Washington's only direct communication with General Schuyler at Albany. Near where the George Washington Bridge now leaps the Hudson, toiling soldiers sank large stone-laden frames called chevaux-de-frise. Atop these bulky objects were protruding points capable of cracking the hulls of vessels.

Even as these ambitious structures were being lowered, some of the timbers joining their elements separated, creating a passage. A few weeks later two British warships and three tenders felt their way up the river, found the opening, and moved through.

In still another effort to deny the Hudson to the enemy, the Americans threw up a five-sided earthwork on a dark limestone hill slightly north of where 180th Street now meets the river. Fort Washington, as this safehold was called, was designed to operate in conjunction with an older one, recently given the name of Fort Lee, on the Jersey shore almost directly opposite.

Sir William Howe and his brother, the admiral, came to New York with instructions to perform a double mission. Their orders made them at one and the same time the leaders of the British invasion and peace commissioners. As peace commissioners they were authorized to offer the Americans certain concessions, provided they laid down their arms.

On a torrid July morning a British naval officer docked at

New York under a flag of truce. In his hand was a message inviting the American commander in chief to confer with the British peace commissioners.

Washington's aides noted that the message was addressed to "George Washington, Esq. &c. &c." They refused it, saying that if Commissioners Howe and Howe wished to communicate with "His Excellency, *General* Washington," they must send a message so addressed. A few days later a second officer came bringing a second message addressed to "George Washington, Esquire." This too was refused. Finally a high-ranking British officer arranged to lay the British peace proposal before *General* Washington in person.

The commander in chief heard him out and shook his head. He failed to see any peace in the British peace offer. He pointed out that the powers of Commissioners Howe and Howe were severely limited. They could offer pardons to the rebels only on condition that they stop rebelling. Washington said that Americans were not rebelling; they were defending their liberties. For this they needed no pardons.

Commissioners Howe and Howe could not lay their peace proposals before the Congress. In British eyes that organization had no legal status. But in London Admiral Lord Howe and Ben Franklin had become friends, had played chess at each other's homes. The admiral described the peace proposals in a letter to Franklin. Congress, informed of its contents, authorized Franklin, John Adams, and Edward Rutledge of South Carolina (brother of the governor) to confer with Lord Howe at his headquarters on Staten Island.

The three-hour conference ran a genial and soft-spoken course. The delegates from Philadelphia said that when England recognized American independence the war would end. Until then, it would go on.

Admiral Howe looked pained. He said that he had always loved America as he would a brother. He would grieve, as for a brother, if she were to fall.

"My lord," said Franklin with a benign smile, "we will use our utmost endeavors to save your lordship that mortification."

On this note the peace conference ended.

Meanwhile, the war had continued.

On the wind-lashed morning of August 22, Lord Cornwallis and fifteen thousand redcoats landed along the Gravesend section of Long Island. Two days later General Leopold von Heister and five thousand blue-coated Hessians followed. Cornwallis pierced inland, swiftly flushing out American sharpshooters whose hiding places in the cornfields of Flatbush had been revealed to him by local loyalists. Von Heister lunged north in the direction of the rebel works on Brooklyn Heights.

Sir William Howe, in overall command of the British invasion, had learned a lesson at Breed's Hill. During the Battle of Long Island on the night of August 26–27, he avoided direct confrontation with the defenders. He attained his ends by a series of flanking maneuvers.

On the British side the bloody encounter was brilliantly executed. On the American side it was marked by ineptitude, by a recurrent failure of communication among the commanding generals, Israel Putnam, John Sullivan of New Hampshire, and William Alexander of New Jersey, more often addressed as Lord Stirling because of his claim to a lapsed Scottish earldom. By noon of the twenty-seventh fifteen hundred Americans were dead or captured.

The others fell back to the fortifications on Brooklyn Heights. From New York Washington rushed four thousand troops to their assistance, only to realize immediately that even with reinforcements the situation on Long Island was hopeless. Behind and below the now almost twelve thousand Americans in the forts of Brooklyn Heights lay the East River. In front of them stretched the British camp, only six hundred yards away.

Sir William Howe's generals urged him to attack the American survivors at once. Howe refused. A direct assault on the entrapped Americans was bound to succeed, but only at a terrible cost in lives. The British commander opted for a siege-like procedure. He began laying down parallels (series of trenches) with the idea of gradually closing in on the Americans, eventually forcing them to surrender. Behind this humane decision was Howe's conviction that he had plenty of time, that the men holed up on Brooklyn Heights could not possibly get away.

But they did. Washington saw to that.

As at Dorchester Heights the elements came to his aid. The night of August 29–30 was one of droning rain, gusty winds, and black skies. All through the dark hours and into a murky dawn, rowboats manned by Colonel John Glover's Marblehead fishermen plied the East River between New York and the foot of Brooklyn Heights. It was 4:30 A.M. before the British realized that their prey was escaping. It was 7 A.M. before a red-jacketed patrol reached the shore of the river, just in time to see the last rowboat vanish northward into a rolling fog. A round of British musketry was ineffective—happily for the American cause, as the last man to leave Long Island that morning was George Washington.

In a splendidly planned and coordinated maneuver he had snatched more than half of his army from certain capture.

But he could not save New York. On September 12, reluctantly, he let it be known that the city was to be evacuated. His announcement frightened the citizens. Thousands of them took off, lugging their belongings with them, stripping the city of the conveyances needed to transport the army's cannon and stores. When the British arrived they would fall heir to most of Washington's heavier equipment and much of his gunpowder.

On the whole, the soldiers exhibited as little dignity as the citizens. Many of them departed without waiting for orders to do so. For three days the highways running up the island were a creeping jam of wagons loaded with household goods, of distraught civilians, and of fleeing soldiers. Terror and confusion were everywhere when under the searing midday sun of the fifteenth the British landed from the East River at Kip's Bay and probed westward along a line roughly parallel with what is now East Twenty-third Street.

Panic seized the Connecticut militiamen assigned to the American trenches in the Kip's Bay area. Some fled, others froze. Washington, suddenly appearing in the vicinity, fell into a rage. He was seen to rip the three-cornered hat from his head and slam it to the earth. He was heard to shout, "Are these the men with whom I am to defend America!" Blinded with fury, he might have been seized by the invaders had not a fellow officer hustled him away.

A few American units were caught south of the invasion line. Most escaped to Paulus Hook (Jersey City) on the western bank of the Hudson. One unit, including a company of artillery under Captain Alexander Hamilton, made its way up Manhattan along hidden woodland pathways, guided by a handsome twenty-year-old major named Aaron Burr.

On Harlem Heights Washington emplaced his men in three lines northward of present-day West 130th Street. General Howe and the vanguard of the invasion force pursued as far as Vandewater (now Morningside) Heights. Nightfall of the fifteenth found the two armies within hallooing distance of one another, separated only by the Hollow Way, the then-wooded ravine where West 124th and 125th Streets now run.

Shortly after dawn the next morning, a battalion of Connecticut Rangers, 150 men under Lieutenant Colonel Thomas Knowlton, slipped into the Hollow Way and prodded westward. Their orders were to encircle the British encampment, determine the disposition of its outposts.

As Knowlton and his rangers trooped toward the Hudson, two enemy battalions were seen coming toward them across the slope that now supports the tomb of General Ulysses S. Grant. Buglers marching with the British blew the fox hunter's call that tells the members of the hunt that their prey has gone to earth.

On Harlem Heights, Washington's recently appointed adjutant, Colonel Joseph Reed of Philadelphia, was "mortified" at this melodic insult. He begged Washington to send reinforcements to the aid of Knowlton and his now-threatened battalion. "Reluctantly," according to Reed, the commander in chief did so. Later he sent in more men and put in motion a scheme that during the afternoon lured a large detachment of British into a disastrous ambuscade.

In his official report General Howe described the six-hour clash that ensued as a mere "scrape," an "affair of outposts." More accurate was the American term for it, "the Battle of Harlem Heights." Within an hour 4,900 Americans and a somewhat larger number of British redcoats and green-clad German Jägers were engaged. The hostilities ranged widely, from the shores of the Hudson eastward into the fields of buckwheat ripening in the valley where later the tenements of the Harlem section of New York would rise.

Heretofore the Americans had done practically all of their fighting from behind barricades. Now, for the first time, they faced the best that England could offer in open combat.

On Long Island the inexperienced defenders of New York had fumbled every opportunity, fallen into every British trap. At Kip's Bay they had turned tail. Here, on the plains of Harlem, the spirit was that of men determined to atone for past weaknesses.

The casualty figures tell the story: 70 Britishers and Hessians killed and 200 wounded, as against 30 Americans dead and 90 wounded. By mid-afternoon Howe's redcoats and Jägers were fleeing to their lines. George Washington, observing the action from Harlem Heights, felt his spirits lift and his faith reviving in "the men with whom I am to defend America." As the afternoon waned he called his triumphant troops home. At this point his job was not to win battles but to preserve a disorganized army from the clutches of a superior force.

Sir William Howe was shaken by the outcome. It could be that the excessive caution which marred his conduct of the English campaigns in America was born that day. A typical product of the leisurely and gentlemanly war-making of eighteenth-century Europe, Sir William in the months ahead would exhibit more timidity than ever. To Washington the small victory in the buckwheat fields of Harlem was heaven-sent. It gave him a badly needed breather—a few weeks in which to put his ragged forces in order.

It was a frustrating period for the British. On September 20 they came close to losing the city they had seized to a fire that gutted hundreds of homes and was probably set by the patriots still in New York. An inkling of Howe's troubled state of mind is found in an incident of the following day. When on Long Island his soldiers picked up a Connecticut captain disguised as a teamster, the British commander acted with uncharacteristic harshness. He ordered the captured spy hanged at once and without trial. The British troops summoned to witness the execution were impressed by the young American's calm as he walked to his doom. His last words sped northward, to be repeated with awe by Washington's soldiers and cherished by their descendants.

"I only regret," said Nathan Hale as the noose draped his shoulders, "that I have but one life to lose for my country."

# 19

# General Turns Admiral

THUS IN THE FALL of 1776 stood the War of Independence, on the spinning top of uncertainty. In smoking, half-burned New York the British settled into a city they would hold for seven years. On Harlem Heights a grateful commander in chief lavished praise on the victors of the battle in the buckwheat fields below and made the most of a brief lull in the hostilities. And far up in the lake country northeast of where the Hudson River takes its first trickling glide, the American effort to conquer Canada was grinding to a bizarre conclusion.

All during the stormy northern winter Benedict Arnold and his ragtaggle troops had hovered on the outskirts of Quebec. To the Canadian governor and military leader, courtly Sir Guy Carleton, their presence beyond the gates of his city was more of a nuisance than a threat. Sir Guy had sixteen hundred soldiers to guard the stout walls of his citadel. In the roadstead of the St. Lawrence River below lay a British frigate, a sloop of war, and several smaller ships. Barring a substantial enlargement of the starving army hanging on his flanks, the English governor-general could wait in comfort until a spring sun melted the ice in the river and permitted ships from home to bring him soldiers and supplies.

In April old and ailing Brigadier General David Wooster of Connecticut came downriver from American-held Montreal, bringing sufficient forces to lift to two thousand the besieging army before Quebec. Enough to lure Sir Guy Carleton into the open where the Americans could get at him? No one could say. Perhaps the two thousand could have accomplished something had Arnold remained on the scene. But Arnold was in pain. A recent fall from his horse had aggravated the injury to his leg. He retired to Montreal, and General Wooster plunged at once into a frenzy of ill-considered activity.

A furious American bombardment of the fortress withered before the greater firepower of its defenders. A daring but futile attempt to burn the British ships in the river cost Wooster more than half his men. He was happy to leave when in May capable Major General John Thomas of Massachusetts came north to replace him as commander of the American forces in Canada.

That did bring out Sir Guy Carleton—suddenly, with nine hundred men behind him and four snorting field guns. Caught unawares, Thomas and his troops sped across the river and stumbled westward. They had put a hundred miles of Canadian farm country between themselves and Quebec when on June 1 they pulled up at Sorel. This little settlement stood at the mouth of the Richelieu, the swift north-flowing stream that connects the St. Lawrence to Lake Champlain seventy-five miles to the south. Here General Thomas died of smallpox even as reinforcements arrived, six thousand Continentals and militia under Brigadier Generals John Sullivan and William Thompson.

Sullivan took command. A skillful but often impetuous soldier, the New Hampshire general had come north with a mandate from Washington. "The misfortune of Quebec," the commander in chief told him, "must be repaired." The great fortress must be assaulted again—and quickly before additional troops could reach Sir Guy Carleton.

Intelligence drifting into the American camp indicated that Carleton had established an outpost at Three Rivers. This small trading center stood on the northern shore of the St. Lawrence, about halfway to Quebec. Eight hundred soldiers, mostly Canadian volunteers, were said to be entrenched there.

Sullivan ordered General Thompson to take two thousand men and wipe them out. That done, Sullivan would follow. Then the rebels would march in force to Quebec.

It was a spirited and hopeful body of Americans who went across the St. Lawrence with General Thompson, but the situation toward which they were marching was not what they had been led to expect. When in the dawn of a brooding June morning Thompson and his followers crawled out of a deep swamp near Three Rivers, they found in front of them not a small body of Canadian militia but eight thousand British regulars. Commanding them was Sir Guy Carleton, assisted by Gentleman Johnny Burgoyne.

The reinforcements from England had arrived.

Burgoyne had brought them. The handsome playwright-general had left Boston shortly after the Battle of Bunker Hill, had hastened to London to propose glittering schemes to Lord Germain. Now he was back in the New World, bursting with ideas for crushing the rebellion.

At Three Rivers four hundred Americans died in a fierce running battle before Thompson and his troops were able to beat their way back to Sorel.

By this time the English were threatening Montreal, and Arnold and his forces had abandoned that city to join Sullivan. In mid-June the American Army began a frantic withdrawal southward, traveling up the rapids-infested Richelieu in heavy bateaux. A large fleet of British river transports pursued. At one point the entire American force would have been captured had not a sudden blow of adverse winds held back the enemy.

No winds could stay the smallpox scourging the fleeing troops. It was a pestilence-ridden rabble who at the end of June reached the southwestern shores of Lake Champlain. There they halted, safe for the moment behind the walls of Crown Point, a small American fort twelve miles north of Ticonderoga.

Express riders had rushed news of their plight southward. Alarm gripped Congress. The size of the British pursuing force—the presence of Burgoyne at Carleton's side—these circumstances shouted that the objectives of the British were not confined to chasing the Americans out of Canada. The enemy had his eyes on Crown Point and Ticonderoga. Seizure of those strongholds could open the way to a British invasion of the Hudson River valley. Implored by Congress to put the best officer he could spare in charge of the situation on Lake Champlain, Washington rushed English-born Major General Horatio Gates to Crown Point.

In the summer of 1776 "Granny Gates," as his men called him, looked older than his forty-eight years. His slight, stooped figure; his ruddy cheeks and round, bespectacled eyes; his thinning hair—these added up to a bland exterior that masked both very real military abilities and an unfortunate capacity for pettiness. Like Charles Lee, he brought to his revolutionary endeavors a long and laudable service in the British regular army. Like Lee, he had moved to America on the eve of the war, purchased a Virginia plantation, and cast his lot with the patriots. And like Lee he would go through the war convinced that Congress had made a mistake, that he not Washington should be the supreme leader of the Continental Army.

Unlike high-born Lee, Gates had begun life under what in class-conscious England were handicaps. His father was a minor government official, his mother a one-time housekeeper to the Duke of Leeds. Still, the frequently offered picture of him as rising solely on his own merits appears to be an exaggerated one. His mother's service to the duke attracted the attention of Horace Walpole, titled London wit and son of a prime minister. The patronage of the powerful Walpole family opened doors to young Horatio. His father's hard-scraped savings purchased him the commission that launched his military career.

Sent to the New World during the French and Indian War, he suffered a severe wound early in the conflict. His injuries kept him off the battlefield and put him in posts where he quickly mastered the details of military administration. This was exactly the experience needed on the southern shores of Lake Champlain in the summer of 1776. Relieving Sullivan, whose orders were to report to Washington at New York, Gates quickly rallied the spirits of the shattered army, halted the desertions that were riddling it, and discouraged the spread of smallpox by issuing extra rations of rum and starting huge bonfires to combat the dampness of the region.

Schuyler joined him at Crown Point, and a council of war on July 5 yielded two decisions. One was to move the bulk of the army from Crown Point to Ticonderoga. Another was that a navy be created to delay the advance of the British, hopefully until the coming of cold weather made it impossible for them to move on to the Hudson River valley.

Months before, Schuyler had anticipated that any invasion from the north would be by way of Lake Champlain. He had already overseen the fabrication of three small armed vessels. Now Gates proposed that Benedict Arnold, the only officer on hand with saltwater experience, direct the construction of additional warships and assume the duties of an admiral.

Arnold built his navy at Skenesboro (now Whitehall, New York) at the foot of Lake Champlain. Wood for the ships was plentiful in the area, but not the skills for building them. Hurried calls for workmen went out. An unusually high wage—$5.00 an hour—attracted carpenters, blacksmiths, sailmakers, riggers, and oarmakers from as far south as Philadelphia. Under Arnold's driving leadership a navy swiftly materialized, a little fleet of round-bottomed row galleys and smaller flat-bottomed gondolas.

It was not only at Skenesboro during the late summer and fall that saws screeched and hammers clanged. Having failed to capture the American Army on the Richelieu River, the British were compelled to halt at the northern end of the lake and construct a battle squadron of their own. Their resources were infinitely greater than those of the Americans. The largest of their vessels, a floating battery christened the *Thunderer,* would carry more firepower into Lake Champlain than all of Arnold's galleys and gondolas combined.

On October 4 the British flotilla, headed by the eighteen-gun sloop *Inflexible,* a three-masted square-rigger, stood out from the mouth of the Richelieu and worked south. Arnold was waiting halfway up the lake, his ships arrayed in a half moon near the western shore behind Valcour Island. A less dauntless commander, seeing the British armada approaching on the eleventh under a vast spread of sail, would have withdrawn.

But withdrawal was not "Admiral" Arnold's way. All day the heavily armored British ships boomed and the American boats piped back. Arnold was everywhere, bellowing commands and directing maneuvers. It would be written later that in the face of certain defeat he conducted the Battle of Valcour Island as though an American victory were inevitable.

As twilight closed in, he counted eighty men lost, two ships destroyed, three captured, the rest wrecks. During the dark hours he and his soldiers gave the British the slip. Next day they rammed their remaining ships against the rocky western shores of the lake. Then, hustling south by land to Crown Point, they burned the fortress there and moved on to Ticonderoga.

The British had won the Battle of Valcour Island, but they had lost the campaign. The American delaying action, initiated by Schuyler and Gates and executed by Arnold, had succeeded. The hard northern winter was setting in. For a short period the British lingered amid the ruins of Crown Point. Then they retired northward to spend the coming months in Canada.

Another year would pass before they would be able to attempt a second invasion of the Hudson River valley. By that time the military arm of the United States would be in a far better position to cope with them.

# 20

# "These are the times . . ."

B Y THE TIME the news of Valcour Island reached the New York area, George Washington was no longer on Harlem Heights. British ships had moved up the East River into Long Island Sound, had begun landing an attacking force on Pell's Point (now part of Pelham Bay Park, New York) on the shores of Westchester County. Fearful of being entrapped on Manhattan Island, Washington had moved northward across the Harlem to the mainland, leaving 2,800 men behind to garrison Fort Washington.

The onus of impeding the British invaders fell to Colonel John Glover (soon to be Brigadier General Glover), commanding his own and three other Massachusetts regiments at Pell's Point. Standing on a hilltop on the morning of October 18, 1776, Glover trained his telescope on the approaching enemy transports. He could see that the troops piling ashore on the rocks below outnumbered his own ten to one. His job was to delay them as long as possible. This he must accomplish with 860 men and three small fieldpieces.

Stocky, red-haired John Glover was frankly scared. He did not fancy himself a military genius. He knew what he was—a hard-working Marbleheader who months before had led his men to Cambridge because a parliament three thousand miles away had threatened to take the bread out of his mouth and out of the mouths of his fellow fishermen.

"Oh! the anxiety of mind I was then in for the fate of the day," he would write of that cloudy autumn morning at Pell's

Point. "I would have given a thousand worlds to have had General [Charles] Lee, or some other experienced officer present, to direct, or at least to approve of what I had done."

But John Glover was a better tactician than he realized. He had studied the surrounding terrain. He knew that to get at the main American Army General Howe and his men must begin their march north through a narrow defile between the rough Westchester hills.

Along the rocky ridges to either side of this trough Glover strung out his regiments, forcing the enemy to run a gauntlet of musketry. There was a limit to how long the Marblehead colonel and his little force could last—but while they lasted they did damage. When at dawn on the following morning they cut and ran, they had held up the invaders long enough to let General Washington throw up strong redoubts on a string of hills north of the village of White Plains, New York.

Here on the twenty-eighth the major encounter erupted. A week later the guns were still yammering. Washington had pulled back five miles to more commanding ground at North Castle, but the relative position of the two armies was little changed. The Battle of White Plains was ending in a standoff.

On the fifth day of November the Americans awakened to a surprise: General Howe and his army had vanished.

Where? Hastily dispatched scouts brought back word that the British had moved first to Dobbs Ferry, New York, a village about half a dozen miles to the west on the shores of the Hudson. Some of the Hessians were still there, but Howe and most of his men were marching south toward Manhattan.

What were Howe's intentions? At a council of war Washington and his aides canvassed the possibilities. Was the British leader contemplating an attack on Fort Washington? Or a jab across New Jersey to seize Philadelphia? Or both?

The consensus was that Washington should cross the Hudson and join forces with Nathanael Greene at Fort Lee. The Rhode Island general had gone to New Jersey in September to command an aggregation of Jersey, Delaware, Maryland, and Pennsylvania militia known as the Flying Camp. From Fort Lee the commander in chief could easily speed reinforcements across the river if Fort Washington was attacked. There too he could deal with an invasion of the Jersey should one occur.

Before leaving North Castle Washington tried to meet all contingencies by splitting his forces. He sent William Heath and four thousand troops up to Peekskill, New York. Heath was to keep an eye on the Hudson River highlands in case Sir William Howe decided to move in that direction.

Charles Lee had returned from South Carolina. He and seven thousand troops were to remain at North Castle. They were to oversee the transportation across the Hudson of the equipment and supplies that the Americans had assembled on the North Castle Heights. This task accomplished, the English-born general and the three divisions assigned to his command were to join the commander in chief in New Jersey.

Washington crossed the river on the morning of the twelfth. In New Jersey he encamped his army—not quite 2,400 men—at Hackensack. He himself hastened to nearby Fort Lee, standing on the Jersey shore across the Hudson from Fort Washington.

Disappointment awaited him there. He had hoped to pick up an additional five thousand men at the New Jersey stronghold. He found that its garrison had shrunk to less than two thousand. Desertions and the expiration of short-term enlistments had all but destroyed the Flying Camp that Nathanael Greene had been sent across the Hudson to command. Frantic efforts by Greene to bolster his dwindling regiments with recruitments had failed.

From the ramparts of the New Jersey bastion Washington could observe the activities of the British on upper Manhattan Island. By the morning of the fourteenth General Howe's objectives were clear. He was massing his troops for an assault on Fort Washington.

Could that hastily erected earthwork hold? There was still time to rescue its 2,800 defenders, to bring them by boat to the safety of New Jersey. But that would mean giving the stronghold to the enemy. So long as it remained in rebel hands the British were in trouble. Its presence on Manhattan Island would tie up thousands of soldiers, making it difficult for Howe to invade New Jersey. On the other hand, if Fort Washington fell, its garrison would fall with it.

Greene urged the commander in chief to leave the Fort Washington garrison where it was—faulty advice, as it turned out, from an officer whose military judgment was usually sound. But if Greene's counsel was bad, Washington's vacillation was worse. In after years he would speak of the "warfare" that raged in his mind as he struggled to reach a decision.

Greene extolled the virtues of Colonel Robert Magaw, the officer in command at Fort Washington. He conceded that the fort itself was not strong, but pointed out that it stood on a 260-foot hill whose summit was almost inaccessible from three sides. On the fourth and weakest slope the Americans had set up extensive breastworks. Greene was certain that Magaw and his men could hold out indefinitely. Doubtful but unable to make up his mind, Washington crossed the river for a firsthand look at the situation—a reconnaissance trip from which he returned still locked in the toils of indecision.

On the sixteenth the assault on Fort Washington began with hand-to-hand fighting along the breastworks at the northern foot of the hill. During the morning the commander in chief made another trip to the threatened earthwork. He had only just returned to New Jersey when the news reached him. A column of helmeted Hessians under General Wilhelm von Knyphausen had gained the hilltop. Surrounded and outnumbered, Colonel Magaw had surrendered. Even now arrangements were being made for marching his men to New York City, where during the next few months hundreds of them would die in the festering holds of British prison ships.

For the rebels the loss of the Fort Washington garrison was a catastrophe. For the commander in chief it was a personal defeat, as his bad judgment had helped bring it about. Nor was the blow softened by the information, reaching him a few days later, that Colonel Magaw might have repulsed the British on-slaught had not hundreds of his soldiers simply refused to fight.

By the time this troubling intelligence arrived at Fort Lee and at Hackensack, all was furious movement at both sites. The now-inevitable British penetration of New Jersey had begun. Lord Cornwallis had crossed the Hudson six miles upriver from Fort Lee. He was marching southward with four thousand soldiers and a formidable train of artillery.

No indecision marked Washington's response to this crisis. He gave no thought to defending the Fort Lee-Hackensack line with a shadow of an army. He ordered the area abandoned at once—and the most spectacular chase of the war began.

Lord Cornwallis moved twenty miles a day. Washington moved faster. Capture of his little army would leave the way open for a British march to Philadelphia. His only hope lay in putting the big Delaware River between himself and his pursuers.

The weather was vile: an icy rain one day, swirling snow mixed with sleet the next. Hard to travel even in good weather, the narrow roads were ribbons of mud. As Washington's ragged forces slogged out of Newark, New Jersey, to the south, Corn-wallis's German Jägers, their green coats dark with moisture, slithered in from the north. As the rear guard of the American Army touched the southern shores of the Raritan at New Brunswick, New Jersey, the vanguard of the British Army materialized out of the mist on the northern bank.

Fortunately for Washington, Cornwallis spent the next six days in New Brunswick—held up by a message from New York. Cautious Sir William Howe was fearful of overextending his lines. His orders were for Cornwallis to stay where he was until Howe could join him with reinforcements.

Washington put the six days to good use. He saw to it that trees were felled and bridges destroyed along the roads to Trenton, New Jersey, standing on the eastern shores of the Delaware only thirty miles above Philadelphia. He ordered every boat on the river along a seventy-mile stretch to be brought to the Trenton docks.

At two o'clock on the afternoon of December 8, Cornwallis and the advance units of the enlarged British Army marched into Trenton—just in time to see the last boatload of Americans approaching the shores of Pennsylvania across the river. Orders from Cornwallis to pursue immediately were reluctantly withdrawn as word reached the British commander that no shipping of any sort remained on the New Jersey side of the Delaware.

Several times during the dash across New Jersey, Washington had rushed express riders to North Castle, New York, requesting General Charles Lee to bring his divisions and join the fleeing army. Washington sent a similar appeal to Philip Schuyler up in Albany. That conscientious general promptly dispatched twelve battalions southward; but for several weeks Lee did not budge.

He was heard to say that under some circumstances "treason can be a beautiful and necessary thing." Lee was given to wild and whimsical remarks. Perhaps he laughed as he spoke of treason, assuming that his listeners would know that he was joking. Perhaps he was. Perhaps not.

He was convinced that Washington was incompetent. He seems to have reasoned that the sooner the commander in chief and his army were seized, the better. Then the Congress would see the wisdom of putting a professional soldier—Lee, that is—in Washington's place.

Three thousand of Lee's troops had recently walked off, their terms of enlistment ended. Lee wrote General Heath at Peekskill that he himself could not leave North Castle for the time being. Nor could he spare any of his remaining troops. He told Heath, his inferior in rank, to send two thousand of his men to Washington. Heath wrote back that his orders from the commander in chief were to keep his soldiers where they were.

On the last day of November, Lee appeared at Heath's headquarters in Peekskill, his army with him. He demanded a cup of tea. Refreshed, he repeated his request for two thousand of Heath's soldiers. Again Heath pointed out that he could not release men unless ordered to do so by Washington.

Lee thought that over. "In *point of law*," he told Heath, "you are right, but in point of policy . . . you are wrong. I am going into the Jerseys for the salvation of America. I wish to take with me a larger force than I now have."

When Heath once more refused to detach any of his men, Lee issued the necessary orders himself. On the next day, however, he canceled them. A capricious gentleman was Charles Lee. When on the first day of December he finally crossed the Hudson and set out to join Washington, only his own divisions were with him.

Once on his way, Lee seemed to be in no hurry to accomplish "the salvation of America." He was still considerably above Newark on December 8, the day that saw the flight of Washington and his soldiers across the Delaware a hundred miles to the south.

The thirteenth found the English-born general at Vealtown, a Jersey village west of Newark. Leaving his army under General John Sullivan, Lee himself rode three miles into the country to spend the night at a comfortable tavern at Basking Ridge. We are told that a pretty lady entertained him there. If so, she did not receive all of his attention. He spent part of the night writing a letter to General Horatio Gates, complaining that the supreme commander of the Continental Army was "not fit to command a corporal's guard." His letter seems to have reached Gates, but the author of it did not get to Washington.

During the night a British cavalry detachment under Lieutenant Colonel William Harcourt learned of Lee's presence at the tavern. About ten o'clock the next day, with a newly fallen snow glistening in the morning sun, Harcourt and his scarlet-coated dragoons overwhelmed the general's guards. A few minutes later the savior of America, clad in dressing gown and slippers, was a prisoner of the enemy.

The news of this development distressed Washington profoundly. He had counted heavily on Lee's assistance. He wrote his brother at Mount Vernon that "the game is up." Without Lee's help he was not certain that he could protect Philadelphia. That city, as he knew, had become a swirl of confusion and fright. Patriot families were fleeing. Tory families were getting ready to assume charge. The members of the Congress had taken themselves and their records to Baltimore, Maryland—an act that some subsequent historians would call cowardly but that Washington viewed as simple common sense. Seizure of the government at this point would have been an intolerable blow to the American cause, already in mortal danger.

Moving a few miles inland from the Delaware, Washington established his headquarters on the commons of Newtown in Bucks County, Pennsylvania. For the moment he and his little army were safe—but only for the moment. With the coming of colder weather the Delaware would cease to be a barrier. Frozen over, it would be a highway for the enemy.

But the British had no intention of using it. Sir William Howe was a creature of habit. At Long Island he had mistakenly assumed that the twelve thousand Americans entrapped on Brooklyn Heights could not escape. Now he erroneously assumed that Washington was pinned down on the western shores of the Delaware until spring. Time enough then, Sir William decided, to assemble boats at Trenton and ferry his army across the big river.

Back went the bulk of his forces to New York and upper New Jersey. A few mostly Hessian regiments set up outposts at Trenton and other western New Jersey points. Lord Cornwallis's wife was ill. With Howe's consent, his lordship began making preparations to spend the winter with her in England. As for Howe himself, he hastened to New York, to enjoy the pleasures of the gaming table and the lively company of his mistress, Mrs. Joshua Loring, Jr., wife of a Boston loyalist.

In the neighborhood of Washington's new headquarters badly needed reinforcements were gathering. From Philadelphia came dashing Colonel John Cadwalader and his Associators. From Albany came Schuyler's battalions, led by Benedict Arnold. On December 20 General Sullivan arrived, bringing Charles Lee's troops. Washington's army now numbered well over six thousand, but it was miserably equipped and thinly clad. Even after bundles of old clothes arrived from Philadelphia, most soldiers remained in tatters. A camp humorist remarked that the buff and blue of the regulation Continental uniform had become "mostly buff."

Washington realized that were his army to remain idle during the rest of the winter, cold, disease, and boredom would destroy it. By mid-December he had drawn up a plan of action.

Intelligence reports concerning the condition of the Hessian garrison at Trenton dictated its details. In command of the three German regiments and other units at that little river-front town was Colonel Johann Rall, a plump and strutty little man, described by one of his diary-keeping aides as "self-indulgent and heavy-minded."

Rall had seen the Americans in action at Long Island. He had watched them fleeing in disorder from New York City. He had decided that the rebel soldiers were "a pack of old women." The colonel's orders from his superiors were to fortify Trenton, but he saw no reason to bother. Repeatedly warned by Tory spies that an American attack was imminent, he shrugged the information aside. "Let the dogs come," he said. "We'll beat them off with bayonets."

On the other side of the river the "dogs" were about to be unleashed. The sallow-faced author of *Common Sense* had tramped across New Jersey with the retreating Americans. At bivouacs stretching from Newark to Newtown, Tom Paine had composed a second propaganda pamphlet. At Newtown Washington read the manuscript before Paine sent it to Philadelphia to be printed. The commander in chief's directions were for the finished copies to be distributed to every soldier in his army.

On Christmas Eve, at campfires all along the Pennsylvania shores of the Delaware, men read and memorized Paine's opening words:

These are the times that try men's souls. The summer soldier and the sunshine patriot will, in this crisis, shrink from the service of his country; but he that stands it *now*, deserves the love and thanks of man and woman.

Seldom has the word so directly supported the sword. Neither warm clothes nor better rations could have done as much for tired bodies and sunken spirits.

On Christmas Day Washington's horsemen were speeding his last-minute orders up and down the river. His plans called for a two-headed drive on Trenton itself, along with a diversionary strike at the smaller enemy garrison at Bordentown, New Jersey, a few miles downriver. With the coming of darkness the commander in chief and 2,400 picked men were to cross the Delaware at McKonkey's Ferry and move on Trenton from the north. Brigadier General James Ewing and a small force of Pennsylvania militia were to push directly over to the Trenton docks. Cadwalader and his Associators were to take care of Bordentown. The cold winter night came on thick and starless with a flaky snow whirling in a clawing northwesterly wind. Ten miles south of headquarters, Cadwalader sent only a few of his soldiers across, holding the rest back on learning that huge and dangerous cakes of ice were floating in the river. General Ewing, after a quick reconnaissance, made no effort to dispatch his militia. Only Washington and his men completed their mission.

John Glover and his valiant fishermen manned the oars. Durham boats—flat-bottomed bargelike river craft for transporting ore—carried the eighteen cannons. Rowboats ferried the men. The classic picture "Washington Crossing the Delaware" barely outlines the rigors of the passage. Before the Jersey shore was gained, two soldiers were dead, frozen where they sat.

Shoes were scarce. The heavy rags wrapping the men's legs made their nine-mile trudge to Trenton a tedious stumble. Bloody footprints recorded their progress in the snow. Washington had hoped to attack at dawn, but the bright winter sun had been up for two hours before the northern outskirts were reached.

Colonel Rall had passed a convivial evening at the home of friends, had stuffed into his pocket unread a message rushed to Trenton by a Tory farmer who had spotted the Americans on the river. The colonel was still abed when the shooting began at the edge of town and a spreading wail rent the morning quiet: *"Der Feind, der Feind. Heraus! Heraus!"* "The enemy, the enemy. Turn out! Turn out!"

The groggy Hessian commander slid from his bed, fumbled into his uniform, and turned out—too late!

Brigadier General Adam Stephen and his Virginia Continentals were pushing south on King and Queen Streets, sweeping Rall's bewildered soldiers before them. Artillery Captain Alexander Hamilton and his guns commanded the southern end of town. From east and west troops under Greene, Sullivan, and Stirling were smashing inward. An hour later Colonel Rall lay on the whitened earth, mortally wounded. Twenty-two of his soldiers were dead. About 430 had fled. The rest—948—were prisoners of war.

Informed by Major James Wilkinson that the garrison of Trenton had grounded arms, George Washington lifted his head sharply. "Major Wilkinson," he said, "this is a glorious day for our country."

It was. Dark days, dark months, even dark years lay ahead for the American cause. But never again would it sink to the depths from which Washington's surprise attack on Trenton had lifted it.

The rebels did not tarry at the scene of their triumph. The failure of General Ewing and Colonel Cadwalader to bring their components across the Delaware meant that Washington and his men were alone in western New Jersey, vulnerable to counterattack by enemy units in the region. By nightfall of the twenty-sixth the commander in chief, his army, and his prisoners were on Pennsylvania soil. On the following day Wash-

ington invited the twenty-three captured Hessian officers to
dine with him at headquarters. The Germans agreed among
themselves that their host was "imposing and cultivated." Some
of them, however, got the impression that he had "a rather
crafty look about him."

Even as Washington was entertaining the prisoner-officers at
Newtown, Colonel Cadwalader was going into action at Bristol,
Pennsylvania. Messengers that morning had brought word that
Washington had crossed a river that the Philadelphian had
concluded only the night before was too much for his men. The
news was a slap to Cadwalader's vigorous ego. If Washington
could do it, so could he.

Over the Delaware he went, his troops with him. Finding the
British outpost at Bordentown deserted, he forged west to
Crosswicks, New Jersey. Suddenly surrounded by the enemy at
that point, he got off a plea for help to Washington.

The commander in chief was annoyed at Cadwalader's un-
authorized venture, but he had no choice but to go to the Philadelphian's assistance. Once more he and his army traversed the
icy Delaware.

The British meanwhile had reacted. Jolted by the American
victory, Lord Cornwallis had abandoned his plans to spend the
winter in England. He was marching toward Trenton at the
head of eight thousand troops. The first day of 1777 found him
a few miles north of Trenton at Princeton. Leaving a small
garrison there, his lordship continued southward.

While Washington dealt with Cornwallis's main army near
Trenton, Sullivan and a small detachment sped on to Princeton.

The redcoats there had billeted themselves in the college
building, Nassau Hall, the largest man-made structure in
America. A cannonball from one of Captain Hamilton's guns,
breaching the building's stone walls, flushed the British soldiers
into the open. Twenty minutes later all of them were fleeing,
killed, or captured; and Sullivan's soldiers were racing through
the lanes of the little college town, nabbing enemy stragglers
and alternately chanting "God save George Washington, God

damn the King" and "These are the times that try *British* souls."

Apprised of the rout of his troops at Princeton, Cornwallis quickly disengaged from Washington and retreated north to protect the English stores at New Brunswick. With Philadelphia out of danger, Washington made ready to lead the bulk of his army into winter quarters at Morristown, among the protective hills rising steeply above the Passaic River in north-central New Jersey.

News of his coup at Trenton and of Sullivan's success at Princeton nine days later spread quickly. To the drooping spirits of patriots everywhere it came as spring rain after drought. The Continental Army's recruiting officers began getting results after months of unbroken failure. Desertions from the armies in the field registered a marked decline. The paper money that Congress had printed, viewed as worthless only a few weeks earlier, started circulating again. Congress itself, miserable in the cramped quarters of a roughhewn tavern in Baltimore and weary of slugging through the mud on which that little tobacco port stood, packed up its records and hastened back to the cozy inns and civilized distractions of the City of Brotherly Love.

# 21

# The Follies of 1777

I N THE LONDON OFFICES of Colonial Secretary Germain that
winter worried men tore up old blueprints for suppressing the
American rebellion and drew up new ones.

Gentleman Johnny Burgoyne was in town again. So was Sir
Henry Clinton. Both generals, it would seem, had scurried
across the Atlantic for the same reason. In America the com-
mand of Sir William Howe extended roughly as far north as
Albany. Above that the governor-general of Canada, Sir Guy
Carleton, was in charge. And it was common knowledge in the
British capital that Carleton was out of favor with Lord Ger-
main. In other words, the stately Canadian governor-general
was about to be relieved of his high post—and Burgoyne and
Clinton were the logical candidates to succeed him.

Clinton had the edge in rank, but General Burgoyne had
vigor, enthusiasm, and charm. In addition he had a plan. He
called it "Thoughts for Conducting the War from the Side of
Canada." Burgoyne's "Thoughts" contemplated a second and
more elaborate attempt to isolate New England from the rest of
America by occupying the Hudson River valley.

Lord Germain liked Gentleman Johnny's Thoughts. His Majesty liked them, from which it followed that Prime Minister
North liked them too. In April the word was out: Clinton was
returning to New York to resume his position as second in
command to Sir William Howe. Burgoyne was on his way back
to Canada. There, having replaced Carleton as commanding

officer in that area, he would launch his carefully planned invasion by way of the Richelieu River and Lake Champlain.

General Howe was also having thoughts. During the winter Lord Germain and his aides found themselves studying not one but three different plans submitted by Sir William. The one selected called for Howe to move south from New York by water with the idea of invading Pennsylvania and seizing Philadelphia.

Sir Henry Clinton objected violently to this idea. He said that with Burgoyne thrusting down from Canada, Howe should move not south but north. Clinton envisaged Howe and Burgoyne joining forces near Albany and operating together against the Hudson River valley. He feared that without assistance from New York, Burgoyne's invasion from Canada could not succeed.

Time was to prove Clinton's warnings correct, but his arguments fell before an implacable combination of bureaucratic inanity in London and military egoism in America.

Lord Germain knew that Burgoyne might need Howe's help, but all the colonial secretary did was send overseas a mild request that Howe complete his Pennsylvania campaign quickly so as to be free to support Burgoyne if that gentleman needed him. Germain was slow about dispatching this message. By the time Howe received it, he was on his way south and no longer in a position to give Burgoyne substantial aid.

Not all of the blame for the follies that ensued can be laid to Germain's ineptitude. Some of it was an outgrowth of the fatal vanity that often clings like their shadows to ambitious men. Howe was jealous of the talented playwright-general and averse to doing anything that might further Burgoyne's already shining career. Burgoyne, on his part, exuded confidence. He was convinced that he could manage the invasion of the Hudson River region on his own. He was not really too eager for help. After all, to receive the assistance of Sir William Howe would be to share the glory with him.

A spring breeze was nibbling away the ice floes in the St.

Lawrence River when on the morning of May 6 the frigate bearing General Burgoyne dropped anchor in the roadstead of Quebec. Within a few weeks the battle fleet that had defeated Benedict Arnold the year before was in shape, and Burgoyne and his army were making ready to move up the Richelieu River on the first lap of their expedition.

In New York General Howe, busily preparing for his Pennsylvania campaign, proceeded with his usual thoroughness. When he finally sailed past Sandy Hook on July 23, his armada consisted of 266 ships, carrying seventeen thousand regular soldiers, an impressive train of artillery, and enough provisions for three months. Sir Henry Clinton remained behind with seven thousand troops to guard New York.

George Washington's intelligence service had informed him of Burgoyne's invasion plans even before they were approved in London. By late May he was aware of the intensive preparations in Canada and correctly assumed that the British general was about to move. Leaving his winter quarters at Morristown, the commander in chief settled sixteen miles away at Smith's Clove, New York, on the western banks of the Hudson. In this stone-ribbed declivity at the southern entrance to the Hudson River Highlands, he was close enough to Manhattan to keep an eye on General Howe's movements. From here too he could easily move north should General Schuyler, charged with coping with the anticipated invasion from Canada, require his assistance.

In July strange reports began reaching Smith's Clove. It was no secret to the Americans that the British were embarking soldiers on their ships at New York. Washington had taken this activity to mean that as Burgoyne pressed down from Canada, Howe would sail up the Hudson River to meet him. But the reports flowing in now were that Sir William and his ships were on the Atlantic. The British commander was moving not north but south!

What could this maneuver mean? Was it a feint, a trick? Was the British leader hopeful that Washington would shift his forces to Pennsylvania to protect Philadelphia? If Washington did so, would Howe then turn around and rush north to join General Burgoyne?

Toward the end of the month messages were on hand from a frightened Congess. Howe's armada had been sighted off New Jersey, seemingly headed for the capes guarding the bay at the mouth of the Delaware. The delegates were convinced that an attack on the Quaker City from the river could be expected at any moment.

Washington sent every unit he could spare to Schuyler. Then reluctantly, his mind laced with misgivings, he moved south. By August 10 he was encamped on Neshaminy Creek only twenty miles northeast of Philadelphia.

Here one morning a nineteen-year-old Frenchman reported for duty, bringing with him a recently issued commission as major general in the rebel army. From the beginning of the war, soldiers of France and other Continental European countries had been hurrying across the Atlantic and talking the Congress into commissioning them as general officers. Most of them had proved far more trouble than they were worth. But there was something about this homely, awkward, overgrown youth that gave the commander in chief the feeling that his services might be of some use. The new major general's name was Marie Joseph Paul Yves Roch Gilbert du Motier, Marquis de Lafayette.

Forbidden on pain of imprisonment to leave France to join the American Army, the marquis had slipped out of his country on his own ship. Thomas Jefferson detected in him a "canine appetite" for admiration and fame, but few men ever labored more assiduously to justify the popularity he craved. His captivating personality, military aptitude, and diplomatic skill would be invaluable to the rebel cause.

Further information concerning the movements of General Howe only increased Washington's bewilderment. One day the report was that Sir William's fleet was in Delaware Bay and about to sail upriver to Philadelphia, some seventy-five miles to the north. A few days later the word was that the fleet had disappeared from the bay. Where had it gone?

Not until August 22 did Washington know the answer to that question. The British armada was in Chesapeake Bay. Howe was preparing to land his troops at the top of that body of water along the shores of Head of Elk, Maryland.

At last the mystery of Sir William's strange behavior was solved. He was going to lead his soldiers some one hundred miles overland and attack Philadelphia from the southwest. But the question of why he was taking so circuitous a route to his objective would still be a subject of speculation two hundred years later.

He had decided against moving up the Delaware on learning that the two little forts flanking the river a few miles south of the Quaker City were well defended. But he could have got around the forts by disembarking his troops below them and marching to Philadelphia along the western banks of the river. This route would have required about half the time that the trip from Head of Elk was going to take. Indeed, Howe probably could have gotten faster to Philadelphia by routing his troops across New Jersey, notwithstanding the difficulties involved in ferrying them over the broad Delaware.

Washington was in action at once. The inspiriting effects of Tom Paine's propaganda pamphlets had taught him the value of show. To reassure the nervous patriots of Philadelphia, he marched his army through the streets of that city. Only a handful of his ten thousand men had the official blue and buff uniforms. Most wore whatever garments had come their way. To give his parading troops an appearance of unity, Washington had each soldier put a sprig of green in his hat. Another of his orders for the occasion was that the women traveling with the army must keep out of sight during the procession. Another instructed the bands to play a "quick-step . . . but with such moderation that the men may step to it with ease, and without *dancing* along or totally disregarding the music, as has been too often the case."

Southward along Front Street, bands playing and colors flying, and westward up Chestnut, past the statehouse, the little army marched. Not all of the onlookers were impressed. An elderly Philadelphian was heard to complain that "our soldiers . . . don't hold up their heads quite erect, nor turn out their toes exactly as they ought." But at least one observer was thrilled. Congressman John Adams found the spectacle "inspiring."

Westward across the Schuylkill River the army made its way. Washington had decided to confront the oncoming enemy along the banks of Brandywine Creek, a few miles north of Wilmington, Delaware. Here on the morning of September 11, at a rocky twist in the stream called Chadds Ford, a driving charge from the western bank by Hessian General Knyphausen and five thousand men opened the Battle of Brandywine.

General Howe had planned it well. Mistaking Knyphausen's action for the main thrust of the British advance, Washington concentrated his forces at Chadds Ford. Not until two in the afternoon did he realize that Howe had tricked him. While the Americans struggled to repel Knyphausen, Lord Cornwallis and eight thousand men crossed the creek at Trimble's Ford, some distance to the north, and were fast massing to the east and rear of Washington's main lines.

As darkness fell over the Brandywine, Washington and his army retreated. Casualty records for the encounter are a confusing muddle. Apparently about two hundred Americans were killed, seven hundred wounded, four hundred taken prisoner. British losses: only eighty-nine killed, 488 wounded, six missing.

For the next two weeks, with the British slowly closing in on the Quaker City, units of the two armies dashed and slashed at one another in the rolling country between the Brandywine and the Schuylkill. On the morning of September 26, Mrs. Elizabeth Drinker of Philadelphia noted in her diary that the day was "fine but cool." She added that "Well! here are ye English in earnest; about 2 or 3000 came in through Second street . . .

Cornwallis came with those troops today—General Howe is not yet come in."

The Quaker City was in the hands of the enemy. Marching down the eastern banks of the Schuylkill, Washington made a desperate effort to dislodge them by attacking Howe and the main British Army at Germantown, eight miles above the city. It was a bold stroke. Catching the enemy by surprise, it might have worked had it not been for errors of judgment on the part of some of the American officers. In the late afternoon of October 4 the rebels withdrew, but the Battle of Germantown could not be listed as a clear-cut British victory. Sir William Howe was impressed by the daring of the Americans in attacking his stronger and well-entrenched forces. Abandoning earlier plans for setting up outposts some distance from Philadelphia, the timorous British commander pulled his forces into the city itself. During the next few weeks he reduced the American forts on the Delaware. Thereafter he contented himself with controlling only Philadelphia and the river to the south of it, leaving the rest of Pennsylvania to the patriots.

For a month or so Washington hovered close to Howe's outer fortifications. Then, convinced of their impenetrability, he led his army into winter quarters at Valley Forge, a rugged hammock of land on the shores of the Schuylkill, twenty-five miles northwest of the conquered city.

Months before, Ben Franklin had gone to France to head an American commission to the court of His Most Christian Majesty, King Louis XVI. Informed by a French official that Howe had taken his hometown, the aging savant shook his head. "I beg pardon, sir," he said. "Philadelphia has taken Howe."

It was a good summation. Howe had reached the City of Brotherly Love in time to enjoy the winter social season—but what else had he got for all his exertions?

Perhaps Sir William equated Philadelphia with London. Everyone knew that to capture London was to capture the British government. But in 1777 the American government was as mobile and elusive as a cat. It was not a place. It was a bundle of records and the Continental Congress. On the very day that Cornwallis led the English vanguard into the city, the records were moving up the Schuylkill on a shallop.

As for the Continental Congress, it was a hundred miles away, doing business as usual in the little frontier town of York, Pennsylvania.

# 22

## *Saratoga*

SIR WILLIAM HOWE'S TOUR of the coastal waters off New Jersey, of Maryland and Delaware—his defeat of Washington at the Brandywine—his seizure of Philadelphia—his repulse of the Continentals at Germantown—these were the highlights of the Revolutionary War in middle America during the summer and fall of 1777. Throughout this same period, another drama was being enacted hundreds of miles to the north.

In the spring of 1777 no officer of the British forces in Canada looked forward more eagerly to the arrival of General Burgoyne than Major General the Baron Friedrich Adolph von Riedesel, commander of the Hessian troops that King George had hired from the duchy of Brunswick in north-central Germany.

The baron was on the verge of forty, short and stubby, with a long upper lip, a tilted nose, and bright blue eyes. He thought well of Burgoyne, but that was only a minor factor in his elation that spring. What brought a lift to his heavy chin was the knowledge that coming with Burgoyne's fleet was the baron's little wife, his "Fritschen" as he called her, the Baroness Frederica von Riedesel.

Months before, the baron had written home that he was perishing of loneliness in the Canadian wilds. Fritschen and the children must join him. Not one thought did the little baroness give to the hardships of the journey ahead or to those she would encounter traveling with Burgoyne's army. The minute her husband's plea arrived, Fritschen closed her comfortable home in Wofenbüttel in Brunswick, and piled herself and her three daughters—the youngest not yet a year old—into a servant-driven carriage.

There were dangerous moments en route to London, an embarrassing one after they got there. The baroness was invited to court, and stout Queen Charlotte was kind to her. His Majesty went further. He kissed her. "I was much amazed . . . since it came to me quite unexpectedly," the baroness would write later in her endearing memoirs.

There were heartbreaking delays in England. Months passed and it seemed that there would never be a ship to America—at least not one willing to carry Fritschen and her three small charges. Then came word that Burgoyne was returning to Canada, and there was no gainsaying the entreaties of the baroness to be taken along.

At last, in the deep-breathing Canadian woods in the vicinity of Three Rivers, the long-postponed reunion took place. Suddenly Fritschen was there, stepping out of a calash, babe in arms, and hurrying to her husband, with the other children trotting at her heels. The journey had aged her. She had left Wofenbüttel a little flower of a girl. She arrived in Canada a woman. It can be taken for granted that the baron did not mind, if indeed he noticed.

Love had conquered, but would Burgoyne? His invasion plan was scheduled to begin with a sweeping double movement. The general and his main army were to move up Lake Champlain, overcome Ticonderoga, and traverse the intervening land mass to Albany on the Hudson River. Simultaneously a smaller force under plump and bustling Lieutenant Colonel Barry St. Leger was to move eastward from Lake Ontario across the 150-mile-long Mohawk Valley. St. Leger was to chase all American soldiers out of the Mohawk region, thus eliminating the possibility of an attack on Burgoyne's extended right flank. This mission completed, St. Leger would join the main army at Albany. From there, with no enemies to the north or west, Burgoyne could proceed at his leisure down the Hudson, reducing the American forts perched on its steep banks as he went.

By late June Burgoyne's mile-long fleet was moving grandly up Lake Champlain, its ships and bateaux weighted with 7,500 soldiers, small mountains of baggage and ammunition, and 138 siege guns.

On the hot, insect-noisy morning of July 5, units of the expedition splashed ashore at Ticonderoga. Occupying that American stronghold were three shrunken and poorly equipped Continental regiments and a scattering of mostly green militia.

General Schuyler, as commander of the Northern Department, had begged Congress for more men. Congress had made little effort to help him. New Yorker Schuyler was unpopular with the influential New England delegates. Their dislike of him was largely the outgrowth of an old feud between Massachusetts and New York, both of whom laid claim to the territory then known as the Hampshire Grants, now the state of Vermont. In addition, the haughty bearing of the aristocratic Hudson River patroon was offensive to the New Englanders' democratic sensibilities.

Realizing the importance of Ticonderoga, Schuyler had asked Horatio Gates to take command in that area. Gates had refused, preferring to linger where he was—in Philadelphia. There he could further his own personal ambitions by ingratiating himself with Schuyler's enemies in the Congress.

Tall, bulky, shaggy-browed Philip Schuyler did the best he could with what he had. He placed all of the men he could spare, about three thousand, at Ticonderoga. He put his ablest officer, British-trained Major General Arthur St. Clair, in charge of them. A less-knowing soldier might have tried to hold the fort against Burgoyne's superior forces. When St. Clair saw that the British were implanting siege guns atop a nearby mountain, he took the only strategically sensible course open to him. He ran.

Burgoyne would have been happier if the American commander had remained where he was and fought. The capture of the Ticonderoga garrison would have left the invading British with one less army to contend with. On the British commander's orders two detachments—one of Britons and the other of Hessians—chased the fleeing Americans as far as Hubbardton, Vermont.

Near this tiny crossroads, the rear guard of St. Clair's army turned about and faced its pursuers. The entry "Hubbardton, Battle of" rarely appears in the indexes of Revolutionary histories, but this brief and bloody brush in the steamy dawn of July 7, 1777, was not unimportant. Only technically was it a British success. The little holding force under Seth Warner of the Green Mountain Boys stood its ground long enough to permit St. Clair and most of his troops to reach Schuyler and the main army at Fort Edward on the upper reaches of the Hudson.

Joining forces there, Schuyler and St. Clair pulled slowly back, blocking the wagon tracks behind them with felled trees as they moved, ripping up bridges, putting the torch to grain fields, chasing off cattle that might help feed the oncoming British, and rolling boulders into streams to divert their waters across the route that Burgoyne must take.

The end of the month found the two American generals at Stillwater, New York, a village on the western rim of the Hudson, fifteen miles below Saratoga (now Schuylerville), New York, an equal distance north of Albany.

The significance of St. Clair's escape was lost on Congress, viewing the northern campaign from its comfortable meeting room in Philadelphia. All that made any impression there was the report that Ticonderoga had been given up without a struggle.

A roar of indignant oratory swept the assembly. The New Englanders blamed Schuyler, and Congress relieved him of his northern command. Washington admired the New York patroon. He refused to take any part in the choice of a successor. To no one's surprise, Congress selected Horatio Gates, who was soon on his way north to Stillwater.

It is a measure of Philip Schuyler both as a man and a patriot that he took his demotion gracefully. Retiring to his old head-quarters at Albany, he worked around the clock seeing to it that whatever troops and supplies General Gates demanded went to him in a hurry.

When the news of the fall of Ticonderoga hit London, Burgoyne was the man of the hour. We are told that George III burst unannounced into the Queen's dressing room, waving a report of the conquest and shouting, "I have beat them! I have beat the Americans!"

But the Americans were not yet beaten. Having toppled Ticonderoga, Burgoyne seemed in no hurry to tackle the remaining seventy miles to Albany. For sixteen days he lingered at Skenesboro at the south end of Lake Champlain, mulling over his plans and enjoying the chatter of the pretty wife of a commissary who, according to that superb war correspondent, the Baroness von Riedesel, "loved champagne" as much as he did.

When Burgoyne finally left Skenesboro, his progress was slow, thanks to Schuyler's scorched-earth policy. Burdened with fifty-two pieces of artillery (and gallons of champagne), he took five days for the relatively short trip to Fort Edward. Another seven days had gone before he reached Fort Miller, a crumbling little post across the Hudson from Saratoga.

As Burgoyne inched down the eastern bank of the river, the American Army on the other side enlarged. Hundreds of newly recruited militia and Continentals reported for duty. From the south, sent by Washington, came bright and devoted Major General Benjamin Lincoln, Benedict Arnold, and Daniel Morgan (no longer a prisoner of the British) with his riflemen.

By August 20 the British commander was beginning to sense that his dream of conquest was turning nightmare. His army included a large component of Indians, and the British policy of using the redskins as allies was one of their major mistakes. The Indians were interested in plunder and scalps. Impatient at Burgoyne's slowness in making contact with the enemy, many of the braves had drifted off. Some of Burgoyne's Tory units had also left, sensing that the patriot star was in the ascendancy.

In truth, Burgoyne's troubles were greater than he knew. Far to the west, the right wing of his army, the force under Colonel St. Leger, was encountering difficulties.

Acting according to plan, St. Leger had left Oswego, New York, on July 25, had struck boldly across the Mohawk Valley in the direction of Albany. His army consisted of 750 Canadians and Tories and a thousand Indians. His first objective was Fort Stanwix, a ramshackle earthwork manned by 450 Continentals under a couple of stouthearted Dutchmen, Colonel Peter Gansevoort and Lieutenant Colonel Marinus Willett.

Reaching Stanwix in advance of his siege artillery, St. Leger set up camp and dug parallels while waiting for the guns to catch up. He was thus engaged when word reached him that a body of New York militia under General Nicholas Herkimer was coming from the east. Hastening forward with most of his troops, St. Leger ambushed the enemy at Oriskany, New York, mortally wounded Herkimer, and dispersed his followers. On St. Leger's return to Fort Stanwix, however, he found his bivouac a shambles. During his absence a detachment had sortied from the fort, overcome the British guards, and destroyed supplies and tenting.

Still in command on the Hudson, General Schuyler called for volunteers to go to the relief of Fort Stanwix. Benedict Arnold undertook to lead them.

Arnold's relief force was small, but circumstances presented him with a solution to that problem. One of the prisoners in the American stockade at Stillwater was a half-witted New Yorker named Hon Yost Schuyler. Hon Yost had been caught up in a Tory plot. He was under sentence of death. Arnold agreed to spare his life if he would hurry to Stanwix, tell St. Leger that he had escaped from the Americans, and inform him that Arnold was approaching with an "enormous army."

Perhaps St. Leger believed Hon Yost, perhaps not; perhaps he was more persuaded by the running quarrel that had broken out between his restive Indians and the other elements of his command. In any event, he marched his forces back to Oswego. Uncompleted then was that part of the British invasion scheme that called for St. Leger to clean out the Mohawk Valley and join Burgoyne at Albany.

At Fort Miller, on the eastern bank of the Hudson, General Burgoyne's woes were multiplying. Scorched earth neither feeds an army nor grows the horses needed to drag its heavy guns. Scouts informed the British commander that in the vicinity of Bennington, Vermont, there were horses, cattle, and grain for the taking. Burgoyne ordered Lieutenant Colonel Friedrich Baum and seven hundred soldiers to get them, and near Bennington that able Hessian officer ran into serious trouble—fifteen hundred newly raised New Hampshire militia under John Stark and five hundred Continentals commanded by Seth Warner.

On August 16 the coming of night dropped a curtain on the four-day Battle of Bennington. Baum was dying of his wounds, and incredible news was racing south to Philadelphia, jittery at the approach of General Howe. In the sunny pastures of Vermont an American force had killed, wounded, or captured one tenth of General Burgoyne's invasion army.

The British commander kept moving. On September 13 he crossed the river to Saratoga. Once on the western bank, he dismantled the pontoon bridge behind him. "Britons never retreat," he declaimed.

Baroness von Riedesel was thrilled by this pronouncement. Very likely her soldier-husband saw it in a less rosy light. By destroying his escape route Burgoyne had committed himself. He must now either conquer the foe awaiting him to the south or suffer decisive defeat.

Gates had encamped three miles north of Stillwater on Bemis Heights, a plateau two hundred feet above the river. His army now numbered close to seven thousand. His fortifications—designed by the talented Polish engineer, Thaddeus Kosciusko—were formidable.

Slowly Burgoyne felt his way southward, halting a few miles above Gates along the upper fringes of a fifteen-acre clearing called Freeman's Farm. His movements were groping and uncertain, for he was ignorant of that terrain and almost wholly in the dark as to the strength and disposition of the enemy.

When on the morning of the nineteenth he sent a body of soldiers to prod at Gates's outposts, he had nothing more in mind than a reconnaissance in force. A furious American response turned the action into the full-scale encounter interchangeably known as the Battle of Freeman's Farm or the First Battle of Saratoga.

Benedict Arnold had returned from his excursion into the Mohawk Valley. His performance at Freeman's Farm was brilliant, but the effort of the Americans on the whole was faultily coordinated, and a spirited last-minute movement led by General von Riedesel gave the British a victory of sorts. To be sure, it was a costly and indecisive one: Burgoyne's casualties were twice those of his opponents, and at nightfall the relative position of the two armies was unchanged. As firmly entrenched as ever on Bemis Heights, General Gates still blocked the road to Albany.

In the early days of the invasion Burgoyne had shown little concern over the inability of the British at New York to come to his assistance. Now he bent hopeful eyes on a message from Sir Henry Clinton. Reinforcements from England had reached New York. No longer pinned down there, Clinton was moving up the Hudson with four thousand transport-borne troops and three armed frigates.

During the first week of October it must have seemed to the Americans manning the little river forts across from Peekskill that Sir Henry and his troops were everywhere. Two of the forts fell quickly. A third would have suffered the same fate had not its defenders burned it before the enemy could arrive.

It is not clear what Clinton's overall plan was. Burgoyne got the impression that he meant to keep moving north, that eventually he would fall upon General Gates's rear at Bemis Heights. If Sir Henry had some such idea in mind at the beginning of his Hudson River campaign, he abandoned it following receipt of an urgent plea from General Howe, then in the process of solidifying his position at newly conquered Philadelphia. Howe demanded more troops, and Clinton scuttled back to New York to take care of his superior's request.

His last message to his worried fellow general at Freeman's Farm expressed the hope that "this little success"—meaning Clinton's seizure of the forts near Peekskill—"may facilitate your operations." Burgoyne's eyes never fell on this cheery sentiment. By the time it was written and sent off, the playwright-warrior's dream of conquest had gone up in the smoke of the Battle of Bemis Heights, known also as the Second Battle of Saratoga.

The knowledge that Clinton was coming up the Hudson reached Burgoyne at Freeman's Farm on September 21. Giving up plans for an immediate second jab at Bemis Heights, he dug in where he was and waited.

Delay took its toll. Food diminished, medicine for the wounded gave out. A trickle of provisions from the northeast closed off when one morning General Benjamin Lincoln and two thousand Americans slashed into Skenesboro and captured the British supply depot there.

Every day Burgoyne scanned the Hudson for a sight of Sir Henry and his flotilla. Every night he realized that the moment was fast approaching when he must either brush the Americans off Bemis Heights or give up his invasion plans.

As the situation of the British worsened, that of the Americans improved. En route from Skenesboro to the Hudson, one of Burgoyne's Indian scouts had slain and scalped twenty-three-year-old Jane McCrea, a New York farm girl and the fiancée of a Tory soldier serving with Burgoyne. News of the outrage, swiftly coursing the countryside, was worth regiments to the rebels. Angry New England and New York militiamen hurried to Bemis Heights.

During the opening days of October, Gates's muster rolls steadily lengthened, soon adding up to over eleven thousand men. Only one disagreeable factor afflicted the American camp. Benedict Arnold was furious at Gates for clinging to his rocky eyrie instead of hurling his swelling power at the enemy. Gates refused to budge. His reasoning was that Burgoyne was a gambler. Sooner or later he would attack Bemis Heights. When he did, the Americans, working out of their well-fortified base, would be in the stronger position.

For days Gates and Arnold exchanged angry words and wrote one another insulting notes. When on the morning of October 7 gambler Burgoyne—unable to wait any longer—launched his attack, Gates sent Arnold to his tent with orders to keep off the battlefield.

Toward the end of the afternoon Arnold disobeyed him. Seeing that an important American unit was moving to the attack too slowly and by the wrong route, he galloped onto the field. Quickly he speeded and redirected the faltering column. Even as the inspirited men moved in for the kill, a Hessian bullet knocked Arnold from his horse, badly fracturing the leg that had been wounded at Quebec. In many other parts of the battlefield that afternoon, the performance of General Gates's troops was valiant and effective.

The autumn dusk was thickening into night before the firing ceased and the British—six hundred of their men dead—began a slow retreat in the direction of Saratoga.

"This moment," Baroness von Riedesel would remember, "was the beginning of our unhappiness!"

Ten days later, on October 17, 1777, Burgoyne surrendered. The terms of surrender, a document known as a "Convention," did not compel the defeated British general to turn over his troops—five thousand in all—but agreed to let him ship them to England. Quickly realizing that every soldier returned to the homeland would release one to fight in America, the Continental Congress contrived by various quibbles to ignore this part of the Convention. In later years attempts would be made to whitewash this action, but to be bluntly accurate "the Honorable Congress" simply went back on its word.

In time Burgoyne and his officers—von Riedesel included—would be allowed to go home. Not so the unfortunate private soldiers. For a year they would be confined near Boston, after which they would be moved in turn to Charlottesville, Virginia; to Lancaster, Pennsylvania; and to other places. A few would be exchanged back to their own army, but at war's end the bulk of those who had survived would melt into the American population.

# 23

# From Versailles to Savannah

NOWHERE WAS THE REPORT of Burgoyne's defeat received with more satisfaction than at the glittering village of Versailles, home of the court of King Louis XVI of France, twelve miles southwest of Paris.

Gallic sympathy for the patriot cause was an outgrowth of the Old French Wars. Not that France was overly upset by the loss of Canada to England during the last of those struggles. On the contrary it was somewhat relieved. Experience had taught it that overseas dominions are hard to manage.

What most irked the French rulers about the Treaty of Paris that in 1763 ended the Old French Wars was that it left England predominant in the affairs of Europe—a position that the ambitious gentlemen at Versailles coveted for their own nation.

As early as 1765, Étienne-François, Duc de Choiseul, energetic chief of the French Foreign Ministry, was watching with interest England's efforts to tighten the reins on her subjects across the Atlantic. Shrewdly assuming that the colonials would rebel, Choiseul discerned in the forthcoming revolution an opportunity to humble the English and attract to France the rich American commerce then going to Great Britain and her possessions.

During the ensuing decade, French agents drifted about America. Carefully they measured the growth of anti-British sentiment there. Two of them were lodged at Buckman's Tavern when in the crisp dawn of April 19, 1775, the opening shots of the rebellion crackled above the little green of Lexington outside their windows.

By this time Choiseul was no longer in office. Happily for the rebels, his successor as the Foreign Minister of France—Charles Gravier, Comte de Vergennes—was equally convinced that his country stood to gain by helping the Americans. As France was now at peace with England, the assistance had to be given secretly.

To Versailles, at Vergennes's bidding, came Pierre Augustin Caron de Beaumarchais, clockmaker, dramatist, and master of backroom intrigue. With funds from the King's purse Beaumarchais organized a commercial enterprise called Roderique Hortalez and Company. Through this fake firm he was to purchase munitions and sell them to the patriots.

The kingdom of Spain helped finance the scheme. That country too had reason to want Great Britain brought low. Early in the century England had seized some of its most valuable possessions, including the fortress of Gibraltar, which from its high rock on the southern fringe of the Spanish peninsula guarded the strait linking the Mediterranean Sea to the Atlantic.

During the opening months of the war, Congress made no effort to avail itself of the help waiting in Europe. The desire for reconciliation with England still ran high among the delegates. Only as that sentiment died, did Congress act.

Even then it moved reluctantly. France and its Spanish ally were England's traditional enemies. As such, for 150 years, they had been America's enemies too. It took time for the delegates to throw off their distrust of countries with whom they had been long at odds. Not until the closing months of 1776 did Congress finally arrange to establish in Paris an American commission headed by Ben Franklin. The commission was to cooperate with Beaumarchais. In addition, it was authorized to offer certain favors to France on condition that the government of Louis XVI recognize the United States of America and enter the war on its side.

Even before Ben Franklin brightened the Parisian scene with

his presence, Vergennes had convinced himself that France should enter the war. But the adroit Foreign Minister was slow to implement his decision. He had no desire to commit his country to the open support of a loser, and for months the American performance on the battlefield was not encouraging. Washington's seizure of Trenton raised French hopes, but his defeat on the Brandywine and the British occupation of Philadelphia dashed them.

Then on December 4, 1777, Versailles learned that an entire English army had surrendered to the Americans at Saratoga. Two months later, on February 6, 1778, King Louis XVI signed two treaties.

Under the terms of these agreements France continued to provide the rebels with guns and money, eventually bringing her monetary investment in the patriot cause to 8 million eighteenth-century dollars. France also recognized the new nation and promised it military assistance in the form of ships and troops—an action that quickly brought from George III a declaration of war on Louis XVI.

When on May 6, 1778, word of the French intervention reached the stone house at Valley Forge where Washington had made his winter headquarters, a mellow sun was dropping behind the rounded hills to the west. In a hastily issued general order, the commander in chief gave no credit for the developments in France to King Louis or to Benjamin Franklin. Having noted that "the Almighty Ruler of the Universe" had come to the defense of "the cause of the United States . . . by raising us up a powerful friend, among the Princes of the Earth," he announced that the following day would be "Set apart . . . for fully acknowledging the Divine Goodness, and celebrating the important event . . ."

Accordingly, on the breeze-swept morning of the seventh, eleven thousand Continentals and militia swung across the open turf in front of the grimy "hutts" of the encampment. Smartly they stepped to the throb of drums, crisply wheeling and turning in response to the commands of their officers. Their uniforms were as patched and motley as ever, but an observer having last seen these men on parade three months before would have stared in disbelief.

During the icy hell that was the winter of Valley Forge a new American Army had been born. Many men deserved a place on the list of its midwives, but by common consent its "mother" was a thickset, reddish-haired German soldier of fortune, the Baron Friedrich Wilhelm Ludolf Gerhard Augustin von Steuben.

Like many of the foreign officers serving with the Americans, von Steuben had found the peace then prevailing in his part of Europe an affliction to his spirit and a bar to his career. In Paris he offered his services to America via Benjamin Franklin.

The dossier he handed to Franklin listed him as a lieutenant general in the army of the warrior-emperor, Frederick the Great of Prussia. His actual rank at the time of his dismissal from the emperor's forces fourteen years earlier was captain. Franklin knew the facts, but he liked the baron and reasoned that his trumped-up dossier would impress the members of the Continental Congress.

It did. When the baron offered to serve without rank or pay, the delegates were delighted. So was Washington. The commander in chief was not in the least taken aback when von Steuben arrived at Valley Forge wearing on his red and blue uniform an enormous silver star, a medal that the ruler of his little German duchy was in the habit of handing out to almost any man who could fire a musket.

What counted with Washington was von Steuben's knowledge of military drill and field maneuver and his ability to teach those arts. Within a few weeks the baron had converted the awkward American Army into a precisely moving combat machine. It would be said later by a qualified commentator that if the commander in chief's men had undergone von Steuben's drill sessions at an earlier date, the outcome of the Battles of Brandywine and Germantown might have been different.

Whatever the soldiers learned from the baron came none too

soon. In late May, Valley Forge buzzed with intelligence concerning changes in the situation of the enemy. Piqued by mounting criticism in London of his conduct of the war, Sir William Howe had resigned and gone home. Sir Henry Clinton had come down from New York to replace him as supreme commander of the British forces in America. Realizing that French military aid for the Americans would soon be on hand, Clinton decided to evacuate Philadelphia and strengthen his position by concentrating most of his troops at New York.

Early in June British ships began falling down the Delaware, carrying loyalist families fearful of staying in a city about to return to patriot hands. On the eighteenth Clinton crossed the river and moved northeastward. Ahead of him went a twelve-mile baggage train. Behind him trudged the seventeen-thousand-man army that for nine months had occupied the Quaker City.

Washington followed, hoping that somewhere in New Jersey a chance to hurl his newly honed forces at the withdrawing British would present itself. The chance did come—near Monmouth Court House (now Freehold); and the question still hovering over the Battle of Monmouth on June 28, 1778, is what would have happened to Clinton and his army had it not been for the inexplicable behavior of Washington's second in command.

General Charles Lee had been released to the Americans in exchange for a captured British officer. The self-styled savior of America was riding alongside the commander in chief when on June 27 scouts reported that Clinton and a large contingent of his troops were in a highly vulnerable position at Monmouth Court House.

Washington ordered Lee to take an appropriate force and enage the enemy "at once." Lee moved forward, but he placed his own capricious interpretation on his superior's "at once." He did not move against the British until the following morning. Even then he proceeded without plan. No sooner was he within shooting distance of Clinton's outposts than he thought it best to retreat.

As though to pile muddle on mystery, he made no effort to distribute his order widely. He simply told the units nearest him to turn back. The result was a hopelessly disorganized withdrawal with British infantrymen in noisy pursuit.

Washington was in the dark as to what was going on until he encountered Lee riding calmly toward him.

"What, sir, is the meaning of this?" demanded the startled commander in chief.

Lee faltered out something to the effect that he had found himself on unfavorable terrain near Monmouth and had considered it best to move back. Observers of the altercation later agreed on only one point: The commander in chief was in "a towering rage." One eyewitness said that he labeled Lee a "damned poltroon" and laced him with "a terrific eloquence of unprintable scorn."

The incident could not have been time-consuming. Almost at once Washington initiated one of those lightning strokes that belie the popular picture of him as a "Fabian general," effective only on the defensive.

In a swift maneuver marked by "admirable firmness and coolness," according to Alexander Hamilton, he turned Lee's fleeing soldiers around. Before the blistering sun of the day had exhausted both armies, Clinton's infantrymen were hastily pulling back. Thanks, however, to Charles Lee's faulty judgment or intentional malingering—whichever it was—the Battle of Monmouth was far from the smashing American victory it might have been. During the night Clinton stole away. Within a few days his damaged but still-formidable army was behind the ramparts of New York.

As for Charles Lee, he insisted that Washington had treated him "abominably." He demanded and got a court-martial. The officers of the military board convicted him on three charges and suspended him from the service for one year. There the strange case of Charles Lee might have rested had not that articulate gentleman sent a letter to Congress so insulting that the delegates dismissed him from the army.

Washington encamped on the western shores of the Hudson and considered various plans for attacking Sir Henry Clinton once the eagerly awaited forces from France arrived.

On July 8 the good news came. A French fleet had appeared at the mouth of the Delaware—twelve ships of the line and four fast frigates. The commander of the fleet, Admiral Charles Henri Théodat, Comte d'Estaing, was an experienced sailor— but his efforts to assist his new allies produced only disappointments.

Washington proposed a joint land-sea assault on New York, but at Sandy Hook d'Estaing discovered that his warships, larger than those of the British, could not maneuver across the bar and into the harbor.

Washington put forth another proposition. Early in the war the British had occupied the little seaport of Newport, Rhode Island. The American commander proposed that d'Estaing move on Newport from the sea. Simultaneously a Continental army under General John Sullivan would attack from the land side.

Again nature, not strategy, dictated results. D'Estaing had no sooner dropped anchor near Newport than the horizon to the south went white with the sails of a pursuing British armada. Before either admiral could put his seagoing wagons into battle array, a sudden storm scattered them.

The British fleet crept back to New York, the French fleet to Boston. There, having refitted his vessels, D'Estaing announced that his services were required in the West Indies, where France and England, once more at war, were maneuvering for position.

Following the unsuccessful Franco-American attempt to remove the British from Newport, the war underwent a drastic change. The focus of activity shifted from the North to the South. Elsewhere, for a considerable period of time, an uneasy stalemate prevailed, broken by small but often significant developments.

On another excursion up the Hudson River, Sir Henry Clinton seized an unfinished American fort standing on a cliff called Stony Point along the western shores of the river about forty miles south of West Point. Leaving a skeleton garrison behind, Sir Henry returned to New York under the impression that he had established at Stony Point an "impregnable citadel." The cliff in front of the fort was sheer, the hill behind it all but unclimbable. When one of Washington's brigadier generals asked leave to attack the area, his proposal so startled his fellow officers that they gave him the nickname he would bear thereafter, that of "Mad" Anthony Wayne.

On the night of July 16, 1779, Mad Anthony and his corps—about thirteen hundred men—scrambled to the top of Stony Point from the land side. No shots were fired. Quickly moving in, the Americans silenced the British pickets by bayonet, killed sixty-three members of the garrison, and wounded another seventy in the same manner, and captured 543. The seizure of Stony Point jolted the English, previously convinced that they held a monopoly on the art of eliminating an enemy force by bayonet.

Inspired by General Wayne's coup, Virginia's dashing Colonel Henry (Light-Horse Harry) Lee staged a hit-and-run attack on Paulus Hook, directly across the Hudson from New York and made off with its British garrison—an action that Sir Henry Clinton, always fearful of attacks on his Manhattan base, found "distressingly unnerving."

Virginia was the springboard for the great land leap of the war. In 1777 George Rogers Clark obtained permission from Governor Patrick Henry to recruit a small force and move across the Alleghenys in an effort to reduce the forts held by the British at scattered points throughout the West. It would take Clark six years to accomplish his mission. He and his men would march for miles through unyielding forest and clinging swamp. Half a dozen times starvation and exhaustion would come close to burying them all. But in the end the enemy would be gone from most of the vast area that ranges from the blue-grass country of Kentucky on the south, to the Great Lakes on the north, to the Mississippi on the west. During the negotiations leading to the treaty of peace, England's efforts to retain these rich lands would falter before the fact that most of them belonged to the United States by right of conquest.

On the sea the navy sired by Washington and sanctioned by Congress made itself felt. Short, skinny, homely, Scottish-born Commodore John Paul Jones was the only American officer to carry the war into the homeland of the enemy. During much of 1778 Jones and his small fleet raided the west coasts of England and Scotland, terrifying the inhabitants and jumping the maritime insurance rates on shipping between England and Ireland from 1¼ to 5 percent. The French gave Jones a decrepit East Indiaman called the *Duras*. Jones renamed the vessel the U.S.S. *Bonhomme Richard* ("Poor Richard") in honor of Ben Franklin, transformed it into a warship, and acquired a fleet to accompany it. On June 19, 1779, in the encounter immortalized by his "I have not yet begun to fight," he captured the British warship, H.M.S. *Serapis*. The exploits of Jones, Commodore John Barry, and other American sailors were annoying to Britannia, proud of her reputation as "ruler of the waves."

At New York, during the early phase of the long stalemate in the North, Sir Henry Clinton fixed tired eyes on a plethora of proposals pouring in from distant London.

Burgoyne's surrender and France's entry into the war had driven Lord Germain and his aides to reconsider their whole strategy. Their orders to Clinton were to hold his actions in the North to a minimum. He was to concentrate henceforth on the South in an effort to divide the American union along an east-west line by seizing Georgia, the Carolinas, and Virginia.

Sir Henry had no argument with Germain's new strategy, but in plaintive letters to Whitehall he listed his difficulties. One dispatch from London ordered him to send the cream of his army south; the next called on him to rush five thousand of his troops to the West Indies. Did Lord Germain really expect him to hold New York and conquer the South with a corporal's guard? He must have more soldiers, more guns, more ships, more everything.

Back from Germain came long replies, loaded with advice. But the new supreme commander of the British forces in America did not need advice. He needed help. "For God's sake, my Lord," he exploded in one of his letters to Germain, "if you wish me to do anything leave me to myself . . ."

Unhappy Sir Henry! He had come to his high post at a bad moment. France's intervention put a new complexion on the situation in the eyes of the British warlords in London. They were now more interested in battling the French than the Americans, and the arena of that struggle lay in the West Indies, where both nations had sugar-rich possessions to defend.

To some extent Whitehall's decision to move the American theater of operations southward was motivated by this fact. Every British unit sent from New York to Georgia or the Carolinas was that much closer to the West Indies, that much more available for use there. In the summer of 1778 Sir Henry Clinton had reason to feel like the player left without a seat in a giant game of musical chairs. The fall of that year had come before Germain at last grudged him a few reinforcements and Sir Henry could launch the second southern campaign of the war.

On November 20, 1778, a Royal Navy squadron convoyed a string of transports past Sandy Hook and through the choppy coastal waters off New Jersey. Aboard the troop carriers were 3,500 British regulars under Colonel Archibald Campbell. Their destination was Savannah, the little seaport of Georgia that from its palm-studded plateau looked down on the mouth of the Savannah River, boundary line between Georgia and South Carolina.

In command of the not quite nine hundred American soldiers in Georgia was Major General Robert Howe. The Battle of Savannah on December 29 was an uneven contest. Within a few hours after the first British gun boomed from the river, Howe and the remnant of his army were fleeing northward into South Carolina.

Knowing that if the British kept Savannah, they would soon control the whole of Georgia, Washington acted at once. At his bidding the Congress put fat, modest General Benjamin Lincoln in overall charge in the South. The delegates could give Lincoln only a thousand Continentals, but by the time he reached the northern shores of the Savannah River in January 1779, he had accumulated another two thousand men, mostly Georgia and North Carolina militia.

General Lincoln was an adept tactician—but he was up against an equally skillful foe. Major General Augustine Prevost had assumed command of the British forces in Georgia and had pushed up the river 125 miles to Augusta.

There were sharp skirmishes between boat-borne units of the opposing armies, intermittent artillery duels across the Savannah. Then Lincoln received substantial reinforcements, including a body of South Carolina militia under William Moultrie, hero of the Battle of Sullivan's Island, now a brigadier general.

Emboldened by this development, Lincoln went on the offensive. Moving his army to the southern shore of the Savannah in February, he marched on Prevost at Augusta. As he did so, Prevost crossed the river in the opposite direction and headed north for Charleston.

Alarmed at this threat to the "London of the New World," Lincoln recrossed the river and raced after him—only to discover on reaching Charleston that the British general had tricked him. Having lured Lincoln away from Georgia, Prevost had quickly piled his troops into flatboats previously assembled off the shores of South Carolina. He was now in Savannah, where he and his men were supplementing the already strong fortifications of the Georgia seaport.

At this point Moultrie and Governor John Rutledge of South Carolina sped a message to D'Estaing, still in the West Indies. They implored the French admiral to bring his warships to the mouth of the Savannah River. They promised him that Lincoln and a large army would be waiting for him. They expressed confidence that together the French and the Americans could pry Prevost loose from his rocky stronghold.

D'Estaing obliged. On the morning of September 8, 1779, his armada filled the river below the Georgia seaport—twenty-two ships of the line, eleven frigates and nearly one hundred transports carrying five thousand troops. Lincoln had encamped on the southern bank, and preparations for a siege began at once.

The allied Franco-American force was overwhelming. Soon Savannah would have been in patriot hands again had d'Estaing not insisted on following his own timetable. Nothing could induce the stubborn and testy French admiral to hurry his preparations.

He was still dawdling away when word arrived that a British fleet had been sighted coming south from New York, heading for Savannah. On the receipt of this intelligence, d'Estaing went to the other extreme. Although his siege preparations were far from completed, he ordered an immediate assault on the Georgia seaport.

Five days later, after an intensive but ineffectual cannonading, the allies lifted the siege. Two days after that, on October 20, 1779, d'Estaing sailed back to the West Indies, never to be seen in American waters again.

VIRGINIA
MD.
DEL.
Baltimore
Potomac River
Fredericksburg
Hanover
Charlottesville
James River
Richmond
Petersburg
Williamsburg
Yorktown
Chesapeake Bay
Portsmouth
Norfolk
Roanoke River
Hillsboro
Salem
NORTH CAROLINA
Salisbury
Cape Fear River
Neuse River
Cowpens
Cross Creek
(Fayetteville)
Pedee River
SOUTH CAROLINA
Wilmington
Hills of Santee
(Greene's Camp)
Augusta
Savannah River
Orangeburg
Eutaw Springs
Santee River
Georgetown
Ogeechee River
Charleston
GA.
ATLANTIC OCEAN

Ashley River
Mt. Pleasant
LONG ISLAND
Wappoo Creek
Charleston
SULLIVAN'S ISLAND
Fort Johnson
JAMES ISLAND
ATLANTIC OCEAN

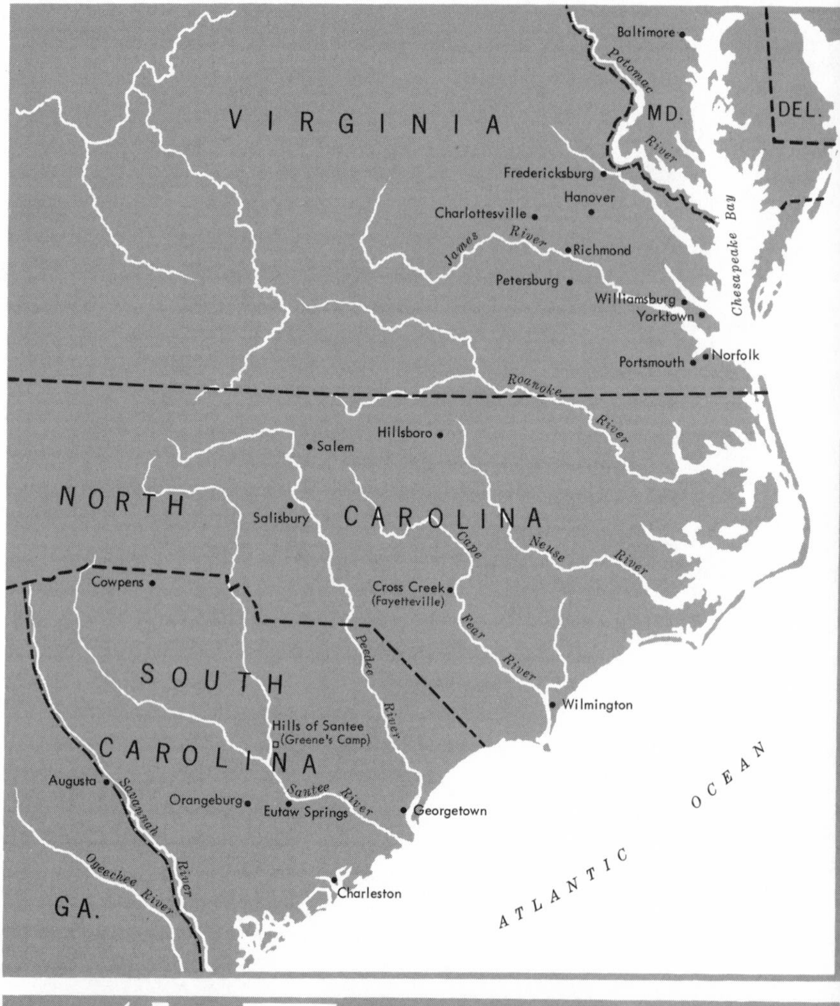

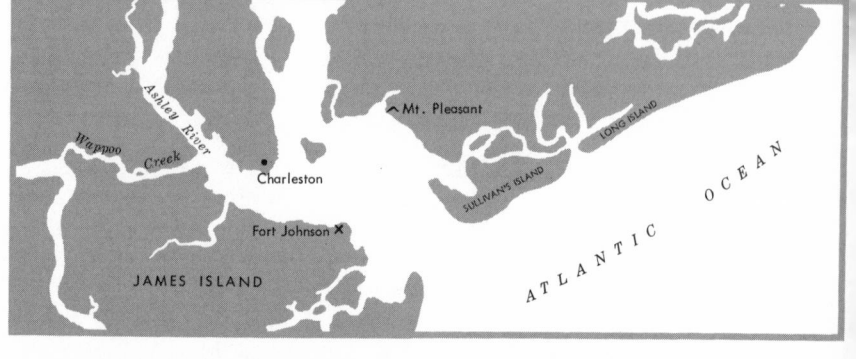

# 24

# Southern Willows Weep

S IR HENRY CLINTON was on the high seas when the siege of Savannah ended. During the summer the British commander had received further reinforcements and had begun making preparations to take personal command in the South.

One of his last steps was to remove the British garrison from Newport, Rhode Island. This action gave him 3,800 more troops at New York, the better to guard that vital base during his absence. Leaving Hessian General Knyphausen in charge, Sir Henry on September 26 sailed for Savannah. With him went an impressive fleet under Vice Admiral Marriot Arbuthnot and 8,500 picked fighting men.

The voyage south was slowed by wintry storms—and brightened in late October by the news that General Prevost had repulsed the allies at Savannah and that d'Estaing had taken his fleet back to the West Indies.

At Savannah Sir Henry lingered only long enough to assure himself that both that seaport and all of Georgia were now firmly fastened to the royal apron string. On February 10, 1780, he moved north and disembarked his troops on Johns Island, thirty miles south of Charleston. From here, operating partly by sea and partly on land, he began investing the London of the New World in accordance with the classic rules of siege warfare.

Sir Henry worked slowly, methodically. He had not forgotten how on his previous visit to Charleston he and his troops had idled uselessly on a myrtle-clad island while from a little log cabin of a fort William Moultrie and a few rebels fought off the mighty British Navy. The memory rankled. Sir Henry had no intention of letting Charleston slip from his hands again.

It didn't. On May 12, after a long and damaging bombardment, the city capitulated, with General Lincoln and six thousand men marching out as prisoners of war.

Clinton at once rushed troops into the interior with orders to secure South Carolina for the crown. One column established itself in the southeast, another in the west. A third and far larger column under Lord Cornwallis headed north to wipe out an American position at Camden, a lumber-mill center huddled under the longleaf pines of north-central South Carolina.

Soon after setting out from Charleston, Cornwallis learned that the garrison at Camden—350 Virginia Continentals and a few cavalrymen under Colonel Abraham Buford—had fled. He gave the task of chasing them to Major Banastre Tarleton.

In command of a Tory outfit called the British Legion, this handsome English officer was a daring horseman and a magnetic leader. He caught up with Buford close to the North Carolina border.

When a military body is taken by surprise, it often hollers "Massacre!" In this instance, the charge appears to have been well founded. First Tarleton compelled Buford to surrender. Then, on the pretext that some of the Americans had fired their guns following formal submission, he and his 270 dragoons waded in, sabers drawn.

Little remained of Buford's troops when it was all over. His mission ruthlessly accomplished, Tarleton rejoined Cornwallis, who by this time had occupied Camden.

Down at Charleston exuberant Sir Henry Clinton sent a report to Lord Germain in London. "I venture to assert," he wrote, "that there are few men in South Carolina who are not either our prisoners or in arms with us." This was Sir Henry's modest way of saying that the state was well on its way to becoming a crown colony again. Satisfied that all was proceeding nicely, he transferred command of his southern army to Cornwallis and sailed back to New York.

In the Congress, meeting again in Philadelphia, the fall of Charleston unloosed a fury of cantankerous oratory. From Washington came a request that Nathanael Greene be relieved of his duties as quartermaster general and sent south to replace captured General Lincoln. Greene had given ample evidence of military competence, but in the summer of 1780 the Congress was not listening to George Washington. Blandly ignoring his recommendation, the delegates gave the job instead to the hero of Saratoga, Horatio Gates.

In recent months many members of the Congress had come to regard the commander in chief as "that bumbling general" who had failed to keep Sir William Howe from occupying Philadelphia. In striking contrast to Washington's dreary record in Pennsylvania was Gates's victory over Burgoyne on the Hudson. Among some of the delegates and in portions of the high army command, the word now was that the time had come to return Washington to the comforts of Mount Vernon and give his post to Gates.

To this prolonged attack on the commander in chief historians have attached a melodramatic name. They call it the "Conway Cabal" after one of Washington's most outspoken critics, Major General Thomas Conway, an Irish-born soldier who had thrown in his lot with the patriots after long service in the army of France.

The word "cabal" conjures up a picture of dark and secret plotting, or organized conspiracy. Actually the Conway Cabal was simply one of those upsurges of discontent with the man at the top common to all human enterprises. Delegates John Adams and Benjamin Rush grumbled about the commander in chief's "inadequacies." The Hero of Saratoga told anyone willing to listen that were he summoned to lead his country's forces he would not shirk the responsibility. Throughout the entire row, however, the power structure remained unchanged, save that for a time the Congress was deaf to some of Washington's requests.

The call on Gates to assume command in the South found him enjoying a furlough at Traveller's Rest, his Virginia plantation. As he prepared to join the army awaiting him at Hillsboro, North Carolina, his old friend and neighbor, Charles Lee, came by to see him off.

The Savior of America was in good form. His parting words were, "Take care, Horatio, lest your Northern laurels turn to Southern willows."

Lord Cornwallis had placed a garrison at Camden and had returned to Charleston. He found plenty to do there. He was perfecting his plans for the pacification of South Carolina when word arrived that Gates was bearing down on Camden. Cornwallis moved in that direction at once.

Two routes to Camden lay open to the American commander. Knowing that speed was necessary, Gates chose what appeared to be the shorter one. Unfortunately it led his little army, mostly raw militia, through desolate pine barrens and scummy swamps. Gates had no transports. His men had to live off the land, and the land yielded next to nothing.

The collision with Cornwallis near Camden on August 16, 1780, scarcely deserves being called a battle. It was the spent force careening into the immovable object. The late-afternoon sun burned down on at least six hundred American dead, one thousand captured, the rest in flight.

Gates himself was nowhere to be seen. Of the fifty-three-year-old general's headlong dash back to his starting point at Hillsboro, Alexander Hamilton later remarked: "One hundred and eighty miles in three days and a half. It does admirable credit to the activity of a man at his time of life."

The American catastrophe in South Carolina was a blow to George Washington—and another followed it. Only a few weeks later came the revelation that one of his ablest generals had gone over to the enemy.

The reasons behind Benedict Arnold's treason remain a mys-

tery. Greed? The British paid him a sum equivalent to at least
$55,000 in modern purchasing power. Self-pity? Arnold brooded
like a spoiled child over what he took to be the failure of the
Congress to show proper appreciation for his valor on many
battlefields. The influence of the pretty Philadelphia aristocrat
who became his second wife in 1779? Some historians romanti-
cally paint golden-haired Peggy Shippen Arnold as a gay mad-
cap, but her voluminous correspondence suggests a serious and
determined young woman, quite capable of persuading her
much older husband of the rightness of her Tory viewpoint.

All of these factors appear to have entered into Arnold's
decision in May 1779 to send a secret message to Sir Henry
Clinton in New York, offering his services to the British. Handling the treason negotiations at the New York end was handsome and gallant Major John André, Clinton's youthful adjutant
general.

In the summer of 1780 Arnold persuaded Washington to put
him in command of the American forts erected earlier in the
war on the plateau of West Point on the western bank of the
Hudson, across the river from Fishkill, New York. In coded
letters to British headquarters, the traitor offered to deliver
West Point to the enemy in return for £20,000. In September
André went upriver on the British warship *Vulture* to close the
deal. He and Arnold met on the western shores in the country
home of a loyalist farmer. Even as they were conferring, the
commander of an American outpost on the river opened fire on
the *Vulture*, forcing the warship to withdraw downstream.

Unable to return to New York as he had come, André donned
civilian clothes, crossed the river, and moved on horseback in
the direction of the British lines below Tarrytown, New York.
He had almost reached his destination when seven patriot
outlaws waylaid him.* Their original motive seems to have been
robbery. Then a chance remark from André prompted them to
question the validity of the pass Arnold had given him—a

---

* The names of only three of them are known, but four others were on
hand.

document identifying him as John Anderson, Merchant. Stripping "John Anderson," the outlaws discovered incriminating papers in his stockings and hustled him off to the nearest American commander.

Word of André's capture reached Arnold at his headquarters only a couple of hours before the expected arrival of George Washington and his staff for an inspection tour. Throwing himself onto his personal barge, the traitor fled downriver to the warship *Vulture*. It was late that afternoon—Monday, September 25, 1780—before Washington learned what had happened. Arnold meanwhile had gained the safety of New York.

André, convicted of spying by a military court, went to his death on the gallows with a dignity that brought tears to the eyes of his captors and earned him a monument at Westminster Abbey in London.

The defeat of Gates at Camden had one beneficial result. It quieted forever the mutterings associated with the Conway Cabal. A chastened Congress turned in despair to George Washington.

The commander in chief responded by putting his quartermaster general in Gates's place. South went Nathanael Greene in December 1780, to begin a cat-and-mouse game with Lord Cornwallis. During the next ten months this remarkable campaign would render the cat—his Lordship—utterly frustrated. It would elevate the uncatchable mouse—Greene—to a secure place on the honor roll of military strategists.

Greene's major handicap in the South was his army. At all times it was small and ill equipped. His major asset was that his second in command was Brigadier General Daniel Morgan. At forty-four Morgan was racked with rheumatism, but the spirit that had lighted Benedict Arnold's men through the "direful howling wilderness" of Maine still burned in him.

On his side, Cornwallis, although supported by a larger and far-better-equipped army, also labored under handicaps.

Lurking behind the decision of the London warlords to concentrate on Georgia and the Carolinas was the conviction that once the British gained a foothold in those areas, brawny loyalists would spring from behind every tree fully armed and ready to chew up any patriot showing his face below the Potomac. We have no real knowledge of the actual extent of Tory sentiment in the upcountry South. We only know that it might have been strong enough to tip the scale in favor of His Majesty had the British not made the same mistake there that they had made in other American areas.

The officers in charge of the British rural posts in South Carolina exerted no real effort to stop their men from plundering. The Hessians were particularly enterprising thieves. These men were professional soldiers. Most had volunteered to serve in America with the understanding that rich spoils would be available to them there.

When a South Carolina farmer pledged allegiance to the King, the British gave him a document identifying him as a loyalist. To the Germans these documents were meaningless. For one thing they couldn't read English. For another, they weren't interested in the politics of the local farmers, only in their removable possessions.

As the Hessians and their redcoated allies raided and robbed, Tory sentiment ebbed in the upcountry South. Many Tory landholders turned neutral. Others hastened to join the patriot partisan or guerrilla bands roaming the pinewoods.

The caliber of the leaders of these rifle-toting irregulars provided Cornwallis with one of his worst headaches. There was frail, dark, eagle-beaked Colonel Francis (Swamp Fox) Marion who had fought under Lincoln at Savannah and had escaped capture at Charleston by being on sick leave. There was handsome, recklessly brave Colonel Thomas Sumpter, the "Gamecock." There was daring Colonel Andrew Pickens. These backwoodsmen knew every trick of those strike-and-vanish tactics that are guerrilla warfare.

Ordinarily the partisan bands moved in quickly, delivered their sting with the speed of a wasp, and as swiftly vanished into the forest. But on the drizzly morning of October 7, 1780, on the flat, footprint-shaped surface of Kings Mountain in north-central South Carolina, two opposing guerrilla groups clashed in open battle.

Commanding the Tories was Major Patrick Ferguson, an English regular. Among the patriot leaders were Colonels Isaac Shelby and John Sevier, tough North Carolina mountaineers.

When the encounter opened, the somewhat larger loyalist force held the hilltop and the patriots were scrambling up the steep slopes. When it ended, Kings Mountain was patriot territory. Quickly traversing the countryside, the news of this small but important American victory kept on the farm many a Tory who might otherwise have joined the royal colors.

Easily the most troublesome of Lord Cornwallis's problems stemmed from the strained relations between himself and his superior at New York, Sir Henry Clinton.

Soon after the British evacuation of Philadelphia, Earl Cornwallis had hurried home to the bedside of his invalid wife. In England he had given thought to resigning from the service, under the impression that the mistakes of the English military in America could never be rectified. Following the death of his wife in February 1779, he experienced a change of heart. A vision seized him, a conviction that there was one man who could reverse the tide in America—himself.

On his return to the New World in late 1779, the earl's orders not only made him Clinton's second in command but specified that, in the event of Sir Henry's leaving his post, Cornwallis would automatically succeed him. From the minute he learned of this arrangement, Sir Henry began looking on Cornwallis as a schemer trying to get his job.

From time to time, to be sure, Clinton had tried to resign. Eager as he was to quit, however, he had no intention of letting Lord Cornwallis force him out. By the time Sir Henry departed from Charleston, leaving the earl in charge in the South, the once reasonably cordial feelings between the two men had chilled into rancor.

Clinton's final words were for Cornwallis to make no "substantial" incursions northward of South Carolina until that state was securely pacified. Cornwallis regarded these instructions, not as orders from a superior, but as the mere recommendations of an equal. Once Sir Henry was on his way to New York, the earl began making plans for the subjugation of North Carolina and Virginia—a campaign that he was certain would crush the rebellion and win him everlasting glory.

In the closing days of 1780, in short, Lord Cornwallis entered upon his grueling duel with Nathanael Greene blinded by the same fatal ambition that had brought General Burgoyne skimming up Lake Champlain and lunging across upstate New York to Saratoga.

A small American army awaited Greene at Charlotte, North Carolina. Immediately on his arrival there, he divided his command. He himself and the larger portion of his forces moved southeast to a more defensible position at Cheraw, South Carolina. Morgan and the remaining troops hurried southwest in the direction of a fortified enemy post at Ninety Six, a South Carolina hamlet near the Saluda River. Morgan's mission was twofold. He was to rally the local patriots as he moved along and threaten Ninety Six.

From his newly established headquarters at Winnsboro, South Carolina, Lord Cornwallis observed these operations with satisfaction. Greene's action in splitting his tiny army in two struck the earl as sheer insanity. He had anticipated trouble in eliminating the American force as a whole. Now Greene had presented him with the opportunity of picking it off piecemeal—a much easier task.

Cornwallis sent Tarleton and his legion after Morgan. "Push him to the utmost," he told the hard-riding cavalry leader.

Tarleton struck north along a route that put him on a collision course with Morgan. By the fifteenth day of the new year, 1781, the two armies were within striking distance.

On the sixteenth Morgan encamped at a rural market center called Hannah's Cowpens, a few miles below the upper South Carolina border. Tarleton had about twelve hundred men.

Morgan had perhaps eleven hundred, but many of his troops were newly recruited partisans. He was aware that under the sustained fire of open battle soldiers of this stripe were likely to break and run. With this possibility in mind, he positioned his men with their backs to the Broad River at a point where the stream was unfordable. He reasoned that if they couldn't retreat, they would go forward.

Forward they went when on the morning of the seventeenth Tarleton and his dragoons attacked. On the rebel side few engagements of the war were better planned. None was more successfully executed.

As Tarleton's dragoons hit the American center, Morgan hurled his left and right wings against the enemy's flanks. The resulting double envelopment was so tight that Tarleton had difficulty finding a hole through which he and a few of his stunned horsemen could escape. Of the men engaged on the British side, 110 were killed, eight hundred captured. Tarleton's losses included also two cannons, eight hundred muskets, one hundred horses, and a baggage train of thirty-five wagons, heavy with ammunition. Morgan's losses were twelve killed, sixty-one wounded.

Smashing as his victory was, Morgan knew better than to remain at Cowpens or to continue southward toward Ninety Six. Cornwallis was nearby and would be on the move the minute word of the British disaster reached him. Morgan plunged northeastward, crossing the Little Catawba River just in time to keep the earl from cutting him off at that point.

Greene meanwhile had sized up the situation and had moved northwest. On January 30 he joined Morgan on the Little Catawba in south-central North Carolina—and the great chase was on.

Greene and Morgan moved now north, now south, now east, now west. Cornwallis pursued. At one point, to gain speed, his lordship destroyed his baggage train. For a brief period this drastic maneuver helped. In the long pull it hindered: soldiers must eat.

All along the way there were skirmishes and lively bushwacking operations. There was one full-scale encounter—the Battle of Guilford Court House in upper North Carolina on March 15.

Every engagement was a British victory, but the increasingly exasperated British commander realized that he was not winning the campaign. By mid-March he had lost more than a fourth of the almost eight thousand regulars with whom he had started out. Efforts to recruit loyalists along the way had been only moderately productive. Supplies and ammunition were dwindling. In far-off England a London wit noted the heavy British losses at Guilford Court House and quipped that "another such victory would destroy the British Army." General Greene, in a letter to an acquaintance, summed up his own tactics graphically: "We fight, get beat, rise, and fight again."

Leaving Colonel Lord Francis Rawdon in charge of the British positions in the Carolinas, Cornwallis invaded Virginia. As he did so, Greene moved quickly in the opposite direction. Plunging into South Carolina, he took on Lord Rawdon's forces. Again he lost encounter after encounter. Again he annoyed the enemy beyond endurance.

In an effort to bag the elusive American general, Rawdon abandoned his upcountry bases and concentrated his forces along the Tidewater in the vicinity of Charleston. In this area, on September 8, 1781, Greene fought his last full-scale battle, a fierce contest at Eutaw Springs, thirty miles east of Orangeburg, South Carolina. Rawdon, seriously ill, had sailed for England. Colonel Alexander Stewart commanded the. British regiments. The day ended with neither side in a position to claim victory. American losses were 139 killed, 375 wounded, 8 missing. Stewart's casualties were 85 killed, 351 wounded, 430 missing.

By mutual agreement both armies withdrew, and Greene led the bulk of his troops into the nearby High Hills of Santee. It was cool and safe in these leafy uplands. Here the American general and his men recuperated for a few days before returning to the coast to establish a blockade around Charleston. They deserved the rest; they had fought a unique campaign. Without winning a single tactical victory, they had cleaned the enemy out of all but a small section of South Carolina.

Miles to the north, above the Dan River, Cornwallis was grabbing patriot military stores in Virginia and skirmishing indecisively with an American army under the Marquis de Lafayette. Even more of his lordship's energy was going into a long paper battle with his superior in New York, Sir Henry Clinton.

The correspondence between the two generals was marked by hostility and confusion. The supreme British commander was convinced that Cornwallis would have succeeded in the South had he heeded Sir Henry's advice to secure South Carolina before moving northward. Instead his lordship had allowed Greene to lead him a merry chase. Worst of all, Cornwallis had operated for the most part far from the coast where he might have had the assistance and protection of His Majesty's navy.

The British commander at New York thought Cornwallis had made a mistake in coming into Virginia at all. Now that he was there, Sir Henry saw no reason why his lordship shouldn't move still farther north. Sir Henry was toying with various schemes. In one letter he proposed that the earl join him in Rhode Island for a movement against the enemy positions there. In another he spoke vaguely of a joint action in Pennsylvania, with the idea of once again occupying Philadelphia.

Cornwallis had no interest in these notions. He wrote that he had come to regard Virginia as "the key to winning the war." He wanted to stay where he was until every rebel soldier had been swept from the Old Dominion. One senses in Cornwallis's statements the agony of a desperate man. Badly outmaneuvered in the Carolinas, he now hoped to refurbish a sinking reputation by conquest in Virginia.

Suddenly, in early July, the whole tenor of Sir Henry Clinton's letters changed. Forgotten were his ambitious plans for carrying the war to the foe. Developments in the North had convinced him that an enemy assault on New York was in the offing. Always fearful of losing his Manhattan base, he now demanded that Cornwallis send him three thousand men.

Cornwallis sputtered. In an angry letter to his superior he reiterated his belief that Virginia was "the key to winning the war." He wrote that he needed every man he had to continue there.

Before Sir Henry could get around to repeating his demand for reinforcements, Lord Germain cut the ground from under him. Writing to Clinton from London, the colonial secretary blandly observed that he agreed with Cornwallis. He, too, thought that "the war on the side of Virginia" should be pushed "with all the force that can be spared until that province is reduced."

Reluctantly Sir Henry permitted Cornwallis to keep all of his army for the time being. He went one step further. He endorsed a procedure that Cornwallis had proposed. This plan called for the earl to shift as quickly as possible to the Virginia coast, where he could keep an eye on the largest inland waterway along the Atlantic, the Chesapeake Bay.

For years the British had given thought to creating a base on the Chesapeake. A stronghold there would serve many purposes. It would help seal off the American South. It would deny the big bay to ships sent across the sea by the patriots' friends in Europe and open it to British vessels.

On several recent occasions Clinton had sent expeditionary forces into Virginia, one of them commanded by his new brigadier general, Benedict Arnold. These raiding parties had failed in their major objective. No base on the Chesapeake had been set up, but the invaders had spread havoc through large sections of the Virginia countryside.

Washington had responded by sending into the area a number of divisions under Lafayette and other generals. In late July Cornwallis passed up an opportunity to seize Lafayette's little army, then at Richmond, Virginia. The earl's explanation for this oversight was a less-than-convincing one. Heretofore he had paid scant attention to Sir Henry Clinton's orders. Now he gave out that he could not stop at Richmond because Clinton had directed him to take up a position on the Virginia coast overlooking the capes flanking the entrance to Chesapeake Bay.

On August 1, 1781, Cornwallis's southern rambles came to an end. East of his last stopping point rippled the apple-green waters of the Chesapeake. To the north flowed the York River. His lordship himself later conceded that his choice of a position could have been better. The terrain compelled him to divide his command. To protect his northern flank he had to send Tarleton and his legion across the river to Gloucester Point.

While on that side of the York, Tarleton threw up breastworks, Cornwallis on the other side grimly set about fortifying the sun-struck haven to which he had brought his travel-weary troops.

The name of the haven was Yorktown.

# 25

# From Newport to Victory

T OWARD THE MIDDLE of 1779 the Marquis de Lafayette left
America for a visit to his native land. During a six-month
stay in France he exerted all his charm and influence to persuade
King Louis XVI and Foreign Minister Vergennes to send more
ships and men to their patriot allies.

When at Boston, on April 27, 1780, the young Frenchman
once more touched American soil, his first action was to send a
message to "His Excellency, the Commander in Chief."

In his ardent way he expressed his eagerness to see again a
man for whom he had come to feel the affection of a son for a
father. He added that he had "affairs of the utmost importance"
to communicate. To Washington, worried over the then-alarm-
ing situation in the South, the "affairs" that Lafayette communi-
cated to him at his New Jersey headquarters on May 10 were
important indeed.

France was sending another war fleet, seven ships of the line
and two frigates, commanded by Admiral Charles Louis
d'Arsac, Chevalier de Ternay. Coming with the fleet on thirty-
five transports was a French division—about 5,200 soldiers—
under Lieutenant General Jean Baptiste Donatien de Vimeur,
Comte de Rochambeau.

All this was good news, and there was more. Neither Admiral
de Ternay nor General Rochambeau would be subject to recall
by their government as Admiral d'Estaing had been. Once in

America, they were to stay as long as they were needed. Best of all, the instructions to Rochambeau commanded him to defer to Washington where all military decisions were concerned.

Some historians argue that the patriots could have won the Revolution without France. Perhaps so. One point is self-evident. Without stout, middle-aged, unassuming Rochambeau, France could never have assisted America as effectively as it did.

Little things tell us much about him. The French fleet arrived at Newport, Rhode Island, on July 10, 1780. Rochambeau would have been within his rights if he had asked for an immediate interview with Washington. When young Lafayette urged him to do so, the older man waved the idea aside. He waited patiently until Washington, almost two months later, suggested a conference.

Rochambeau would also have been within his rights had he demanded a chance to inspect the American Army. That, too, subordinates urged him to do; but when Washington failed to invite him to such an inspection, the French officer refrained from requesting one. He sensed, instinctively, that the American commander might not wish to parade his ill-clothed and poorly equipped men before the leader of the magnificently accoutred soldiers that Rochambeau had brought across the ocean.

Circumstances arising soon after his arrival in America held the French at Newport for almost a year. In mid-July a British squadron appeared off the coast of Rhode Island. Commanded by Admiral Arbuthnot, it established a blockade that rendered the French warships inactive. It was still there when in the last month of the year Admiral de Ternay died and was replaced by Admiral Jacques-Melchoir Saint Laurent, Comte de Barras.

In France arrangements had been made for still another French admiral, François Joseph Paul, Comte de Grasse, to bring a second armada to Newport along with another component of fighting men. The news reaching America in August, however, was that like Newport the French seacoast town of

Brest, from which de Grasse was planning to sail, had been sealed off by an enemy fleet.

When on September 20, at Hartford, Rochambeau and Washington met for the first time, the French general explained the import of these events. Granted that his orders were to obey Washington in all military undertakings; those same orders obliged him to work in concert with the French Navy. He could not bring himself to leave Newport until his country's endangered vessels no longer needed the protection of the French land forces.

Washington comprehended the desire of a French general to protect a French fleet. He and Rochambeau confined their discussion to possible future operations.

Both understood, when they parted, that eventually they would join their forces and attack either Sir Henry Clinton at New York or Lord Cornwallis in the South. The Hartford conference yielded no plans for immediate military action. Still it was a fruitful one. It enabled the two commanders to study one another. Each rode back to his headquarters with the warm feeling that he had met a man he could trust and respect.

Rochambeau put the idle months at Newport to good use. The citizens of the little shipping center on Narragansett Bay had not reacted with pleasure to the news that their town had been chosen as the landfall for the French fleet. Like all New Englanders they had good memories. Some had fought in the Old French Wars. Most of them regarded all Frenchmen as "but light, brittle, queer-shapen little mechanisms only interested in frizzing their hair and painting their faces." The feeling about town was that life was going to be pretty disagreeable after those "queer-shapen little mechanisms" got there.

Rochambeau sensed the attitudes of the local citizens. Within a month after his arrival he had altered them. He accomplished this miracle—for miracle it was—by making his soldiers behave themselves and by considerate actions on his own part.

"Under no circumstances," he instructed his men, "are you to take anything that does not belong to you. Do not lay hands on a sheaf of hay for your horse or a cabbage for yourself without paying for it, and only then if the American owner is willing to sell."

During the recent British occupation of Newport, the equipment of the newspaper had been destroyed. The French had brought a printing press with them. Rochambeau lent it to the newspaper owner so that once more the citizens could enjoy the gossipy columns of the *Newport Mercury*.

Rochambeau's conquest of Newport deserves a place among the American victories of the Revolution. It would have long-range effects. The day was near when the French and the Americans would fight together the better for having first learned to live together.

That day drew close when in late March 1781 the French general received a welcome message from his superiors at Versailles. At Brest on the shores of France, Admiral de Grasse and his fleet had eluded the British blockade. The admiral was en route to the West Indies. When he finished his chores in that region, he would sail north to cooperate with the French squadron still hemmed in at Newport.

Rochambeau passed this information to Washington, and on May 21 the two generals held a second council of war, this time at Wethersfield, Connecticut. Here they laid the preliminary plans for a combined Franco-American expedition.

Rochambeau had fortified Newport. He now believed that a small force there could protect Admiral de Barras's blockaded armada. He, therefore, informed Washington of his willingness to remove most of his army from Rhode Island and join the Americans at any site selected by the commander in chief.

During two days of cordial conversation the allied leaders discussed possible actions. Should they try to remove Sir Henry Clinton from New York? Or should they march south and strike at Cornwallis, now operating against Nathanael Greene in the Carolinas?

Washington strongly favored an assault on New York.

Rochambeau just as fervently preferred an action against Corn-wallis. The capture of Manhattan Island would necessitate a complex siege operation. More experienced in the ways of war than the American commander, Rochambeau doubted whether even a combined American-French force could storm that rock-girt fortress.

In the end the two generals left the decision up to de Grasse. Rochambeau was to write the French admiral at once. He was to ask him to bring his men-of-war either to Chesapeake Bay or to Sandy Hook. If de Grasse chose the Chesapeake, the com-manders of the allied land forces would march south; if Sandy Hook, they would assail Sir Henry Clinton.

In Newport again, Rochambeau began preparations for evacuating his troops—a move that the townspeople decried even more vociferously than they had deplored the coming of the French in the first place.

From the docks of nearby Boston, on a stormy May night, a fast French frigate headed for the open sea and turned south. Aboard was a message to the Comte de Grasse—a letter that the French admiral would receive in the harbor of the Haitian seaport of Cap-Français (now Cap-Haïtien) two months later. Written by Rochambeau, the letter described the situation in America. The French general did not presume to tell de Grasse whether to bring his ships to Sandy Hook or the Chesapeake. Neither did he hesitate to offer the purely professional comment that a powerful squadron off the shores of Virginia would better serve the Franco-American cause.

As the note to de Grasse glided southward, its author had no way of knowing that when the French admiral arrived at the capes of the Chesapeake, Lord Cornwallis would be right there—as though deliberately waiting for him. In that bodeful spring of 1781, there was another development that Rocham-beau had no way of foreseeing. During the next few months the fate of the war would hinge on the alertness of the French and English Navies—and at the most crucial moment the vaunted fleets of Great Britain would be found wanting.

When on June 10 Rochambeau and his troops left Newport, all the French commander knew was that Washington had stationed his forces 230 miles away on a large estate called Philipsborough near White Plains, New York. Here on the eastern shore of the Hudson he and Washington reviewed the questions that had come up during their talk at Wethersfield. Should they hurl their combined forces at New York or march south to attack Cornwallis?

Events quickly gave them the answer. During the last week of July, a Franco-American reconnaissance in force against the British outposts along the Harlem River convinced Washington that Rochambeau was right about New York. It could not be taken. The opening days of August brought significant news. At New York Clinton had received reinforcements, making his position even stronger. In Virginia Cornwallis had encamped at Yorktown on the Chesapeake. Finally, on August 14, came a letter from de Grasse.

The French admiral was sailing north with his fleet. He was carrying with him 3,500 fighting men commanded by the seasoned general, the Duc de Saint-Simon. His destination—Chesapeake Bay.

That settled it. Rochambeau wrote at once to de Barras at Newport. That admiral was to place on his ships all of the French soldiers still there and all of the French siege guns. At his first chance he was to slip past the British blockade, fighting his way out if necessary. He was then to sail south to join de Grasse at the mouth of the Chesapeake.

Washington hurried a message to Lafayette, who had emplanted his army, about five thousand men, only sixteen miles from Yorktown at Williamsburg, Virginia. The commander in chief's instructions to his protégé were to try to prevent Cornwallis from leaving Yorktown by land.

Washington's decision to bypass New York and move south was one of the boldest and riskiest of the war. From Philipsborough Manor on the Hudson to Yorktown on the Chesapeake was over four hundred miles. And the allied leaders had no idea what they would find after their hard march across New Jersey, Pennsylvania, Delaware, Maryland, and Virginia. Perhaps de Grasse would reach the Chesapeake and shut Cornwallis in, perhaps not. A British fleet bearing down from New York or up from the West Indies might intercept him. In that case Cornwallis would probably be unconquerable. The whole outcome of the venture rode on the pounding waves of the Atlantic.

Since the end of the French and Indian War, the British Navy had deteriorated. Lack of cash was partly responsible for its decline. Another cause was that the naval ministry, the Admiralty, was in the hands of a money-loving landlubber, John Montagu, fourth Earl of Sandwich.

It was written of Sandwich that he was

> Too infamous to have a friend,
> Too bad for bad men to commend.

The First Lord of the Admiralty was a competent administrator but a dishonest one. Corruption and jobbery dominated his department. Both at the offices of the Admiralty in London and on the ships at sea standards of conduct were low. Many fleet commanders spent more time enriching themselves by seizing cargo vessels loaded with valuables than in battling the foe.

In recent years, on the other hand, the French had enlarged and improved their navy.

Even so, in the summer of 1781, Britannia still ruled the waves. No fears that this situation would ever be otherwise existed either at New York, where plodding Thomas Graves had recently taken charge of the British fleet, or down in the West Indies, where His Majesty's finest admiral, handsome George Brydges Rodney, directed the British naval arm.

Yorktown might have been a different story had Graves and Rodney acted with dispatch and decision. But Graves was poky and dull—and Rodney was greedy.

The waters of the West Indies had become the chief passage-way for vessels bearing ammunition and other war goods from

France and Holland to America. In the summer of 1781 Rodney was so busy seizing these richly laden ships that he neglected to keep close track of what his French rival in the region, Admiral de Grasse, was doing. When early in August de Grasse suddenly left the West Indies, some days passed before Rodney realized that the commander of the French flotilla was on his way to the American coast. At that late date all the British leader could do was hurry a pursuing squadron north under Admiral Samuel Hood.

Hood had no idea of where along the American coast de Grasse was going. On August 27 a long and fruitless search of the Atlantic brought him to the harbor of New York, where he found his superior officer, Thomas Graves, making ready to carry men and guns to Lord Cornwallis in Virginia. Hood's arrival brought the British fleet at New York to nineteen ships of the line. On the last day of the month, all of them set sail for the Chesapeake with Graves in charge.

A desperate race was on. Admiral de Barras had left Newport, the French siege guns lashed to the decks of his vessels. De Grasse was drawing closer to Virginia. If British Admiral Graves reached the Chesapeake ahead of de Barras, the French commander with his smaller fleet would be unable to enter the bay. If Graves got there before de Grasse, Cornwallis would be in a strong position and the allied armies hastening down from the Hudson would be in trouble.

Washington and Rochambeau were unaware of these critical naval maneuvers as in late August they broke camp at Philipsborough.

Under the torrid summer sun, tents fell and rafts moored at the eastern banks of the Hudson grew heavier by the hour with baggage and field guns. From tightly barricaded New York City a few miles down the river, Sir Henry Clinton kept an eye on these activities. But with seventeen thousand men at his beck and call he made no effort to stop them.

One of Rochambeau's diary-keeping aides found the British commander's passivity hard to credit. "An enemy a little bold and able," he wrote, "would have seized the moment of our crossing the Hudson, so favorable for him, so embarrassing for us, for an attack. His indifference and lethargy at this moment is an enigma that cannot be solved by me."

Perhaps it will never be solved. In early June British spies had intercepted a letter from Washington to Lafayette. Writing soon after the conference at Wethersfield, the commander in chief had informed the young Frenchman that he and Rochambeau were going to attack New York. Sir Henry concluded that the letter was authentic. It was, but it is hard to understand Clinton's failure to realize that a decision reached in the spring could easily be changed during the summer.

As the allied commanders prepared to march south, they made elaborate efforts to convince Sir Henry that they were indeed about to besiege him. One trick was to assemble many of their boats along the shores of New Jersey across the bay from the British camps on Staten Island. Another was to build bake ovens on the nearby mainland as though preparing to feed a large body of troops.

Again it is difficult to believe that a warrior of Sir Henry's experience was taken in. One must assume that his failure to waylay the allies as they struggled across the Hudson was not a product of his reading of the situation but of his character. Over the years Clinton had become a prisoner of the fortress he himself had built. Holding on to New York had become a mania with him. To send ships and soldiers up the Hudson to attack the departing enemy was to risk losing it—a risk he could not force himself to take.

Across the big river on June 25 went the allies, Washington and about half of his army, Rochambeau and most of his. They were ferrying the Delaware at the other end of New Jersey before Sir Henry Clinton realized that their objective was not his precious fortress but Cornwallis's uncertain position at Yorktown.

On September 2 and 3 the allied armies paraded through Philadelphia. On both days Washington's general orders were paeans of hope. He assured the troops that they were marching to certain and perhaps final victory.

The commander in chief's words were braver than his thoughts. Reports from the Atlantic coast were that the sails of "many ships" had been sighted far out to sea. But were these vessels flying the Union Jack of Britain or the golden lilies of France? Those who brought the word of them could not say.

In short, where was de Grasse? Was he proceeding confidently toward the Chesapeake, or fleeing before a British armada?

Below Philadelphia the allied commanders parted company for a few days. Washington marched overland to Chester, Pennsylvania. The French general and his aides went by water, to inspect the American defenses along the lower Delaware.

It was as the ship bearing the French staff neared Chester that Rochambeau beheld an unusual sight. Washington was waiting for him on the docks. But this was not the statue of a man whose impassive demeanor in public had become a symbol of strength to thousands of soldiers. This was a boy of a Washington. One hand holding his hat, the other waving a white handkerchief, the 280-pound Virginia aristocrat was dancing.

Rochambeau guessed the reasons for this spectacle well before he could reach the dock and hear them from his friend's lips. The anxiously awaited word had arrived at last. De Grasse and his fleet, General Saint-Simon and his troops—all were in Chesapeake Bay.

Cornwallis was trapped.

Or was he? A week later, as Washington and Rochambeau moved southward in Virginia, a courier dispatched by Lafayette brought them troubling information. De Grasse was no longer in the Chesapeake. He had moved into the open ocean to meet the challenge of a British fleet.

The next few days would have been easier ones for Washington and Rochambeau had they been able to witness the drama taking place in the heavy seas off the coast of Virginia.

De Grasse had barely time to drop anchor in the Chesapeake and disembark Saint-Simon and his troops when shortly after dawn, September 5, a patrol ship signaled the appearance of the enemy. It was Graves and Hood and their nineteen ships of the line.

British intelligence had been faulty. Graves was under the impression that de Grasse had brought only a part of his fleet from the West Indies. He expected to see no more than a dozen French warships. He was confronted instead by twenty-eight, including the 120-gun flagship *Ville de Paris,* the largest and most powerful vessel of its kind then afloat.

For five days wooden hulls quivered under the thud of cannon balls and ships' guns thundered and flashed. On the night of the ninth, the French lookouts spotted still a third fleet in the vicinity. It was de Barras. In a finely controlled movement, de Grasse put his armada between the little squadron from Newport and the British. Amply protected from the fire of the enemy, de Barras and his ten ships slipped into the great bay, carrying the French siege guns. Some twenty-four hours later the British naval commanders, outgunned and outmaneuvered, stole away, and de Grasse turned to the Chesapeake. Thus ended the single most decisive engagement of the American Revolution. Ironically, it was also the only one in which no Americans fought.

And now, like a swiftly unraveling skein of yarn, the war moved toward its conclusion. On the fourteenth Washington and Rochambeau reached Williamsburg. Lafayette crawled from a sick bed to greet them and to introduce them to General Saint-Simon, who had already brought his 3,500 French troops up the James River. On the following day a small French ship came up the James with the news of de Grasse's victory at sea, and on the eighteenth the allied commanders conferred with the French admiral aboard his flagship in Chesapeake Bay.

Fierce headwinds on the James delayed their journey back to Williamsburg, and disturbing information arrived soon after their return there on the twenty-second. Intelligence of the situation at New York had found its way to de Grasse. Additional British ships had put in at Manhattan. Once again Admiral Graves was planning to move south to the Chesapeake, this time with a far-larger fleet. De Grasse had decided against waiting for the British to reach him at the capes. He was about to sail north and fall upon the enemy's warships while they were still bottled up in the harbor of New York.

This news alarmed Washington and Rochambeau. Fearful that Cornwallis would escape if the French fleet left, they rushed a message to de Grasse, begging him to remain in Virginia waters. Lafayette himself acted as their courier, and there was jubilance at Williamsburg when on September 25 the young Frenchman returned. De Grasse had bowed to their wishes. He warned the allied commanders, however, that important business awaited him elsewhere. He could stay in the bay only a short time longer. He urged them to move fast against Cornwallis.

They did. Up the James to Trebell's Landing came the siege guns that de Barras had brought from Newport. With them came the howitzers and fieldpieces that Major General Henry Knox and his artillerists had dragged south from the Hudson, partly by land, partly by water.

Sweating cannoneers manhandled the guns ashore. Ox teams dragged them across the York peninsula to prepared emplacements. To the northern shores of the York River went Brigadier General George Weedon and his Virginia militia—too few men to dislodge Banastre Tarleton and his legion from Gloucester Point, enough to pin them down there.

Finally, on the morning of September 28, the Franco-American army began its dusty sixteen-mile march to the rolling meadows lying to the west and south of the high loaf-shaped plateau at Yorktown where Lord Cornwallis had thrown up his fortifications. From the roof of Moore's house, his hilltop headquarters, the earl watched them come, and realized that unless a British fleet got to him soon, his chances were thin.

The mathematics were all against him. Occupying the white tents mushrooming on the fields below him were 9,500 Americans and 7,500 Frenchmen. His own effectives, including Tarleton's legion across the river, came to only 7,800. Standing in the shimmering waters of the big bay to his left were thirty-six powerful French warships against two British frigates, three transports, and some smaller ships locked into the roadstead of the York River behind him.

On the following day the British commander received an encouraging message from his superior in New York. Sir Henry Clinton informed him of the arrival there of naval reinforcements, assured him that a relief expedition under Admiral Graves would soon be on its way to the capes with troops and supplies. In an effort to hold out until the expedition came, Cornwallis withdrew the soldiers manning his outer redoubts and concentrated his forces behind his central fortifications on the Yorktown plateau.

On the night of October 6–7 the allies began digging their first parallel, a long ditch across the pasture south of Cornwallis's position. By the morning of the twelfth a second parallel had been run, this one only three hundred yards from the outermost elements of the British works. On the fifteenth Cornwallis sent Clinton a message that "the safety of the place is . . . so precarious that I cannot recommend that the fleet and army should run great risque in endeavouring to save us."

But his lordship had not given up yet. Early the next morning he hurled a detachment of 350 picked men at the center of the second allied parallel. Muskets barked as the redcoats overran the trench. They were spiking guns all along the line when a French force noisily counterattacked and flung them back.

With the coming of darkness the main American-French assault began. During the night Cornwallis loaded his garrison on the British frigates and transports in the river. There was little hope that this desperate attempt at escape would work, even if some of the ships managed to reach Gloucester Point on the northern side of the York. None did, a sudden and drenching rainstorm compelling those that had begun the crossing to scuttle back to the Yorktown shore.

By dawn the American attack was at its fullest, with a hundred allied field guns ceaselessly roaring—24-pounders, 18's, 16's, big howitzers, and little trench mortars called coehorns. To one journal-keeping American, "the whole peninsula" seemed to tremble "under the incessant thundering of our infernal machines." Another would remember that for several hours the rising of the sun went unnoticed. Beneath the smoke of battle night lingered on.

On the Yorktown plateau, along about nine o'clock, the British commander seated himself at a desk in the living room of Moore's house. His hand trembled as he wrote the date of what was to be one of the most quoted notes in history. It was October 17, 1781—anniversary of the surrender four years before of Burgoyne to Gates at Saratoga.

"Sir," the earl wrote, having addressed his note to General Washington, "I propose a cessation of hostilities for twenty-four hours, and that two officers may be appointed by each side, to meet at Mr. Moore's house, to settle the terms for the surrender of the posts at York and Gloucester. I have the honor to be, Sir, your humble and obedient servant, CORNWALLIS."

Precisely at 9:30 A.M. a drummer boy appeared on the British parapets. At first his staccato rat-a-tat was lost in the uproar. Then a Pennsylvania rifleman saw the lad there and realized that he was beating out a request for a parley.

Gradually the guns left off. The smoke cleared, and the awful din was succeeded by an awful silence, broken only by the tap-tap of the drum as the boy picked his way across the battlefield. Behind him stepped a heavyset British officer carrying a white handkerchief in one hand and Lord Cornwallis's message in the other.

No more did muskets snarl or howitzers boom. At Moore's house officers conferred. On the field the rival forces buried their dead and tended to their wounded. Although the French had the smaller of the two allied armies, they suffered the larger losses. Rochambeau's casualties were 60 killed and 193 wounded. Washington's were 23 killed and 65 wounded. The British figures were 156 dead, 326 wounded, 70 missing—and 7,247 soldiers and 840 seamen captured.

The ceremony of surrender took place on the sunny, windy afternoon of October 19. At one o'clock the allied soldiers lined up along a sandy road, the Americans on one side, the French on the other.

At two o'clock the British and the Hessians marched out between them, colors cased. It has never been ascertained exactly what songs the English bands played that afternoon. A cherished tradition is that one of them was a lively tune often set to the words of an old ballad called "The World Turned Upside Down."

On that same afternoon Sir Henry Clinton sailed from the harbor of New York with seven thousand troops, convoyed by Admiral Graves's reinforced fleet, twenty-seven ships of the line and eight frigates. Not until the seagoing relief force reached the capes of Virginia on October 24 did Clinton learn that Cornwallis had surrendered. Under the circumstances he prudently decided that an encounter with the French armada still in the Chesapeake would be futile.

Back went the supreme British commander to the now-meaningless safety of his island fortress.

# PART THREE

---

# THE PEACE

---

# 26

# The Confederation and the Constitution

Yorktown was the last big battle. There were a few more engagements, all small; but by the close of 1781 it was understood on both sides of the Atlantic that the war was over. Great Britain had lost an empire. The people of the United States had won the right to govern themselves.

To many Englishmen the news of Lord Cornwallis's surrender was less than painful. They had never liked the American War. Indeed, in recent years it had stirred tensions among them not unlike those that nearly two centuries later would divide the people of America during their long military adventure in Vietnam.

In the summer of 1780 the so-called Gordon Riots had stained London with blood and blackened it with fire. Ostensibly this civilian outburst, the worst in English history, was a protest against parliamentary removal of long-time restrictions on English Catholics. In a deeper sense, readily recognized by Lord North and his war cabinet, it was a cry of rage from a people sick to death of their country's costly and futile hostilities in the New World.

In Parliament Lord Rockingham and other antiwar Whigs made no effort to hide their delight whenever news arrived of an American victory. Repeatedly, openly (treasonably in the eyes of His Majesty), they spoke of George Washington's troops as "our army."

Only the King and his close supporters mourned when on March 20, 1782, Lord North resigned as Prime Minister. So angry was His Majesty at what he considered North's desertion of the cause that he was heard threatening to leave England and live out his days in his other kingdom, the little German principality of Hanover. The gossip in London for several weeks was that the royal yacht was standing in readiness to carry its frustrated owner across the Channel.

Forced to accept the pro-American Marquis of Rockingham as North's successor, George sent an intermediary to inform his lordship of his elevation and refused to have any personal dealings with him. Rockingham died a few months later, but to the chagrin of the King, the next Prime Minister—William Petty Fitzmaurice, second Earl of Shelburne—proved as determined as his predecessor to bring the war to an official close by concluding the necessary treaties.

Well in advance of the American victory at Yorktown, the Congress had sent John Adams to Paris for conferences looking forward to a pact of peace. Adams, however, was too blunt of speech to get along with the silken-voiced officials at the Court of Versailles. At the urging of the French minister in Philadelphia, the Congress appointed four additional peace commissioners, simultaneously getting Adams out of France by sending him on a diplomatic errand to the Netherlands. Of the other four American commissioners, one never reached Paris and another got there late. The bulk of the negotiations in the spring, summer, and fall of 1782 were carried on by seventy-six-year-old Benjamin Franklin and thirty-six-year-old John Jay of New York.

Their job was not easy. In 1779 first Spain and then Holland had entered the conflict against England. Russia, Denmark, and Sweden had banded together to deny the use of the Baltic Sea to British vessels—an action that entitled them to a voice in the discussions at Paris. At the elegant Hotel d'York, where most of the parleys convened, the American negotiators were surrounded by wily European statesmen, each trying to get from the proceedings special advantages for his own country.

Happily for the nation they represented, Franklin and Jay

walked surefootedly on the slippery slopes of Old World diplomacy. It remains an argument as to how much credit for the terms of the final pact—all advantageous to America—should be given to Franklin's persuasive charm, how much to young Jay's bold spirit and alertness.

Reluctantly England acknowledged the independence of its onetime colonies, recognized their governments, and reinstated the right of Americans to fish in the waters off Nova Scotia and Newfoundland. To Spain went the formerly English colonies below Georgia, areas now embraced by Florida and lower Alabama. France retained New Orleans. Nearly all of the rest of North America south of what is now Canada and east of the Mississippi became the property of the new republic.

Once the treaty was signed on September 3, 1783, the British troops in America began leaving, a movement that ended November 25 with the evacuation of New York City. In that city's Fraunces Tavern on December 4 Washington resigned his commission and said goodbye to his comrades in arms. Like all his public speeches, this one was brief. Hardened soldiers wept as the tall Virginian left the room. On smoky battlefields and dreary night marches they had taken the measure of their now-retired commander. They knew that he embodied, as did no other single person, the qualities that had carried the new nation through its fiery testing—tenacity, enterprise, a readiness to make do with the limited resources at hand, and a passion for liberty.

And so peace came to America, and with it all the pangs of adjustment that follow every long war—aggravated in this instance by the kind of national government the American people had built for themselves during the conflict.

A remarkable aspect of the Revolution is that for almost seven years, the war was conducted by a government that, strictly speaking, had no governing powers. The wonder of this becomes all the sharper when one reflects that the war was both a struggle with Britain and an internal or civil war.

No one has yet convincingly disputed the guess of John Adams that throughout the conflict at least one third of the Americans remained loyal to Great Britain. Another third were neutrals, people who didn't much care who won and who never caught the Spirit of '76 until after the definitive American victory at Yorktown in 1781.

The Revolution was carried to its successful end by a mere third of the population. These people made the sacrifices and took the gamble. And gamble it was. Frequently during the war Brigadier General John Glover considered resigning his commission—troubled by the knowledge that back home in Marblehead his wife and children, stripped of their breadwinner, were living on public charity. Representing only one third of the populace, the patriots provided the fighting men and ran the state governments. They saw to it that the laws of Congress were obeyed—even though these decrees rested on nothing stronger than the flimsy Articles of Association drawn up by the First Continental Congress in 1774.

From the beginning, the members of Congress realized that the union could not last long on this shaky basis. Sooner or later the states must confederate. Some kind of national government must be achieved.

The first official move in this direction came in May 1776, when the same resolution that asked the states to declare themselves independent also called on them to confederate. As John Dickinson then foresaw, the actual formation of a national government took time. Several versions of what were to be Articles of Confederation were drafted and debated. Sir William Howe had occupied Philadelphia and Congress was meeting in the little frontier town of York, Pennsylvania, before at last—on November 15, 1777—the delegates adopted the Articles and submitted them to the states.

By the end of 1779, twelve states had ratified them. But the badly needed government remained as far away as ever. Maryland refused to sign.

Maryland was a "landless state." It was surrounded by other

states. It had no access to the vast territories stretching westward of the Appalachian Mountains. On the other hand, some of the "landed states"—notably New York, Connecticut, and Virginia—had already filed claims to large portions of these western areas. Maryland's complaint in 1779 was that under the Confederation the landed states would enjoy undue influence.

Toward the end of 1780 a compromise came to the rescue of the Articles of Confederation. The major landed states agreed to give up most of their western territories. One by one, their legislatures voted to cede these areas to the Continental Congress. Satisfied with this arrangement, Maryland ratified the Articles.

The national government thus brought to life consisted of a one-house legislature, a continuation of the Continental Congress. The Articles permitted the legislators to issue and borrow money, to raise armies and declare wars, and to execute treaties with foreign governments. Aside from these few privileges, they had almost no powers at all.

They could not regulate commerce among the states, a situation that created difficulties for the rich, especially those in commerce and shipping.

They could not levy taxes, a situation that worked a hardship on everybody, rich or poor.

Under the Articles the Congress could ask the states for money, but it could not force them to pay. For the year 1782, it requested $8 million, for the next year, $2 million. By the end of the year after that, it had received in all less than a million and a half. For the remainder of its existence it had barely enough income to pay the day-by-day costs of running the government.

By 1784 the new nation's war debt—the money it had borrowed from friendly nations in Europe—had risen to $35 million and was going up daily. Because Congress could pay nothing on this obligation, it couldn't borrow money either in Europe or at home. Consequently hard money, silver and gold, began to vanish in America, especially among the poor. The country people found themselves unable to pay their debts or to buy seed and equipment for their farms.

Some states tried to help them by issuing paper money, but this seldom worked because the merchants to whom the poor were indebted knew the paper was worthless and refused to accept it. In 1786 the distressed farmers of Massachusetts rose in arms, giving birth to the quickly suppressed disturbance called Shays' Rebellion after Daniel Shays, its leader.

Before the war the British fleet had protected American shippers against the plundering of the Barbary pirates from the northern coast of Africa. The impoverished Congress of the Confederacy could afford neither the guns nor the sailors necessary to defend American vessels.

During the war the Congress had decreed that when peace came every army officer would receive half pay for the rest of his life, every enlisted soldier a bonus based on length of service. All the Congress of the Confederation could do about these arrangements was to give the veterans pieces of paper—promises to pay them in money or in land at some indefinite future date. Rich veterans held on to their paper, hopeful that someday the government would make good on it. Poor veterans, desperate for cash, sold theirs to speculators for a fraction of their face value.

By 1786 even once-ardent patriots were saying that the American experiment in representative government had failed. The time had come to replace it with a monarchy. In New York City former peace commissioner John Jay heard this cry of despair on all sides.

He did not go along with it. Neither did any other major American leader. Washington and Madison in Virginia, Charles Pinckney in South Carolina, Alexander Hamilton in New York —all were convinced that the American people had wit enough to create a national government capable of taking care of the needs of the country and at the same time subject to the rule of law and the will of the voters.

It was with these ends in mind that in late 1786 delegates

from five states met at Annapolis, Maryland. Their avowed purpose was to lay plans that would let Congress regulate commerce among the states. What actually came out of the Annapolis Convention was a call to all the states to send delegates to Philadelphia to draft the document later known as the Federal Constitution, the noble framework of the strong national government under which the people of America have been living ever since.

# 27

# The Revolution Goes On

T HE AMERICAN HISTORIAN Edmund S. Morgan has written that a revolution is such a large affair that no one understands it while it's happening. In truth, no one ever quite understands it afterward.

Concerning the upheaval of 1776, only one flat statement may be ventured. On the world of the eighteenth century the triumph of the patriots had the impact of a wrench in history. It stirred the minds of men everywhere. New thoughts formed in their heads, daring thoughts about the place of the individual in society, about his personal liberties, his civil rights, and his civic responsibilities.

Never before in modern times had a colonial people overthrown its masters. Never in so large an area had a republican government sprung into being.

The significance of these events moved across the Atlantic like a shock wave. The kings of Europe trembled, aware that a threatening new thing called democracy had asserted itself.

England herself was the first of the Old World nations to move in that direction. In 1783 the House of Commons passed a bill calling it "a high crime and misdemeanor" for the King, by bribes or any other means, to try to influence votes in Parliament. Outraged at this legislative rebellion, George III fired his cabinet—an action that availed him nothing, for the next Prime Minister was twenty-four-year-old William Pitt, son of the Great Commoner. Pitt carried the issue to the people by calling a general election, got their endorsement of the Commons curb on royal power, and set in motion the reform movement that in 1832 would give England its present government, under which Parliament rules supreme.

For several generations after Yorktown, most accounts of the American Revolution hewed to what has come to be known as the "Old Whig Interpretation." In the stern colonial policies of King George III the Old Whigs saw a deliberate attempt to set back the clock of progress, a cold-blooded refusal to realize that the hour of human liberty had struck.

Some of the early writers took a somewhat softer line. They accused Great Britain of nothing more wicked than short-sightedness, faulty judgment, and stupidity. To the more fervent Old Whigs, England's handling of its American subjects after 1763 was actual oppression. To others, it was only potentially so. One scholar argued that the uprising of 1776 differed from the one that broke out in France in 1789 in that it was aimed "not at tyranny inflicted, but only at tyranny anticipated."

The Old Whig interpretation dominated writing about the Revolution down to the closing decades of the nineteenth century. Then new interpretations began coming along from the pens of scholars called "revisionists."

Inspired by the work of historian Charles Beard, some revisionists decided that the American Revolution was not so much a fight for political freedom as for economic gain. These writers pictured the patriots as chiefly concerned with resisting those laws of England that restricted their commercial activities.

No sooner was the economic theory in view than it was challenged. One of the sharpest indictments of it appeared in Allen French's fascinating story of the first year of the War of Independence. French wrote:

. . . While it is plain enough to certain modern thinkers that America ought to have fought the war for economic causes, it is equally plain that she did not . . . in British laws controlling commerce and navigation [there was] plenty of reason for American complaint, and complaint there was. But it came in no such volume or vehemence as to lead to war. The theory that all wars rise from economic conditions does not hold in regard to the Revolution. American resistance sprang only from political oppression.

Led by historians Carl Lotus Becker and the elder Arthur M. Schlesinger, another group of revisionists concluded that the outburst of 1776 was really two revolutions. It was both a battle for home rule and a struggle to determine "who was to rule at home."

Critics of the "two-in-one" theory complain that it makes too much of the scrabble for power common to all human societies. They admit that fights over who should rule broke out repeatedly in the Continental Congress. On the larger issues of the Revolution, however, there was more consensus than disagreement.

Nothing better supports this observation than the contrast between the course of the French Revolution of 1789 and that of its American predecessor. The French revolutionaries set out in search of "liberty, fraternity and equality." They ended up with Napoleon and a military dictatorship. Some authorities say the Napoleonic system wasn't a true military dictatorship. Perhaps not, but it certainly wasn't "liberty, fraternity and equality."

The American revolutionaries set out in search of two things. They wanted independence and representative government. They got both.

Such fights as the patriots had among themselves were never intense enough to destroy the cause. "Was there ever a revolution brought about, especially so important as this," mused Sam Adams after it was all over, "without great internal tumults and violent convulsions!"

Whereas the Becker-Schlesinger revisionists say there were two American Revolutions, the members of another group known as the "New Conservatives" say there was none. All the New Conservatives can find in 1776 is "a little colonial rebellion" untouched by any of those profound social shifts that we associate with a true revolution.

One of the most eloquent of the New Conservatives is the lawyer-historian Daniel J. Boorstin. Boorstin confesses that the view that the Revolution was a "mere colonial rebellion" has long been an article of faith among the Daughters of the American Revolution.

So be it, says Dr. Boorstin. "The more I have looked into the subject," he writes, "the more convinced I have become of the wisdom of their [the Daughters'] naïveté."

According to Boorstin, the American rebellion was not a liberal movement at all. It was a conservative one. His reasoning is that the Americans were happy to be subjects of the King so long as British colonial policy was consistent with British constitutional tradition. It was when British policy *changed* that the Americans rebelled. From the colonists' point of view, the Revolution originated in Parliament. It began when the members of that body tried to impose on the Americans a string of laws "for which there was no warrant in English constitutional precedent." Boorstin insists that during the war that followed, the Americans fought "not so much to establish new rights as to preserve old ones."

Thus runs the New Conservative Interpretation. Quite frankly, it doesn't seem to run the course. It is true that during the family quarrel the patriots often resorted to the constitutional argument, to the insistence that the colonial policies of King George III were at variance with British tradition. They also made at least as much use of the natural-law argument. Again and again they reminded the parent country that they were only asking for their "inalienable rights," for those rights that they could not in good conscience allow any government to take away from them.

Another revisionist interpretation derives its support from the political left, particularly among those who extract their understanding of the world from the Communist doctrines of Karl Marx. These historians trace the origin of the break with

England largely to the existence of class conflict in colonial America.

Class conflict there was, but attempts to link it to the outbreak of the rebellion are unsatisfactory. It would seem that if this kind of unrest were a major factor, most of the rich would have stood by England, most of the poor by America. Such was not the case. Support for both sides cut across class lines. Most of the wealthy merchants were either open or secret Tories, but almost to a man the wealthy planters of the South were patriots. The common people constituted the backbone of the Continental Army, but pro-British feeling ran high among two of the most disadvantaged groups in America, the small landholders of the back-country South and the discontented tenant farmers of upstate New York.

All of the revisionist theories are enlightening. They leave us with a healthy appreciation of what an enormous and complex experience the American Revolution was. Like a great river, it had many tributaries. Still, some were more important than others, and most recent accounts of the conflict tend to move back in the direction of the Old Whig interpretation.

At the very least, that view tells us why the patriots thought they had not only a right but a moral obligation to rebel. It accounts for the intensity and persistency with which they did it.

In his collection of essays entitled *The American Revolution Reconsidered,* Richard B. Morris questions whether the "key to the Revolution" can be found in any of the revisionist theories.

"Without denying other important facets of the . . . movement," he writes, "most present-day historians . . . accept the American Revolution for what it said it was—a political and constitutional struggle over sovereignty, a battle where who was right was more important than whose pocketbook was being pinched."

With a few notable exceptions, the early chroniclers of the Revolution concentrated on its political and military aspects.

Then in 1925, on the eve of the 150th anniversary of independence, the Princeton University historian J. Franklin Jameson delivered four lectures later published under the title *The American Revolution Considered as a Social Movement*.

The thrust of Jameson's remarks was that the time had come to try to determine in what ways the Revolution had changed life in America itself. His words started a trend. Recent years have witnessed an outpouring of studies dealing with the social implications of the break with England.

Taken as a whole, these essays bear out the Princeton scholar's contention that although the Revolution was fought for political ends it created a climate of thought friendly to the view that a society can survive only by constantly liberalizing its social institutions.

The patriot leaders never claimed that their job was done. They recognized that like all sweeping changes in history the Revolution left unfinished business in its wake, problems with which the American people have been coping ever since.

In a Fourth of July oration in 1787, Dr. Benjamin Rush told his fellow Philadelphians that there "is nothing more common than to confound the terms of *American Revolution* with the *late American war*. The American war is over; but this is far from being the case with the American Revolution. On the contrary, nothing but the first act of the great drama is closed."

Even as Rush spoke, the Founding Fathers were meeting in the old statehouse on Chestnut Street. There they had gathered to frame the Federal Constitution that they hoped would give the new republic "a more perfect union." With its ratification two years later, the curtain fell on the First American Revolution.

Now the American people had their "more perfect union." Removing their gaze from the past and leaning hard into the future, they set out on the long and difficult struggle to create a more perfect society.

# Bibliography

Abernethy, Thomas P., *Western Lands and the American Revolution*. New York, 1959.

Adams, John, *Diary and Autobiography*, L. H. Butterfield, ed. Cambridge, Mass., 1961. Paperback: Atheneum Publishers.

Alden, John R., *The American Revolution, 1775–1783*. New York, 1954. Paperback: Harper Torchbooks.

———, *General Charles Lee: Traitor or Patriot?* Baton Rouge, 1951.

———, *General Gage in America*. Baton Rouge, 1948.

———, *The South in the Revolution, 1763–1789*. Baton Rouge, 1954.

Aldridge, Alfred O., *Man of Reason: The Life of Thomas Paine*. Philadelphia, 1959.

Allan, Herbert Sanford, *John Hancock: Patriot in Purple*. New York, 1948.

Anderson, Troyer S., *The Command of the Howe Brothers During the American Revolution*. New York, 1936.

Bakeless, John E., *Turncoats, Traitors, and Heroes*. Philadelphia, 1960.

Baldwin, Alice M., *The New England Clergy and the American Revolution*. New York, 1958.

Baldwin, Ernest H., "Joseph Galloway, the Loyalist Politician," *Pennsylvania Magazine of History and Biography*, Vol. 26 (July 1902), pp. 161–91; (October 1902), pp. 289–321; (December 1902), pp. 417–42.

Becker, Carl L., *The Declaration of Independence*. New York, 1933. Paperback: Random House Vintage Book.

Bennett, Lerone, Jr., *Before the Mayflower: A History of the Negro in America, 1619–1964*, rev. ed. Paperback: Penguin Books, 1966.

Bill, Alfred Hoyt, *New Jersey and the Revolutionary War*. Princeton, 1964.

Billias, George A., ed., *George Washington's Generals*. Paperback: Apollo Editions.

Boatner, Mark M., *Encyclopedia of the American Revolution*. New York, 1966.

Bonsal, Stephen, *When the French Were Here*. New York, 1945.

Bridenbaugh, Carl, *Cities in Revolt: Urban Life in America, 1743–1776*. New York, 1955. Paperback: Putnam's.

Brinton, Crane, *The Anatomy of Revolution*. New York, 1957.

Brown, Gerald S., *The American Secretary: The Colonial Policy of Lord George Germain, 1775–1778*. Ann Arbor, Mich., 1963.

Burnett, Edmund C., *The Continental Congress*. New York, 1941. Paperback: Norton Library.

———, ed., *Letters of Members of the Continental Congress*, 8 vol. Gloucester, Mass., 1963.

Burns, Rev. John F., O.S.A., *Controversies Between Royal Governors and Their Assemblies in the North American Colonies*. Boston, 1923.

Chute, Marchette, *The First Liberty: A History of the Right to Vote in America, 1619–1850*. New York, 1969.

Closen, Ludwig, Baron von, *Revolutionary Journal, 1780–83*. Chapel Hill, 1958.

Commager, Henry Steele, and Richard Morris, eds., *The Spirit of Seventy-Six: The Story of the American Revolution as Told by Participants*, 2 vols. Indianapolis, Ind., 1959.

Dickerson, Oliver M., *The Navigation Acts and the American Revolution*. Philadelphia, 1951. Paperback: Perpetua Books.

Dickinson, John, *The Writings of John Dickinson*. Vol. I: *Political Writings, 1764–1774*, Paul Leicester Ford, ed. Philadelphia, 1895.

Du Puy, Col. Richard Ernest and Col. Trevor A., *The Compact History of the Revolutionary War*. New York, 1963.

East, Robert A., *Business Enterprise in the American Revolutionary Era*. Gloucester, Mass., 1964.

Fleming, Thomas J., *Beat the Last Drum, the Siege of Yorktown*. New York, 1963.

Forbes, Esther, *Paul Revere and the World He Lived In*. Boston, 1942. Paperback: Houghton Mifflin Sentry Editions.

Freeman, Douglas S., *George Washington, a Biography*, 7 vols. New York, 1948–1957.

French, Allen, *The First Year of the American Revolution*. Boston, 1934.

Goddard, William, *The Partnership; or, The History of the Rise and Progress of the Pennsylvania Chronicle*. Philadelphia, 1770.

Gottschalk, Louis R., *Lafayette Comes to America*. Chicago, 1935.
————, *Lafayette and the Close of the American Revolution*. Chicago, 1942.
Great Britain, Parliament, House of Commons, *The Examination of Joseph Galloway, Esq*. London, 1779.
Hall, Michael G. and others, eds., *The Glorious Revolution in America: Documents on the Colonial Crisis of 1689*. Chapel Hill, 1964.
Hawke, David, *The Colonial Experience*. Indianapolis, Ind., 1966.
Heath, William, *Heath's Memoirs of the American War*. New York, 1904.
Hoemer, James K., *The Life of Thomas Hutchinson*. Boston, 1896.
Ives, Mabel Lorenz, *Washington's Headquarters*. Upper Montclair, N.J., 1932.
James, Sir William M., *The British Navy in Adversity: A Study of the War of Independence*. London, 1926.
Jameson, John Franklin, *The American Revolution Considered as a Social Movement*. Princeton, 1926. Paperback: Princeton University Press.
Jensen, Merrill, *The Articles of Confederation*. Madison, Wis., 1948. Paperback: University of Wisconsin Press.
————, *The Founding of a Nation: A History of the American Revolution, 1763–1776*. New York, 1968.
Johnston, Henry P., "The Campaign of 1776 Around New York and Brooklyn," *Memoirs of the Long Island Historical Society*, Vol. 3. Brooklyn, 1878.
Jones, Thomas, *History of New York During the Revolutionary War*, Vol. 1. New York, 1879.
Knollenberg, Bernhard, *Origin of the American Revolution: 1759–1766*, rev. ed. New York, 1961. Paperback: Free Press Paperbacks.
————, *Washington and the Revolution, A Reappraisal*. New York, 1940.
Labaree, Benjamin Woods, *The Boston Tea Party*. New York, 1970. Paperback: Oxford University Press Galaxy Books.
Lamb, Martha J., "Historic Homes and Landmarks." *Magazine of American History*, Vol. 21 (January 1889), pp. 1–23.
Lancaster, Bruce, *From Lexington to Liberty*. New York, 1955.
Lowell, Edward J., *The Hessians and Other German Auxiliaries of Great Britain in the Revolutionary War*. New York, 1884.
Mackenzie, Frederick, *Diary of Frederick Mackenzie*, 2 vols. Cambridge, Mass., 1930.

McLaughlin, Andrew Cunningham, *The Confederation and the Constitution, 1783–1789*. New York, 1962.

Malone, Dumas, *The Story of the Declaration of Independence*. New York, 1954.

Miller, John C., *Sam Adams, Pioneer in Propaganda*. Palo Alto, Calif., 1936. Paperback: Stanford University Press.

———, *Origins of the American Revolution*. Palo Alto, Calif., 1957. Paperback: Stanford University Press.

Montross, Lynn, *The Reluctant Rebels: The Story of the Continental Congress*. New York, 1950.

———, *The Story of the Continental Army*. New York, 1967.

Moore, Frank, comp., *The Diary of the American Revolution*. New York, 1967.

Morgan, Edmund S., *The Birth of the Republic, 1763–1789*. Chicago, 1956. Paperback: University of Chicago Press.

———, and Helen M., *The Stamp Act Crisis*. Chapel Hill, 1953. Paperback: Macmillan Collier Books.

Morris, Richard B., *The American Revolution Reconsidered*. New York, 1967. Paperback: Harper Torchbooks.

———, *The Peacemakers; the Great Powers and American Independence*. New York, 1965.

Nickerson, Hoffman, *The Turning Point of the Revolution; or Burgoyne in America*, 2 vols. Port Washington, N.Y., 1967.

Quarles, Benjamin, *The Negro in the American Revolution*. Chapel Hill, 1961. Paperback: Norton Library.

Riedesel, Friedericke C., Baroness von, *Baroness von Riedesel and the American Revolution;* journal and correspondence. Chapel Hill, 1965.

Roberts, Kenneth, ed., *March to Quebec: Journals of the Members of Arnold's Expedition*. New York, 1938.

Robson, Eric, *The American Revolution in Its Political and Military Aspects*. London, 1955. Paperback: Norton Library.

Rush, Benjamin, *The Autobiography of Benjamin Rush*. Princeton, 1948.

Sabine, Lorenzo, *Biographical Sketches of Loyalists*. Port Washington, N.Y., 1966.

Scheer, George F., and Hugh F. Rankin, eds., *Rebels and Redcoats*. Cleveland, 1957. Paperback: New American Library Mentor Books.

Schlesinger, Arthur M., *The Colonial Merchants and the American Revolution*. New York, 1918, 1939.

Shy, John W., *Toward Lexington: the Role of the British Army in the Coming of the American Revolution.* Princeton, 1965.

Smith, Justin H., *Arnold's March from Cambridge to Quebec.* New York, 1903.

Stille, Charles Janeway, *The Life and Times of John Dickinson.* Philadelphia. 1891.

Stryker, William S., *The Battle of Monmouth.* Princeton, 1927.

Thayer, Theodore G., *Nathanael Greene.* New York, 1960.

Watson, John S., *The Reign of George III.* Oxford, England, 1960.

Wiederhold, Capt. Andreas, "Colonel Rall at Trenton," diary extract. *Pennsylvania Magazine of History and Biography,* Vol. 22 (1898), pp. 462–7.

Willcox, William B., *Portrait of a General: Sir Henry Clinton in the War of Independence.* New York, 1964.

Wright, Esmond, ed., *Causes and Consequences of the American Revolution.* Chicago, 1966. Paperback: Quadrangle Books.

Wrong, George M., *Canada and the American Revolution.* New York, 1935.

# Index